DATE			

A CASE OF CHILD MURDER

A Case of Child Murder

Law and Science in Nineteenth-Century Tuscany

Patrizia Guarnieri

translated by Claudia Miéville

Polity Press

This English translation © Polity Press 1993
First published in Italy as *L'Ammazzabambini*
© Giulio Einaudi editore s.p.a., Turin 1988

First published in 1993 by Polity Press
in association with Blackwell Publishers

Editorial office:
Polity Press
65 Bridge Street
Cambridge CB2 1UR, UK

Marketing and production:
Blackwell Publishers
108 Cowley Road
Oxford OX4 1JF, UK

238 Main Street
Cambridge, MA 02142, USA

ISBN 0 7456 0903 1

A CIP catalogue record for this book is available from the
British Library and the Library of Congress.

Typeset in 10$\frac{1}{2}$ on 12 pt Sabon
by Best-set Typesetter Ltd., Hong Kong
Printed in Great Britain by Biddles Ltd, Guildford and King's Lynn

This book is printed on acid-free paper.

Contents

Abbreviations

ACI	Archivio Comunale di Incisa (Municipal Archives of Incisa)
ACS	Archivio Centrale di Stato Roma (Central State Archives of Rome)
ACTF	Archivio Centro Traumatologico Firenze (Archives of the Trauma Centre, Florence)
AOPF	Archivio ex Ospedale Psichiatrico San Salvi Firenze (Archives of the former Psychiatric Hospital of San Salvi, Florence)
APCLF	Archivio Pia Casa di Lavoro Firenze (Archives of the Charity Workhouse, Florence)
APSA	Archivio Parrocchia di Sant'Alessandro Incisa (Archives of the Parish of Sant'Alessandro, Incisa)
ASF	Archivio di Stato Firenze (State Archives, Florence)
AVF	Archivio Vescovile Fiesole (Diocesan Archives, Fiesole)

Acknowledgements

Funding towards the preparation of this work was granted by the Tuscan Department of Education and Culture. I also received courteous help from the History of Science Institute and Museum and from the Incisan town council, whose archives I was shown by Massimo Tarassi.

The development of such a project would have been impossible without my previous contacts with the historians at the Wellcome Institute for the History of Medicine in London and Roger Smith. I am truly grateful to Arturo Colombo, Nino Dazzi, Renato Pasta and Luigi Tomassini, each of whom read and evaluated the typescript. I am also grateful to Pietro Costa for suggestions concerning the legal aspects of the case, and to Vittorio Donato Catalpano, Antonio De Pascalis and Giuseppe Germano for discussions on the psychiatric aspects.

Finally, I wish to thank the many people I have met during my research who have supported me, particularly Giovanni Levi and Carlo Ginzburg.

This book is dedicated to my father.

Callisto Grandi
« L'uccisore dei bambini »

And as he was going up by the way, there came forth little children out of the city, and mocked him, and said unto him, Go up, thou bald head; go up, thou bald head. And he turned back and looked on them, and cursed them in the name of the Lord. And there came forth two she bears out of the wood, and tare forty and two children of them.

Second Book of Kings 2: 23–4

The truth is hard to know
and is written in bakers' nails.
A mute was singing the Miserere;
A blind man answered: – I have seen a great deal –
I met a peasant on the road.
– What have you got in your sack? – he said – I'm going to the mill.

G. Moroni (illiterate), Florence 1879

1

Events and Enquiry

Alarm in Incisa

At just after eleven o'clock in the morning of Thursday, 10 October 1895, at the former monastery of the Murate in Florence, two guards called for the heavy door to be opened and entered the prison. They reappeared not long after, with 'a short little man' walking between them. He was dressed in dark clothes and 'used a handkerchief to keep wiping' his bald head. He had just finished paying what is called his debt to society: more than twenty years behind bars, including almost two years in Florence, almost twelve in the fortress of Volterra, and the last seven as a convict on the island of Capraia, from which he had just returned.

Callisto Grandi, forty-four years old, was now a free man. His mother still lived in his home town, as did his brothers and sisters and many nieces and nephews, some of whom had never met him. He had 700 lire in his pocket, which he had earned in prison by working as a blacksmith, but he wanted to keep only 38 lire for himself. He intended to give the rest of his savings – so the chronicler in *La Nazione* informed his readers – to his seven little orphaned nieces – not that they were truly orphans, since his brother was not dead; nor did he have so many daughters. On the other hand, those who followed the news in *Fieramosca – The People's Newspaper* learned that he had already sent the money to some of his aunts. At any rate, the ex-convict was hoping to find a job soon. He had a trade and was not afraid of hard work, and he had already sought assistance from the ex-convicts' benevolent society.[1]

At that point it was hard to say exactly when and where he was to be settled. At police headquarters they would have liked to have seen him admitted, for a while at least, to the charity work house – but the director, Carlo Peri, would not take him in that morning. Rosso and Ridolfi, the two policemen who had accompanied their charge to the Montedomini workhouse, had to take him away again.

On their way from Via Ghibellina to Via Malcontenti, in the Santa Croce area, they met a man from Incisa called Gobbino ('Hunchback'), a porter by trade, who recognized the former prisoner. Grandi signalled his fellow townsman to keep quiet, but Gobbino immediately began pointing him out to passers-by. The word quickly spread, and the man who was no longer a prisoner, still accompanied by the two guards as well as by Brigadier Miniati, 'was followed through the streets by a crowd of people, most of them children, who' – added the *Nazione* reporter – 'gazed at him in terror'. This was his first walk as a free man, and it soon ended towards midday in the Via dei Ginori, where at the central police station they took him in and locked him up again.

Where on earth 'can this wretch go?' asked the anonymous reporter on the Florentine daily paper. Anyone who had served the sentence imposed on him by the courts should then have the right to enjoy his freedom, and Grandi could certainly claim that right. But no one in his home town of Incisa, in the Val d'Arno, wanted him back, and there was great consternation at the prospect. The municipal council believed that he should be forever 'kept far away from those places which still held the extremely sad memory of the ghastly crimes and of his poor victims'.

Certainly there was no lack of sympathy, at least 'among all decent people' in the district, for the wicked wretch's family who had suffered so much misfortune. Beyond that though, everyone agreed that Grandi's crimes were too horrible and too notorious for his return not to constitute a danger to others and even to himself. 'The slightest incident could push some lawless type into extracting atrocious revenge', they warned.

The general unease had already been expressed a week earlier, when the moderate Tuscan daily newspaper *La Nazione* had urged the authorities to address the problem: 'The return to Incisa of this human beast is not in any way appropriate.' Everyone regarded him as 'an object of fear, especially fathers and mothers'. What would happen if he was 'seized once more with an obsession for murdering children? And it really was a true obsession,' diagnosed the journalist, 'because Carlino Grandi . . . made great efforts to lure them into his trap, then killed them and buried them under the earth floor of his workshop.' He had strangled five children, an article published on 4 October 1894 misinformed its readers, 'and was discovered when he had almost finished killing the sixth'.

'It's true that I killed four children,' declared the murderer in an interview with *La Nazione*, 'by crushing their heads with a grindstone... then throwing a handful of earth over them.' The journalist believed him to be repentant, but then Grandi added,

> 'And I was a fool... if I had buried them three metres deep they would never have found them. The last boy, whom I think is now a priest or a monk, I didn't catch him properly with the grindstone, it slipped out of my hand and wounded his cheek. While I was just about to finish him off, a woman, a big woman, saw it all through a hole in the door of my workshop and so...'

The murderer had been discovered and the child saved.[2]

Normally, people met and married only others from the same town or at least from not far away. Unusually, though, Amerigo Turchi, a railway worker, the son of Incisan parents, born and bred and at the time still living in Incisa, paid his addresses – as was said of someone on the point of getting married – to a girl from the North. On 12 April 1891 the young man presented himself at the Town Hall and answered the questions put to him by Archimede Bellini, the acting deputy mayor, resplendent in full regalia. Yes, he intended to marry the girl present there with him, Luigina Senerica, daughter of the late Luigi, who was still living at home and had been born and lived all her life at Pizzighettone.[3]

The young bride was twenty years old when she joined her husband. She left behind Padana, that ancient Cremona town carved out of the Adda, the sanctuary which held 'el turrin', where Francis I had been imprisoned, and the Blessed Virgin of Roggione Full of Grace, before whom the people of Pizzighettone marched in procession every third Sunday in Lent. Everything was different in the Val d'Arno. The landscape was unfamiliar, uneven and hilly with narrow fields and rows of vines edged with trees. The food and herbs were not the same as those which her mother had taught her to cook. And most different of all were the habits of both town and country people, their way of talking, the brusque and slightly arrogant manner of the Tuscans, even when joking. They were a people she hardly understood, and didn't know at all.

The local people, on the other hand, almost all knew each other and certainly knew the husband whom Luigina quickly made a father. First came two girls: Vittoria in the winter of 1892 and Gina

in the spring of the following year. Then, finally, the son named
Gaetano after Amerigo's brother, a knife grinder who had died in
1881 at the age of eighteen. Gaetano was barely fourteen months
old in June 1895, when another girl arrived.[4] To bring four children
into the world within four years of marriage was no small matter,
but the young Turchi couple had no financial worries. The head of
the family no longer appeared on his children's birth certificates as a
railway worker but as a property owner. But even so, how could
any parent feel secure at that time in Incisa?

It was common knowledge that the 'childkiller', as the newspapers
called him, was to be released from prison in October 1895 and that
unless an alternative was found, he would be returning to his old
neighbourhood. There, once again, the talk was all about those
wicked crimes. People either remembered them vividly or had heard
the stories and told them over again in their own versions. It can't
have been easy for Amerigo to make his wife, who was not from the
area, understand exactly what had taken place there twenty years
earlier, on 29 August 1875. He had been a child of nine at the time
and possibly didn't remember events very clearly. On that day his
mother had fainted and he had been swept into his father's arms and
carried away from that place, covered in dirt and scratches, and
with a frightening amount of blood on his face. Everyone had come
running and there was total confusion. There had been hundreds of
people at the trial in Florence a year later as well. They had all
talked a great deal and it had been impossible to understand everything
all those doctors and lawyers were saying. The facts were really very
simple. He had explained everything properly and Carlo Grandi had
confessed, so the mystery of children disappearing without trace was
solved. Grandi had killed them and the bodies had been found in his
workshop.

But after such a long time it was hard to tell the story. And it
must have been difficult for Luigina to overcome her fear and
understand. How was it possible that no one had suspected for more
than two years? And how was it possible that the killer was someone
well-known to everyone in the neighbourhood? And how could it
have happened every time right there in the main street, the Via
Petrarca, close to the church and the Town Hall?

In Luigina's memory of the North, where she had grown up, there
had always been order and security. The Austrians had made sure of
that after 1815, by stationing a garrison of fifty men right there in
Pizzighettone. The countryside had been cleared of bandits, who
were all hanged, street lights had been installed in the via Postale,
and from 1823 there had been schooling even for the girls. The

2500 inhabitants had their magistrates' court, their customs office, their carabinieri* – as well as the prison with its convicts.[5]

At Incisa, on the other hand, a town of 3460 inhabitants at the last count in 1873, there was no prison, nor were any carabinieri stationed there. When needed these had to hurry from Figline, despite the fact that the town, formerly called Ancisa, had been granted autonomy *motu proprio* on 2 August 1851.

The presence of a force of carabinieri was no longer merely a desire, but a necessity, explained the mayor of Incisa in a letter to the Prefect in Florence dated 30 April 1875.[6] In previous years crimes had been less frequent, 'apart from ill-founded grudges', but the situation had deteriorated. Property was being stolen and public order disrupted, and the sparse patrols of carabinieri stationed six kilometres away were ineffective. The only way these 'very grave incidents' could be avoided was to establish a permanent force of carabinieri at Incisa. In March 1876 the general in charge of the legion confirmed that it was impossible to provide permanent patrols in the environs of Figline, which alone had almost 10,000 inhabitants. The Prefect's reply was the same as that with which he had answered all such previous appeals: that unfortunately there was a shortage of personnel, and while a brigade of carabinieri at Incisa would certainly be useful, it could not be provided. The Incisans continued to insist. They claimed that the region was full of criminals and that armed strangers had been seen in both their own town and in neighbouring Regello.

And it was not only thieves who were threatening public order. Unknown agitators had been deliberately deployed by a branch of the First International, held in Florence in 1872. In fact, in the following year a small group was apparently formed at Incisa itself, and held meetings in Cioni's bakery.[7] All this must certainly have worried the local authorities who, to satisfy the current income requirements for election, all belonged to the elite group of land-owners. The hard lives led by ordinary people were not subject to the same threats or fears – people like the agricultural labourers and sharecroppers in the country and the artisans and shopkeepers in town, people who formed the backbone of the community and lived their lives without great changes, often passing their trades from father to son.[8]

Judging from the file of 'Querele e denunzie' (legal actions) for the year 1873 (the only copy left from that decade), not many crimes or

---

* Carabinieri are members of the Italian Army corps who act as a police force.

misdemeanours occurred which resulted in any action being taken by the Incisan authorities. This scarcity of cases served to justify the response which was communicated by the Prefect in Florence on behalf of the Minister of the Interior on 13 June 1877: that it was not possible to establish a contingent of carabinieri, both because of a constant shortage of manpower and 'because public security in Incisa, as demonstrated by the small number of offences having occurred between 1 January and 31 May last year, does not justify the establishment of a permanent force there.'

The refusal came for the umpteenth time and called on statistics and official figures alone to deny the insistent appeal. From the evidence, however, it was reasonable to deduce that very few people in Incisa turned to the authorities for justice. Those who did often waited some time after the offence to declare themselves victims of the theft of a pig or a bale of hay. Most cases concerned simple quarrels, insults or threats. The municipal tax office messenger had been attacked by three individuals whom he could not describe. The same thing had happened to Brother Lucio, who had been attacked in the street by a well-dressed stranger who had stopped him on the pretext of asking for a drink. Someone else, unidentified according to the municipal usher, had accused the municipal employees of being 'a load of cheats'.[9]

The man who recorded those few denunciations and legal actions in 1873 was the landowner Venanzio Ceccherini. As mayor of Incisa it was his duty, according to Article 62 of the Penal Procedure Code, to 'take note of whatever crime, offence and contravention occurring in the place' under his jurisdiction, particularly since there was no Public Security official in the town and the mayor had also to assume those duties under direction of the Prefect in Florence (law of 20 March 1865).

In that same September, Ceccherini recorded that 'the town was alarmed'. The reasons for the alarm are not sufficiently explained by the archive material, although the relevant documents (category IV, 'Urban Police and Public Security') do include a special section which appears to have been lost. This is Section I, Class 3, devoted to 'The Disappearance of Children'.[10]

The disappearance of the children

Family and friends had searched everywhere for them. The two children seemed to have disappeared into thin air one after the other between Saturday and Sunday, 21 and 22 August 1875. Finally, after hours of fruitless effort, the mayor of Incisa decided on the second night to telegraph the magistrates at Figline. On the following day the magistrate received two reports, one running to three pages from the locally stationed carabinieri and the other from the Public Security official. Having been informed of the event and the alarm which had arisen among the people of Incisa, they had gone to the town to begin investigations in a somewhat perfunctory manner.[11]

They took details of the missing children, who were eight and nine years old. They found out when and where they had last been seen. Commander Achille Delú, accompanied by private Gaetano Trecchi, relayed the information that one child had last been seen at midday and the other in the afternoon. The Public Security official, however, learned that one had last been seen at three o'clock in the afternoon and the other between eleven and twelve at night. He was assured that more information would certainly be forthcoming from 'the sons of the woman known as Ginora's daughter', but that the hour was too late to press them for details. In fact, the investigation succeeded in finding out only what had already been discovered in the town. The only trace of the missing children was the straw hat usually worn by the child Fortunato, which had been found in an unspecified place 'in the centre of town'.

News of the disappearances appeared in *La Nazione*. Within a few short lines the journalist got the place wrong (he stated that the incident occured at Figline) and he naturally emphasized the sensational, concluding that 'despite the most vigorous investigations, nothing has been discovered by political or local authorities to throw any light on this mystery.'[12]

To judge from his report, the Police Commissioner was disposed to consider the case closed if not solved. The boys had probably 'sadly perished in the weir where they had gone alone recently at nightfall to swim and play other games'. To Baciocchi, the Public Security official, this seemed to be the 'most reasonable' of current theories. But it was not the answer, for the children knew how to swim and knew every inch of that stretch of river. Furthermore, the Arno was dry after a hot, rainless August. And if they had drowned, their bodies would have been found by the two carabinieri who had spent so much time dragging the river bed. So the local people said. Nevertheless, Delú concluded that the two boys must have drowned because they were 'poor swimmers and weak due to their tender years'. Not even the magistrate found this explanation very convincing.[13]

What other explanation could there be? In the frightened town 'the strangest and most unlikely theories' were circulating, 'giving rise to instant fear and rumour'. It was important to the Public Security officials that these rumours should be laid to rest as soon as possible. According to the Florence newspaper, stories were beginning to spread of 'a child killer who feeds on young flesh, and there isn't a single fairy story, including one about an enormous serpent, which isn't going around'. The point was that this was a fairy story told to evoke fear of the impossible and a belief in happy endings.

The city journalist chose to make fun of all that peasant credulity, but none of those questioned mentioned anything of the kind. Instead, they reported that prevailing opinion held that a stranger must have been responsible. There was no particular suspect, only conjectures which serve to illustrate the various forms in which a fear of the unknown were expressed, and to show how defence mechanisms were deployed in the face of an inexplicable evil within a small community whose individuals led lives which were hard but who knew, on the whole, what particular pains, deprivations and losses they would have to endure. Children disappearing from the streets for no reason had never happened before. Maybe it was a gypsy or a group of gypsies or some other rascals. Whoever was responsible, it was certainly no one from within the community.

The cartwright whose workshop was near the main square was telling people that he 'had met a bad man' near San Vito a Loppiano. 'This bad man had asked him whether he came from Incisa and if there were any carabinieri there. When he had answered that there weren't any carabinieri the man asked if there was a municipal guard there and when he answered that yes, there was, the wretch disappeared into the countryside. He said he had been very frightened, that he would have followed him' and killed him had he been armed.[14]

Among the group of men who met outside in the evenings to discuss the day's events there were some who believed this story and some who didn't. The women may have been more inclined to believe, since they could not forgive themselves for not having taken greater care of the children.

The boys especially were hardly ever at home. They played out of doors and went to work from the time they were five or six years old. The country people were eager to keep boys and work them hard and some even took in foundlings from the orphanage for the purpose. The employment of 'children in itinerant work' was forbidden by a law of 21 December 1873, but everyone knew that 'the shameful trade had started up again', as the Prefect Montezemolo complained in a letter circulated to mayors on 16 September 1875.[15] Under the circumstances it was not so absurd to believe that a 'robber of children, a gypsy with a bushy beard, was roaming the countryside stealing other people's children' and working them to death. According to the reporter in the *Fieramosca*, such 'tales ended up being believed as solid fact by those worthy peasants.' One journalist on the *Opinione Nazionale* stated that it was quite awkward for a stranger 'to go to Incisa after the disappearance of the two children'.[16]

Nevertheless, no solid facts had actually been discovered. Once the carabinieri had carried out their investigation and gone back to Figline, people would gradually have calmed down. If nothing more had happened beyond the disappearance of those two children the affair would, as time passed, hardly have been talked about. So many, after all, were buried that year. Normally, the annual death rate for the community seldom rose above 100. But in 1875, in Incisa and nowhere else, the death rate was extraordinarily high: 260 people died and, as usual, most of those were the youngest and weakest, who fell ill and simply never recovered.[17]

During the search for Fortunato and Angelino someone must surely have recalled how six months earlier another little boy had disappeared without his parents ever finding a trace of him. And there had been another case of a little boy of the same age, barely four years old, who had disappeared in March 1873. During the days of 21 and 22 August 1875, however, there were probably few people who made any connection between these four mysterious disappearances. There were so many burdens to be borne after all, and life had to go on for those who were left. Other children would be born to the same families and these were sometimes baptized with the same name as the brother or sister they would never know.

Yet certainly during the days following the disappearances at Incisa, parents especially were extra vigilant. Even though they had to go out to work, all the women – the seamstresses and spinners, those who worked in the fields and those who were in service in wealthy houses – all tried not to let the children out of their sight. They were afraid, and they kept a closer watch over their children than ever before, insisting that they were to come home on time, they were not to wander away without telling anyone, and above all, they were never to trust strangers.

Hide-and-seek, Catch, Tag, the children of Incisa had many names for it. You only needed two to play but it was better with lots of people. On that Sunday morning there were 'Narciso Biagi, Alpinolo,

Cecchino . . . Barocchino's little Beppa' and others of Amerigo's age
or a little older. One had to count with his eyes shut while the others
went to hide, and then go to look for them. Amerigo wasn't sure
whose turn it was to be 'it', but he knew that his two older sisters,
Beppa and Lina, had already hidden somewhere 'in the little room in
the workshop'. He ought to get in there quickly himself if he wanted
to play. Did he want to join in the game or not?

The most important thing was to find a good hiding place. Sometimes, though, the hiding place felt so safe that you forgot to look
out and you didn't know what was going on around you. You
didn't know if the person looking for you was creeping up on you
silently, just about to pounce, or if it was the perfect moment to
dash for 'home'. The most difficult of all was peeping out. Then you
had to see without being seen. Sometimes there was one person who
simply never came out at all, as though he only felt safe in his hiding
place. The longer you kept still in your hiding place, your heart
beating, the greater the chance of being caught. The ones who
played like that were usually the ones who couldn't run fast, the
cowardly ones. Or else the very smallest ones. The big ones helped
them sometimes.

Some people knew the area of the game better than others and
had an advantage because they could find hiding places no one else
would ever have thought of. Carlino, called 'Baldy', knew the workshop well. Naturally he did – it was there at number 43 in the main
street that he worked. Amerigo lived at number 45 and that morning,
as on many others, he went into the workshop to hide.

And I went into the workshop with Carlino. Carlino closed the outside
door with the big chain inside and he also closed the shutters inside the
little window looking onto the alleyway. When I was inside the workshop,
which was as dark as night, Carlino led me to the bit of earth dug up near
the wall on the window side. He said he had dug a hole there, but I don't
know when. He said, "get in here", and I got in and he arranged me so I
was lying with my mouth and stomach down, and he said, "now I'll cover
you with the overalls", but he didn't cover me with the overalls, he
emptied a basket of sand over me, but I lifted my head up and I tried to
escape and I screamed, but he grabbed my face with one hand over my
mouth to stop me screaming and he grabbed my neck with the other hand
to strangle me and he wanted to throttle me but I carried on screaming,
and then Carlino dragged me into the little room where the wood is kept
which is under the stairs, and he had both hands round my neck and I
couldn't breath any more nor scream and I was on the ground because
Carlino had thrown me down, and he was killing me. I was biting his
fingers but I couldn't defend myself anymore because I was already down

on the ground, but some people from outside came to help me, and I heard the door in the passage break down and they opened it and some people came in and my father was there too, so then Carlino let me go and opened the door and rushed away into the house, and they carried me away and I had blood all on my face because Carlino had scratched my face.[18]

All this and more took place after 11.45 on 29 August 1875, very near the Town Hall at Incisa. A couple of hours earlier it was in that very building that the magistrate was questioning the parents whose children had disappeared a week before. It was a public holiday and the weather was sultry, but Raffaello Chelini was still at his work. He had not been completely satisfied with the reports he had received from the carabinieri or the Public Security officer, and had decided to take over the investigation of the mysterious events himself.

Raffaello Chelini's industriousness was regarded as praiseworthy by his superiors, though they described his abilities as no more than adequate. His knowledge of the civil and penal codes was fair. He was in line for possible promotion to a position as a judge in chambers or deputy public prosecutor. In fact, his personal files were being evaluated at around that very time, on 2 August 1875, by the president of the Court of Appeal in Florence. Chelini was a Tuscan from Montevarchi, who had gained an honours degree from the University of Siena in 1860 and passed his law exams in 1864. He had been appointed to his present position as magistrate at Figline on 24 August 1873, after having held the same post in various cities in Romagna. He was to stay in that district of the Val d'Arno until September 1878 – more than a year after the end of the judicial processes which, in August 1875, were just beginning in Incisa.[19]

On the morning of 29 August, assisted by a pupil qualified as a deputy clerk of court who wrote the answers on the appropriate forms for 'The Investigation of Witnesses not under Oath', Raffaello Chelini learned more about what had taken place in Incisa. Details were provided by three witnesses who had been officially summoned by the bailiff of the magistrates' court two days earlier.

The father of Fortunato Paladini, 'a young boy of about nine years old', was not questioned, since he lived and worked near La Spezia. The man's wife, Maddalena, 'daughter of the late Alfonso Daviddi and aged about thirty' (she could not be more accurate than that), an illiterate seamstress, born and living in Incisa with her son and two daughters, did not prove to be of much help in the enquiries. She stated that her son had gone out after lunch, 'into town with other children – I don't know which ones – as usual'. Normally, each child would return to his own home for a piece of bread in the middle of the afternoon and later for supper. But on that evening he hadn't. 'About my son's disappearance, I don't know what to think. It's possible he drowned in the Arno but the fact that he hasn't been recovered after so much searching makes it unlikely.' This was the substance of the woman's conclusions, although doubtless her actual words would have been somewhat different from the official record. She signed her testimony with a cross. 'In any case, I can offer no clarification to the officials, since I am not in possession of any relevant facts.'[20]

Half an hour later, the interview with the forty-year-old farm labourer Serafino Martelli, also illiterate and a native of Incisa, reached a similar conclusion: 'I cannot understand how my son can have vanished, and although it is possible that he was drowned in the Arno, the fact that he has never been recovered . . . makes it seem very doubtful. In any case I am unable to shed any light on this matter.' The story was the same: seven-year-old Angelo had not come home. He had been home at about midday and three hours later his mother had seen him at the fair. His father recalled that 'after eleven o'clock, our usual supper time, since the child had not come home, I went looking for him in the streets of Incisa.' His search was in vain. The magistrate then heard nine-year-old Giuseppe Buzzafini: 'From eleven until midnight we were in the main square', until his mother had called him in; Angelo had stayed outside alone to play for a bit longer. Nobody saw him after that. These were familiar details which had already appeared in the Public Security commissioner's report and which the little boy must have told his neighbours a hundred times already.

The investigation started at eleven and by the time it had finished the magistrate had no more clear idea than he had had before. A few minutes later, however, as he himself put it, 'the cause of it all was blindingly revealed.'

Towards midday yesterday I was in my house, which is opposite the workshop of the cartwright Carlo Grandi, known as 'Baldy', and I heard voices coming from inside the workshop itself, which was shut at the time, like a child's voice saying, 'You're killing me! Stop!' And a man whom I knew to be Grandi was answering, 'Keep still!' At first I thought it was my little sister Angiollina, who was in bed with my father, but when I recognized young Amerigo Turchi's voice I ran at once to tell my mother and I said, 'There's a child screaming in Grandi's workshop!'

Then my mother listened and she recognized the voice of the boy Amerigo Turchi too and said, 'Go and tell his parents'. And I ran quickly to their house, which is near Grandi's workshop, and told them to come quickly because their son was being murdered. So then they came running and as both the doors to Grandi's workshop were shut they started shouting his name, calling 'Carlino! Open up!' But nobody answered. So they called the blacksmith, Gianni Cioni, who used pliers to break the chain on the little door leading onto the entrance to the Catolfi house, and when it was open everyone went into the workshop and I stayed outside. After a little while I saw young Amerigo Turchi carried out in his mother's arms. His face was all dripping with blood and he was moaning saying 'Oh God! Oh God!' After a while I saw Grandi come out too and he was all sweaty. He went into the house saying that the Turchi boy had thrown stones at him and that was why he hit him. After a while my mother came out of the workshop too and I went home with her and I didn't see anything else.

This evidence, the first of any real importance, was given by an Incisan child, a girl this time: Giulia Monsecchi, 'twelve years old...spinster, illiterate'. The magistrate naturally wanted to summon the girl immediately to the Town Hall, even before hearing her mother's evidence; the earliest opportunity came at nine in the morning of 30 August. Before then, on the previous evening, Raffaello Chelini had been rather busy.

The murderer is discovered

The magistrate, four carabinieri and Grandi were locked inside the house. Outside, a furious crowd was demanding the murderer, for it was obvious now that it was he who had been responsible for the four missing children of whom no trace had been found until then. He had murdered them and buried them in the workshop where their remains had been discovered.

At four o'clock in the afternoon, while he was still awaiting the arrival of military reinforcements, Chelini compiled a detailed report for the public prosecutor wherein he summarized the recent days' events and described what had taken place that Sunday:

Towards the hour of 11.45 in the morning, the agonized screams of a little boy were heard coming from the ground floor of the building at number 43 in the main street of this town of Incisa. People ran to enter the said building, which was found to have all entrances locked. A small door having been forced open, certain citizens of Incisa entered the room, where they were met by an extraordinary scene. The said Callisto Grandi, son of the late Giuseppe, twenty-four years old, a cartwright by trade, born and domiciled in Incisa, was on top of the boy Amerigo Turchi, son of Sebastiano, whom he was attempting to strangle. The victim having been rescued and the room examined, a small trench was found, which had probably been destined to receive that young boy's body. Near the said trench were soon revealed the remains of one or more children buried in shallow earth.

At this sight the population was immediately enraged and it was a miracle that Callisto Grandi was saved from the fury of the crowd, who wanted to deliver justice on the spot. By the intervention of the clerk, the deputy mayor, the municipal tax collector and other influential townspeople, Grandi was able to be removed to a house in town. Having received the news, the author of this report proceeded to the house immediately with an escort of carabinieri. As news of the affair spread the crowd increased, as did their indignation, which was exacerbated by the sight of the young Amerigo Turchi covered in wounds and bruises and the cries of those parents who had lost their children and were calling out for vengeance. We were obliged to engage in hand-to-hand fighting to control the crowd and at this moment, although the people are somewhat calmer, it is nevertheless unsafe to venture outside the house, where we are besieged together with the accused Grandi and four officers of the royal carabinieri from Figline.

Reinforcements of carabinieri from the posts at Rignani and Pontassieve have already been requested and with their help it is hoped to be able to conduct Grandi to the prison at Figline this evening without incident. Then all the material evidence pertaining to the crime, of which there is a great deal, will be gathered, and legal proceedings will be initiated as soon as possible.[21]

Two mounted soldiers did arrive from Pontassieve to join Brigadier Achille Delú and the other carabinieri – Moroni, Trecchi and Felicione – who had been the first to arrive on the scene from Figline. They attempted to take the accused to prison but became more involved in keeping at bay the 'population not only of Incisa but the whole of the Val d'Arno, who had rapidly gathered there' and were threatening to set fire to the house, turning their threats onto the officials themselves for protecting Grandi's safety. Councillor Venanzio Ceccherini, the town clerk Francesco Forti and a few other of the more influential persons in the town applied themselves for several hours to the task of restraining the people, so as to avoid the worst. It was not until seven o'clock in the evening that reinforcements finally arrived in the form of three carabinieri from Rignano summoned by Ceccherini himself in a telegraph message relayed to all the surrounding carabinieri posts. And it was not until after nine o'clock, or even midnight according to some chroniclers, that by some unknown strategy Grandi was finally slipped into a carriage and transferred with a mounted escort to Figline, where another crowd was already waiting vociferously for him.

Thus the mission was completed, thanks to 'the firm and resolute behaviour of the armed forces', as Lieutenant Tedeschi informed the district commander of Florence who, in his turn, used the same phrase in his report to the public prosecutor.[22]

Sleep did not come easy that night. Exhausted though he was, not even Raffaello Chelini rested much. At four in the morning the conscientious magistrate had already set out for Incisa, which was more than five kilometres from his house, accompanied by the court clerk Antonio Comparini and by Bernardino Giaconi, Figline's municipal doctor. They were joined by Luigi Migliarini, the municipal doctor of Incisa.

In the town's main street, already then called the Via Petrarca, a little way beyond the central square, they entered the ground floor of number 43 and began to make a detailed inspection.[23] Beyond the wide double doors which locked and bolted from the inside only, was a room twelve metres long and five metres wide spanned halfway across by an arch. To the right of the entrance was another small door leading to the building's stairway. At the far end on the left was a window looking onto the alleyway which led to the Piazzale della Fiera. Half the floor was stone flagged but at the far end it was of bare earth, and there they inspected a small, irregular, oblong trench. The hole, twenty-five centimetres deep, had recently been dug, and all around it for about a metre the earth was soft. They only needed to shift the surrounding earth slightly to reveal 'pieces of decayed flesh'.

The news was already out. The day before, when the cartwright had been discovered attempting to murder the child and had taken refuge in the house, some people who had rushed to the spot in consternation were suspicious when they saw the hole where Amerigo was about to have been buried alive. Francesco Somigli reported that people were saying, 'there's something fishy here', and beginning to dig up the earth. A municipal guard who was present – Fortunato Piccioli, himself an Incisan – had ordered three of the men to dig: Somigli, a farm labourer, Torello Degl'Innocenti, a forester, and Ottavio Farsini, a kiln worker. The first shovelfuls brought up something which looked like a shin bone and then, at a hand's depth, they found three little corpses all in a row, which were immediately recognized as the children who had vanished and had so far been searched for in vain. Under the stairs, at a depth of thirty centimetres,

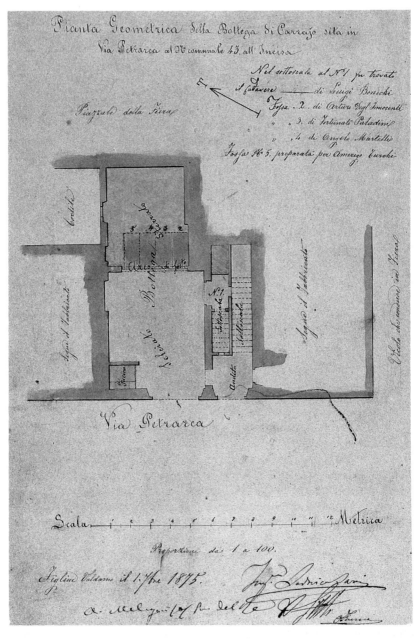

Florence State Archive, *Tribunale di Firenze, Processi. Assise 1875*, b. 818, f. 275.

they found a few bones which together were not enough to make up one body or even a head.

Then it was the turn of the two doctors to examine these remains in the presence of the magistrate. Their presence as officially appointed experts was required by law according to the Penal Procedure Code (Article 125). The code in fact forbade the exhumation of corpses who had died by violence or presumed violence before an official from the criminal police department had submitted a report upheld by 'the absolute declaration of scientific fact' provided by a doctor. Nor could the doctors Migliarini and Giaconi refuse to undertake this official duty, under pain of legal sanction (Article 159 of the Penal Procedure Code). They had to describe the corpses, exhume them and dissect them if necessary to ascertain exactly how those children, whom the Incisan doctor had known personally, had met their deaths. The doctors swore, as they were legally bound to according to Article 299, to carry out their prescribed duties honestly and in good faith and with no other aim than to discover the truth.

There were three corpses lying one next to the other. One lay on its side with the legs bent and the arms stretched along its back. The third was lying face down, the hands tucked under the stomach and the head more deeply buried, as was the head of the middle corpse, which was lying on its back with its mouth full of earth. The position of the corpses together with the absence of any fractures or wounds apart from facial ones, led the experts to conclude that their violent deaths had been caused by suffocation. However, both doctors requested and were granted permission to seek further verification.

There were further legal procedures to be conducted according to the requirements of the code. Thus it was that some three or four hours after the initial inspection, those townspeople who had known the victims personally were summoned and required under oath 'to tell the truth, the whole truth and nothing but the truth'. Degl'Innocenti, Piccioli and the municipal tax collector Pietro Tarchiani confirmed that the first corpse 'had been the boy Angiolo Martelli, son of Serafino and Clementina Bellaci, about nine years old and known as "Paschiarello"...that during the day of 22 August...he had been lost by his parents'. They also identified Fortunato Paladini, of the same age, whom they had also known very well. The boy's parents, Luigi and Maddalena Daviddi, had lost him on 21 August. They could not, however, firmly identify the other body, which was too small and ravaged by time. Nor could

they say anything about the various remains which had been discovered at the end. It was later confirmed and certified[24] that these
were the remains of the children who had disappeared on 18 March
1873 and 2 February 1875, Luigi Bonechi and Arturo Diotisalvi,
both four years old. The remains were then placed in four boxes and
carried with an escort of carabinieri to Incisa's town cemetery.

By nine o'clock the report had been written and signed, and
without stopping for a moment the magistrate returned to the Town
Hall, only a few metres away from the scene of the crime. After
having seen in the workshop how those four poor children had
ended up and what would have happened to the fifth if the alarm
had not been raised, the magistrate Chelini turned his attention to
Giulia's account. Basically it was thanks to that little girl in pigtails
that Amerigo had been saved and that the nightmare hanging over
the town was ended.

> Callisto Grandi, known as Carlino and nicknamed Prospero, a bachelor
> aged twenty-four years, son of the late Giuseppe, a cartwright born and
> domiciled at Incisa, detained and charged with persistent premeditated
> murder committed and attempted, of having treacherously and deliberately
> for motives of vengeance . . . violently taken the lives . . .
>   1. of Luigi Bonechi, aged four, on 18 March 1873;
>   2. of Arturo Diotisalvi or Degl'Innocenti, aged four, on 2 February
>   1875;
>   3. of Fortunato Paladini, aged nine, on 21 August 1875;
>   4. and of Angiolo Martelli, aged seven, on the 22nd of the said
>   month of August.
> Also of having treacherously and premeditatedly for motives of
> vengeance attempted to murder Amerigo Turchi aged nine . . . without
> success . . . in this endeavour contrary to his intentions and due solely to
> fortuitous circumstances.[25]

Approximately forty days after the arrest, on 9 October 1875,
this detailed charge was compiled by the Assistant Attorney General
of the Court of Appeal in Florence in his capacity as public prosecutor.
The charge was then presented at the court hearing when the prosecutor, Sante Dini, explained in language that was both objective
and rhetorical what conclusions he had drawn from the documents
passed to him by the judge's chambers. It was his speech which
provided the evidence to validate the charge and justify criminal
proceedings and to enable the accused to prepare his defence in an
informed and effective manner.

Grandi had been pushed to commit murder by 'the hatred he felt
towards the children of that town, who sometimes mocked his

physical deformities'. This much was clear both from the confession which the accused eventually made, after having initially denied the evidence, and from 'the fact attested to by almost all witnesses that he took it in bad part that he was occasionally the butt of jokes'. This then was the motive. If it appeared to be a slender one, stated the prosecutor, it was enough to bear in mind 'the inclination to arrogance and wickedness' which many people saw in the cartwright's character. He was a brutal man, sometimes even towards those closest to him. The many proofs of his wicked nature were listed: the 'calculated and insidious manner' in which he had lured the children; 'the laboured pretence' he had adopted during the search for the lost children whom he had done to death; the way he himself had spread 'the story that he had met a bad man in the woods . . . with such a sinister look' that people would assume he had come across the kidnapper; and the way in which he had given further credence to his story by an anonymous message which threw suspicion on a certain ex-convict in Incisa. Not only that, but during his interrogation Grandi had tried to explain the discovery of the bodies in his workshop by maintaining that they had been hidden there by certain local people who were jealous of his work and hoped to harm him and his family. All this was put forward as a series of facts to prove both Grandi's wickedness and his 'acute intelligence'. Intelligence which was proved, moreover, by 'his having raised himself to the head of his family', whose interests he apparently guarded 'shrewdly'.

Here then was the motive which justified the charge: that the murders were committed and attempted out of vengeance. It was equally clear that the crimes were premeditated. The proofs of this were his preparation of the holes in the workshop, the fact that he waited for the opportune moment, the threats he made 'to those who mocked him', and the 'obvious indifference' with which he killed the children when the time came. There was also his underhand manner of enticing his victims and his plans for the disappearance of a fifth child, the one he had not succeeded in killing. In the face of such a charge Grandi was likely to face life imprisonment.

The exact nature of the charge was communicated to Grandi in prison, where the court bailiff whose duty it was delivered the prosecutor's summary on 22 October 1875. The grounds for prosecution were not included. In order to establish the legal validity of the charge, the assistant Attorney General of the Court of Appeal had had to consider both the documents relating to the preliminary investigations and the written conclusions presented by the prosecutor, which in turn were based on the findings of the examining magistrate in his investigations at the scene of the crime.

Thus a whole mass of documents, official statements, certificates and reports of interrogations accumulated both on the Attorney General's table and in the chancellery at the Court of Appeal where Sante Dini deposited them along with his summation. Pages and pages covered in handwriting – often tiring to read and couched in tedious and inevitably repetitive bureaucratic language.

This mass of documentation formed the bricks and mortar on which the judicial system was constructed, laying the foundations for the process of public trial and final judgement. Inaccessible to anyone – to the press, to the accused, even to the defence lawyers until the preliminary investigation was concluded – these documents were destined to be consigned eventually to the relative obscurity of the archives. Anyone with access to the paperwork would have been able to predict the outcome of the proceedings without necessarily having to attend all the court hearings. The law seemed to follow its own rigidly established rules, rules which were strange and almost incomprehensible to anyone outside the legal system. In 1890 a magistrate at the Court of Appeal in Turin was to complain that all too often the public criminal trial was merely 'the solemn public performance of the judicial drama' of which the 'dress rehearsal had already taken place in the examining magistrate's office.'[26]

There were many skilled interventions by experts between the initial and final phases of the proceedings but these were all over-shadowed by the secrecy of the process. Despite the fact that they all conformed to the same code, the various stages of the proceedings lacked continuity. The initial evaluation of the truth of events, which could only be assessed by the examining magistrate during the enquiries he co-ordinated as soon as the crime was discovered, tended to be diluted with the passage of time. The initial investigation might contain elements which were subsequently lost among all the legal documentation and were not always recoverable at the trial.

This certainly happened in the case against Carlo Grandi. Among the mass of papers which make up his criminal file, we can only decipher the various narratives and evaluate the subtle differences between them by turning to other sources of information. The important subjective responses and omissions which are meaningful in the light of what was or might have been said inevitably emerge from the weight of the impersonal, legalistic style.

The city magistrates

The train took approximately one hour forty minutes to travel from the station of Maria Antonia in Florence to Figline. A forty kilometre run along the Aretino–Umbra line, which had been constructed as far as Pontassieve by 20 September 1862, had then been extended to Rignano, Incisa, Figline and San Giovanni, and had reached as far as Montevarchi by 5 April 1863. Now the Roman Railroads Company was in deep financial trouble and was abandoning the Terentola-Chiusi line, which was due to have opened in November 1875.[27]

At a little before two o'clock on Monday, 30 August 1875, two distinguished if somewhat overheated gentlemen alighted from the train at Figline station. They were the Deputy Public Prosecutor and the examining magistrate from the Civil and Correctional Court of Florence. Giovanni Melegari and Agostino Satti were directed to the municipal prison, which that year had seen an unusual number of inmates: 136 had entered and 141 had left (nine having already been there on 1 January).[28] The prisoner whom the two magistrates were seeking was Carlo Grandi, whose case had been entrusted to them that very morning.

By this time the legal machinery was in full motion. Between 29 and 30 August the carabinieri commander had despached one report to the captain and another to the magistrate; the police comissioner had also sent one to the magistrate and in turn the magistrate and the commander had each sent one to the public prosecutor in Florence. The whole procedure was in accordance with regulations set out in the Penal Procedure Code which had been in force since 1 January 1866. The next step in the investigation was to gather all the proofs necessary to determine what criminal proceedings the public prosecutor would institute.

On Sunday Grandi had been caught in the act of committing a crime (Article 47) and immediately arrested (Article 64). On Monday all the police reports had already reached the prosecutor's office and had been placed in the hands of a magistrate who was charged with supervising all enquiries during his term as examining magistrate on the case. Included with the documents was the order for him to go immediately 'to the scene together with the public prosecutor's representative, the lawyer Melegari'.[29]

Agostino Satti had been born half a century earlier and was married with children. He had qualified at the Legal College of Reggio Emilia and gained his degree at the University of Modena.

He had been an examining magistrate since 1859, based in Florence since 1871.[30] As required by the regulations, he was first taken to see the arrested man, who was fatherless had neither wife nor any material goods, and was demonstrably a poor man.

> I am Carlo Grandi, son of the late Giuseppe and of Caterina Falugi, twenty-four years old, born and domiciled at Incisa in house number 72, the property of the Branchetti heirs. I am a cartwright, a bachelor, I am nicknamed Prospero, I have never been in prison.[31]

Thus began the first interrogation, within twenty-four hours of the arrest. For legal reasons the magistrate Chelini would not have been able to conduct the questioning. The gravity of the charge was such that if he had, he would have been required to pass the transcript to the public prosecutor, who would have repeated the interrogation himself. The public prosecutor did not have the same authority to repeat the process if the interrogation was conducted by the official examining magistrate alone. In the Grandi case, however, Satti always worked in the presence of the prosecutor's deputy, Melegari. In accordance with Article 231 of the Penal Procedure Code, the first questions were of a general nature, as in the examination of all witnesses: questions to ascertain whether the accused could read and write, if he had any possessions, whether he had completed his military service. Then followed the specific questions regarding the circumstances of the crime and hence the cause of the arrest.

The magistrate questioned Grandi at length. The cartwright at first denied all responsibility, accusing others of the crimes and outlining an alibi for himself. But in the end he confessed. Yes, it was he who had killed the four children and he had tried to do the same to Amerigo Turchi.

A statement running to sixteen pages was compiled by the court clerk, who was obliged to be present for the proceedings to be valid. It was his specific task to write down the whole content of the interrogation, 'both questions and answers ... without any abbreviations' (Articles 85 and 82). But Fiumi, the court clerk, did what was common practice and omitted to transcribe all the questions put by magistrate Satti. He only recorded two of the most crucial questions, and did not transcribe the magistrate's exact words. It is possible, however, to infer what those words probably were; indeed, in this case it is not difficult to guess.

Nevertheless, the omission remains and it is not merely an obstacle to a complete reconstruction of the interrogation. The incompleteness of the report highlights the ambiguity as well as the value of the testimony. The silence and invisibility of the questioner obviously renders what is recorded more problematic. It raises several doubts but at the same time often forces one to see the potential meaning of the recorded answers grow and multiply – meaning which clearly varies according to who was listening and in what situation the questions and answers were spoken and even in the light of further information which would later be added to that context. One particlar answer, for example, can be an appropriate response to several possible questions. One can hypothesize the questions but the ones actually asked by the magistrate may have been quite different. It is impossible to know how often various tricks and methods were employed to make the accused say something that would be better left unsaid, and 'suggestive' questions may have been put to him, although their use was formally prohibited by the code (Article 85).

The lack of coherence in the interrogation is not entirely due to the absence of the questions. One cannot necessarily presume a consequential link between question and answer. It is the very extrapolation of meaning and indefinable reorganization which often confers its own coherence on the words of one who spoke in that particular way in response to being questioned. It is not possible to decide conclusively how clearly each party sustained the respective roles assigned to them outside of the context of the particular interrogation.

Therefore, from a dialogue which was in fact often dramatic, there remain only the words of one of the protagonists, devoid of a voice, of silences, of pauses and variety of tone – words which were written down in the first person, according to the required procedure, so as to appear more realistic. To read them as they are set out, one answer after another, does in fact give one the impression of almost knowing the 'real story' which the accused had to tell, despite his lies. These are remarkable documents. Many records of trial proceedings present the testimony of men, women and in this case even children, who pass by without leaving any trace of themselves in the story. In this interrogation, paradoxically, the words come from the weak while it is the strong who retain the privilege of silence. The court clerk omitted the magistrate's words and left instead the altered phrases of the accused, which we cannot evaluate properly, fossilized in a presumed objectivity. The result is that Carlo Grandi, who confessed to murder on 30 August under interrogation while a prisoner at Figline gaol, becomes more easily understood and ultimately judged, and we gain a greater understanding and knowledge of the tragic events and the people involved.

The confession

'Last night at twenty-three hundred hours I was brought here to the prison by seven carabinieri who took me from my home at Incisa yesterday.'

'The carabinieri arrested me at my house and brought me here because the people wanted to kill me, and they were there in the main street opposite my workshop with pistols and rifles because they wanted to kill me.'

'The people wanted to kill me because they hate me and my family.'

'The people were angry with me about those children, and now I will tell you everything. On Sunday the 22nd of this month Bibi, the mother of Angiollo Martelli, came with a farm worker whom I don't know and they asked me if I had seen Angiolino, the son of Martelli, because he couldn't be found and they said they had lost him. I was involved in searching for that boy, too, and I did search for him; I searched until eleven o'clock at night together with Giuseppe Lodi, and he wasn't found and, Mother of God, I was in tears because he couldn't be found.'

'Angiolino Martelli was my relation because the boy's grandmother and my father were brother and sister.'

'Yes, Fortunato Paladini went missing too. His father is working in Venice as a builder; that boy was seven years old and they say that he too disappeared on Saturday the 21st of this month.'

'They found them all dead in my workshop.'

'I know they found them dead in my workshop; and that carabiniere told me – the smallest of the ones from Figline who brought me here last night.'

'They were saying they had found four of those children and they said they were all dead.'

'The four children found dead in my workshop were Fortunato Burchi, Arturo Degl'Innocenti, Angiolo Martelli and Fortunato Paladini.'[32]

'I knew all four of those children and they all lived near my home in the same group of houses.'

'Sometimes they came to my workshop to hang around, to play, and I used to warn them not to hurt themselves, poor little things, but I didn't send them away.'

'Fortunato Burchi disappeared from the town and was never seen again since the Feast of Candlemas which is in February, and Degl'Innocenti, said to be the son of Baracco, disappeared last Feast of Saint Joseph.'

'I was only related to Angiolo Martelli, not the others.'

'I know Amerigo Turchi as well, he must be six or seven years old. They say that Angiolo Martelli was nine years old, Paladini was seven, Fortunato Burchi's mother said he was exactly seven years old and they say that Arturo Degl'Innocenti was seven or eight years old.'[33]

'Yesterday at midday I was in the workshop in the inner part and that boy Amerigo Turchi was with me and the boy Tito Brachetti was also going to come in but his aunt called him away and I was left alone with Amerigo Turchi, and Amerigo fell down in the saws and he scratched his face all over and I gave him a couple of slaps and he fell and I gave him the slaps because he threw stones at me.'

'It must be a fortnight since Amerigo threw stones at me and hit me in the right knee and he threw them at me because he said I had stolen a nut from him.'

'It was Tito Brachetti who asked me yesterday if they could play "nocino"* in my workshop and I told him and Turchi – you idlers, aren't you ashamed of yourselves? – but so as not to look bad I did let them go and play "nocino" in my workshop.'

'Argenta Monsecchi, who is a thief and lives right opposite my workshop, and both she and her husband wish us harm and they have duplicate keys to my workshop and there were two gimlets missing and a pair of pliers and a lot of other stuff.'

'Yesterday this woman started shouting out to people when Amerigo Turchi was in my workshop and she was shouting that there was a child crying in the workshop, that is my workshop, and people came and opened the door by breaking the latches and they came in and found me and Turchi.'

'The workshop has two doors, one inside and one out and only the inner one can be locked. The outer door is closed by a latch inside.'

'I went into the workshop yesterday morning at half-past eleven by the outside door on the main street, and Tito Brachetti and Amerigo Turchi were there and when I was inside with Turchi I closed the door a little with the bolt and Brachetti went away.'

'Last Saturday evening it was my Aunt Gigia who closed the workshop doors.'

'My workshop is partly stone-flagged and partly an earth floor.'

'During the last month the workshop was half stone-flagged as I said and the boss did not want it all to be flagged and I did want it all to be flagged and Venanzio Ceccherini wanted the stone flags to stop at the arch.'

'There are two spaces under the stairs in the workshop and the first one is for keeping wine in and the second one is for wood.'

'They found three of those dead children in the earth floor of the workshop where the stone flags end and one under the stairs where the wood was kept and I know that because some people were saying it yesterday morning and I heard them telling everyone.'

'Paladini and Martelli were buried in the earth floor of the workshop and so was Arturo Degl'Innocenti. Fortunato Burchi was under the stairs.'

'No, I certainly did not dig that hole, that was made by the one who has the

---

* A children's game played in Italy at the time, similar to marbles but played with walnuts.

duplicate keys to our workshop, whose name is Michele Monsecchi, a cartwright who works at Incisa and lives there near my workshop.'

'And the others, that is Burchi, Degl'Innocenti, Martelli, Paladini were killed in my workshop by Michele Monsecchi and Natale Bruschi of Incisa because they were jealous of my work.'

'Yes, those boys taunted me and were cheeky and called me "Baldy", but I told them that my head is no home for lice.'

'There is great enmity between Bruschi and Michele Monsecchi and us, and they killed all those children in my workshop and even buried them there so that when it was discovered we would all be thrown into jail, but luckily I discovered it yesterday when I went into the workshop with Turchi and saw that hole dug and a great mass of earth, and they would certainly have brought the sand in from outside, that is Argentina, the wife of Monsecchi who called all the people yesterday.'

'There was even a basket there in the workshop full of sand and earth and they had covered it with my overalls to hide it.'

'I haven't done anything, I did not kill those boys and if I had murdered them I would kill myself and I would have thrown myself onto the rails under the train when they brought me here yesterday in the carriage.'

'It is not true that I threw Amerigo Turchi into the hole.'

When it was put to the accused that not only was it true that he had prepared the hole in which to bury the victim alive in his own workshop but that he had already thrown handfuls of earth onto him and had used a basket of earth to cover the boy Amerigo Turchi when the boy's cries alerted the neighbours and thence the people, who forced an entry to the workshop where they discovered the subject of the interrogation intent on burying Amerigo Turchi, and that he would in fact have murdered and buried the boy in that manner as he had previously done to Fortunato Burchi, Arturo Degl'Innocenti and Angiolo Martelli:

'No, sir, I did not murder them, and Monsecchi and Bruschi who have duplicate keys killed them and buried them in my workshop out of professional jealousy and to make us all be sent to prison so that they could get the work at the farm at Pian di Cascia where we are doing the work now.'

'They have the keys to the door from our workshop to the alleyway and they entered our workshop in the daytime and at night when we were away at work.'

'It must be three months since we realized that someone was going into our workshop, because the tools were missing as I have said.'

'No, sir, we did not report the theft because we have others of those particular tools.'

'We had the lock to our workshop changed two days ago by Vannucci, the locksmith at Regello nicknamed Sorcino, and he came to change it last Friday exactly.'

When he was asked how Bruschi and Monsecchi could have entered his workshop the day before to dig a trench and carry earth to where they buried

Turchi, seeing that on Friday the 27th of this very month the lock to the same door had been changed:

'It must be that the old keys open our new lock as well, however different it is.'

'I have no witnesses to show that Bruschi and Monsecchi have the duplicate key to my workshop.'

'I remember definitely that on the day of Candlemas when Fortunato Burchi, son of Boneca and Assunta disappeared, I was at Loppiano seeing to Capraija's cart which needed repairing and the farmer Martino made me paint Capezzoli's cart. I went there at five in the morning and came back home at eleven at night and when I returned I found the women all looking for the child. On the eve of Saint Joseph when the other boy, Arturo Degl'Innocenti went missing, I was at Tracolle painting a cart belonging to a certain Tarchiano Michele, a peasant. I went there at four in the morning and came home at five in the evening. On Saturday the 21st when they were missing and even when Martelli was missing, I was at Prulli collecting wood from the farmer Ottaviano. I went there at three in the morning and returned home at one, and I was accompanied by my brother-in-law Antonio. On Sunday the 28th when Paladini went missing, I was at home and I was reading the Bible, both Old and New Testaments and the Graduals.'

'The aforenamed Bruschi took legal action against us for injuries, saying that we had called him a thief. The case was here before the magistrates and we paid eighteen francs and Bruschi gave us a receipt. I want to make them suffer, suffer, not die at once but suffer a bit, cut their fingers off then set fire to the Bruschis and Monsecchis both husband and wife if I can get out of here.'

'In my workshop Bruschi and Monsecchi must have made the holes like they did yesterday to put Turchi in, when they killed Burchi, Degl'Innocenti, Martelli and Paladini; then they must have put them alive into the holes and forced them down, then covered them.'

'In my opinion Bruschi and Monsecchi took them to my workshop and buried them in the daytime during the hours of rest when we were in bed.'

'Even in February, midday was a time for rest and people went to bed.'

'We stayed in bed for two hours then went back to work.'

'There were three of us working in the workshop – me, my brother Mariano and my brother-in-law Antonio Bellacci.'

'No, no, our workshop was not shut, it was open all day during Candlemas, the Feast of Saint Joseph and Saturday the 21st, and Livia Bellacci of Incisa kept an eye on the workshop. She is eight years old.'

'On Candlemas my brother was at Tracolli and my brother-in-law at Pero; on the eve of Saint Joseph my brother was at Pero and I was with my brother-in-law at Loppiano and on Saturday the 21st I went to Tracolli to fetch the wood.'

'We didn't know anything about those boys being buried in the workshop and under the stairs because in the workshop there's a lot of sawdust scattered everywhere so we didn't see anything.'

'We scattered sawdust over the earth like when you sow grain.'

'We didn't smell any stink in the workshop.'

'I am much to blame for what happened yesterday because I would have killed him if he hadn't screamed and if people hadn't come to free him.'

'Write it down, Master Judge, that I am guilty of everything and I killed them all.'

'I killed them for revenge because one day Boneca, Fortunato Burchi's father, painted my face with Minio's paint brush and my face was marked for three days because it was oil paint and it was the child Fortunato Burchi who painted me and not his father; and at midnight on the eve of Candlemas he came into the workshop and I had dug a hole under the stairs in the workshop so I could put him in it as soon as he came into the workshop. He came, I carried him to the hole, I threw him in and covered him with earth and put the wood on top. Arturo Degl'Innocenti came into the workshop on the eve of the Feast of Saint Joseph and played the trick of throwing three pounds of paint at me. I gave him a blow with a shovel, I killed him and I buried him there in the earth floor of the workshop and I dug the hole quickly because the earth was soft. Angiolo Martelli crapped in my coal, I killed him and I buried him in the hole with his face up and I put earth in his mouth and covered his whole body with earth and I sprinkled sawdust over the earth. On Sunday morning on the 21st of this month Paladini came into my workshop but actually it was four in the afternoon when he came, I had prepared the trench, I made him get into the trench and I covered him with earth but first I had strangled him with a cord and I burnt the cord. That boy pushed me once and then he always called me "Baldy". The Turchi boy always threw stones at me, he always called me "Baldy" and I prepared the hole and I made him get in, I emptied a basket of earth on him to bury him but he lifted his head up, he started to shout, people ran up and I escaped to one corner of the workshop and then into the house and so Turchi was saved.'

'I never told anyone about having buried those boys in the workshop and about having killed them, but yesterday I was discovered and now there is no use in my carrying on denying it, and I have confessed the truth because I am guilty and my family are all innocent and they knew nothing, nothing and I killed them myself without anyone's help.'

'All the boys in Incisa taunted me, mocked me, teased me, called me "Baldy" or "Twenty-one-toes" because I've got six toes on one foot, they called me cross-eyed and a dwarf and they made faces at me and they always played some trick on me when they came into the workshop and then when I had killed four of them they left me in peace.'

'Believe me, I threw two of them down into the hole, I strangled them and I covered them with earth and the other two I killed by throwing them into the hole and dropping a grindwheel onto them, then I covered them with earth immediately. I strangled Paladini and Martelli and I dropped the wheel on Burchi and Degl'Innocenti, then I covered them with earth. That one yesterday was strong and escaped from the hole. I prepared the hole for Turchi on Saturday at midnight.'

'When I did these things, I shut myself alone into the workshop, I made the hole with the hatchet and nobody realized anything because those boys had no time to scream. Now I have confessed they won't condemn me to death, I am afraid of death but not of forced labour because I have always worked and I like working and freedom means nothing to me. Please tell my family to send me my jacket and I repeat that I am happy to do forced labour for life, because if I went back to my town they would kill me.'

'I hit them in the back with the wheel and they were killed outright.'

Read, confirmed and signed

Carlo Grandi

Crime or politics

That evening, when the storm which had been threatening finally broke, Agostino Satti must have been reasonably satisfied. The Grandi case had not appeared to present any particular problems from the moment he first received the files. The murderer had been caught in the act; there were already a number of witnesses' statements which all tallied, especially that of the surviving victim; the dynamics of the crime had been reconstructed and the bodies of the earlier victims identified. The fact that the corpses had been found in the accused's workshop confirmed that he was responsible for the mysterious disappearances of the children and finally relieved the anguish which had gripped the town for over two years.

At that point all that was lacking was a confession. And now Judge Satti had managed to obtain that in the course of his first interrogation of the accused. He had drawn on his twenty years' experience in criminal investigation to wear down the murderer's protestations of innocence and no doubt he had used the innate facility with words for which his superiors paid him tribute.[34] We do not know how it was achieved nor precisely what Satti said. It would appear that at one point he threatened to throw the whole of Grandi's family into prison and to shut down the workshop for good.[35] Whatever he said, the fact is that suddenly the accused admitted everything, gave his motive for the crimes and furnished a lengthy and truthful account of events.

Naturally the magistrate had to check certain details and ascertain further information. He had to fulfil the official requirements, including expert opinion at the scene of the crime, identification of the bodies, autopsies etc. . . . All this involved him in routine work which would keep him busy for several days but was not complicated and not at all controversial.

On various occasions Satti had found himself involved in political and judicial controversies, and things had been particularly difficult for him over the past year. Attacked by populist agitators and under pressure from powerful figures, his name had featured in the Florentine newspapers together with not entirely admiring accounts of himself and his professional work. This gave some cause for anxiety to his superiors at the Court of Appeal, who appreciated Satti's talents and yet would gladly have seen him transferred, as they requested the minister, 'to some other post'. The Procurator General of Florence favoured Satti's transfer to Sicily, 'where the firmness of character and the energy with which he is gifted' could be put to good use.[36] Satti, who had been at Grosseto from 1868 until moving to headquarters in 1871, had attracted a great deal of antipathy in Tuscany, possibly because he had held a fairly delicate position 'for too long' or perhaps because he displayed 'excessive zeal'. He usually came under attack from the more extreme factions, but even the *Opinione Nazionale*, the politically independent daily paper, had criticized him strongly in the autumn of 1874 during the tense pre-election period.

Florence had been in turmoil for months. The police had been informed of insurrections planned by the Tuscan-Emilian internationalists, which were apparently due to take place on 8 August at Pontassieve and on the 12th and 13th at Florence. They acted immediately, carrying out searches which were largely fruitless. The Prefect ordered thirty-two democratic associations to be disbanded and there were about a hundred arrests among people of widely varying social standing and political affiliations.[37]

This proved to be an over-reaction, and many people were unjustifiably imprisoned on the basis of insufficient proof. The *Opinione Nazionale*, like other pro-government newspapers, implied that the political right had taken advantage of the danger from revolutionaries to impose measures which struck not only at internationalist anarchists but also at republicans and democrats. The political trials were awaited with impatience. But in Florence, unlike in other main cities, the investigating stage of the legal process never seemed to advance any further.

The fault was Satti's, announced that same liberal newspaper on its front page. Innocent people were waiting for justice in Murate prison while he was taking more than a month's holiday in the country. There had never been 'such widespread public indignation'.

The magistrate heard all sorts of things said about him: that he had a cold heart, that he was not worthy of his position and that he was trampling on the universal values of justice.[38] At one point it was even revealed that he had a personal interest in the matter: the magistrate wanted to buy some land from one of those accused of the events of August 1874 and had promised to release this Marquis Grifoni, although he could hardly be said to be in sympathy with the insurrectionists.

Satti had an even more serious problem. Ten days before the political elections of November 1874 certain insinuations against him had appeared in the press. The accusation came from a very influential member of the Florentine democratic party, the lawyer Salvatore Battaglia, who had collected several preferential votes, particularly from the College of Santo Spirito, even though he had not correctly presented his candidature. Battaglia stated that Satti was not conducting the legal process honestly but 'to further the contrived police plots'.

Agostino Satti took the matter to court and the affair went on for two years. He had no choice, since Vigliani, the Justice Minister, had personally ordered him to bring the charge in a peremptory telegram of 30 December 1874. Almost simultaneously Battaglia was imprisoned for the events of August after lengthy police enquiries requested by the Ministry of the Interior. At the ensuing trial, however, the public prosecutor had to ask for the case to be dropped for lack of evidence.[39]

On 30 August 1875, when Satti received the file on the Grandi case, the jury in the Florentine court were about to acquit forty-one of the forty-three defendants of 'conspiring against the security of the state and internationalism'. Initiated on 30 June 1875, the last day of August thus saw the conclusion of one of the most important political trials brought by the government.[40]

For the magistrate who had gained a reputation of harbouring secret pro-government leanings, the chance to deal with a country murderer must have come as a relief, almost a diversion from his problems. He would not be coming up against powerful people or ideologies nor have to negotiate with his superiors. He would not be involved in party political intrigues nor would he have to exercise a political balance of which he was incapable. Finally, he would not be given any sleepless nights by an antagonistic press, since he was himself the father of a large family. Indeed, the newspapers which were already focusing their attention on the Incisan crime could not fail to admit that Satti was the one who was seeking the truth and moving the wheels of justice towards the verdict and sentence which the public demanded. They could not fail to agree in condemning the ferocity of the crimes committed by the wretched brute, nor could they fail to be moved by the thought of the poor, innocent victims.

Moreover, it was with this type of crime, in which the evil was obvious and horrendous, that Judge Satti usually displayed the qualities which had distinguished him at the outset of his career, when he was said to be 'distinguished by many fine gifts, particularly his perception and memory ... and for immediately unravelling the crux of the matter.' He was exceptionally hard-working and his moral conduct was 'praiseworthy in both private and public life'. It was for all these qualities and for the fact that 'apart from intelligence he has a great command of his mother tongue and a facility with words' that the president of the court at Parma had 'urged the government to make good use of this civil servant's attitude and great good will while he is still young.' This testimonial made him perfect for Tuscany; nevertheless, in January 1878 they were to dismiss Satti with a consolatory promotion. On 29 August 1875, however, the president of the Court of Appeal in Florence still recognized in a report on Satti his 'distinguished ability ... great knowledge of criminal law and praiseworthy industriousness'.

The witnesses and the child Amerigo

The child used his very best handwriting. First his surname Turchi, then his Christian name Amerigo with curling capital letters. He outlined the edges of each letter in ink to make them look good. It was a slow process, certainly, but those gentlemen from Florence who asked so many questions were kind to him and wouldn't mind waiting until he had finished. The child was satisfied with his third signature, and the men hurriedly added their names to his. Most of the others from Incisa were only able to sign their testimony with a cross. Even his father, whose name was Sebastiano and who was a woodcutter over sixty years old, and his mother Rachele, who worked at home and was a little younger at forty-eight, had both marked their crosses. But he, the youngest in the family, could read and write. He had told the magistrate gentlemen that straight away. He went 'to the teacher's school'.[41]

It seemed that everyone wanted to know what had happened to him two days ago, and when he told his story they all looked at the scratches on his face, neck and hands. It was a good thing he was strong. Even the gentlemen waiting for him in the municipal offices had wanted to hear his story at six in the morning on Tuesday, 31 August. His parents had taken him there but he had gone alone into the room where they questioned him and had told them every detail at once.

He had tried to escape from under Carlino; he had shouted 'Oh, daddy, oh, mummy, he's killing me!' His mother, who had gone out to look for her son in the street, had heard him and had realized where Amerigo's voice was coming from: 'I ran to the door of the workshop and I beat it violently with my hands and I was shouting to people, "Come quickly! My son's being murdered!"' And her husband did eventually arrive but first came Guido Perini, then the blacksmith Giovanni Cioni, who forced the lock and opened the door.

'I found my son lying under the stairs and Carlino was on top of him' stated Sebastiano Turchi, who had hurried to the workshop because of his wife's screams and because little Giulia Monsecchi had come to warn him. 'I asked him something, I don't know myself what it was in all the confusion, and Carlino answered that my boy had thrown a stone at him, but that's not true because my son has said he was dragged maliciously into the workshop.' 'No, it wasn't true at all,' agreed Rachele. That was an excuse Carlino invented because someone asked him, 'What have you done to this child, you scoundrel?'

As soon as the door had been broken open she had fallen down in a faint. But she knew it anyway and she wanted to tell his worship the judge how brave and strong and courageous her Amerigo had been and how when they rescued him he looked just like an 'Ecce Homo'. Satti, out of politeness as well as legal practice, could not interrupt the mother as she declared proudly 'that my son fought bravely and for a long time ... and he made a great effort and bit two of Carlino's fingers. Carlino told him to let his fingers go and my son told him, "You let me go, you're killing me."'

The child still bore the marks of the struggle. The magistrates counted about forty scratches on his face, on one arm and on his hands. They even measured the scratches with a ruler and they looked him over again and again, even more than his mother and the town doctor had done that day. The doctor had told him that all the scratches would be gone in three days' time.[42]

If providence hadn't saved him or rather, added Rachele Turchi, 'if I had gone looking for him one minute later, my son would have been as dead as the others.' Amerigo knew it. Everyone was saying so (the adults had no worries about talking in front of the children); he would have disappeared and been buried alive like his friends. He remembered that last Saturday when they couldn't find Fortunato, and Angiolino had said, 'Poor Fortunato. Strangers have taken him.' And then on Sunday they were together 'playing near the poulterer's'. But that evening Amerigo knew that Angiolino wasn't there any more either, and 'they were saying that he had been taken by strangers too.'

The circumstances and the discovery of the crime as they appeared in the police reports were more or less confirmed by the witnesses. A dozen people were questioned on the same day: the victims' parents, the grave-digger and those who had been the first to find the bodies. Agostino Satti and Melegari listened while Fiumi, the ubiquitous clerk, carried on writing down all the answers and none of the questions.

The Turchis were the first to state separately that Grandi had intended to kill other children – twelve, to be exact. They had 'heard people saying so'. Commissioner Baciocchi took care to inform himself further, and on 31 August he sent a list of presumed victims to the examining magistrate. It was to have been Tito Brachetti's turn on the evening of the 29th, the ten-year-old Franco, son of Giuseppe. He had been with Amerigo that Sunday morning chatting with Grandi, but had not been asked into the workshop. Then Tito had gone home because his aunt had called him from the window. Among others destined to die were supposedly 'Cecchino, Amba's son, known as Cecchia's son and . . . Narciso Bruzzichelli, Vincenzo's son'. But those were only vague rumours and so far there was no proof whatsoever.[43]

The Public Security official discovered something else interesting in the course of his enquiries amongst the townspeople and referred to it promptly in the same report:

> The probable reason which decided Grandi to commit such foul deeds seemed to centre on the fact that he was endowed by nature with an unfortunate, almost ridiculous, shape and on the streets was often the butt of the children's derision, and was so upset by these insults that he decided to take his revenge (by killing) all those who were too weak to resist him.

In fact, the accused had admitted as much during his first interrogation. Satti was able to go deeper into this question with the witnesses. 'We boys used to call Carlino "Baldy", "Dwarf" and "Twenty-one-toes", and he used to chase us and throw water at us with a brush he had in the workshop, but we escaped and he couldn't catch us and he used to throw the broom at us.'

This was related by Amerigo Turchi. His mother confirmed the fact that yes, the children used to mock Grandi, but 'they called him a dwarf and "Baldy" in fun, as a joke and he used to get angry and become pure poison.' He used to chase them in vain, and she had once heard him shouting at a boy who was teasing him, 'If I catch you, you'll pay for it!' But they were only boyish pranks and she had told him, 'Carlino, you're behaving like a child yourself.' Sebastiano Turchi and Giuditta Degl'Innocenti, the mother of one of the victims, both agreed that the children enjoyed teasing him because he was bald. Giulia Monsecchi, who was three years older than Amerigo, knew rather more about it: 'They used to throw his hat onto the ground and up in the air and they used to say "You've got twenty-one toes, aren't you ashamed?" . . . and he used to get irritated . . . and he even threw the broom at them and he used to shout . . . "You'd better not come into my workshop, if I catch you there, I'll have you!" '

Clementina Martelli, on the other hand, the mother of Angiolo, whom Grandi had killed ten days before, claimed that 'the wretch . . . was not tormented by the children.' Another of the victims' fathers, the labourer Anacleto Bonechi, stated that he personally had 'never mocked or scorned him'. Witnesses who were not related to the missing children confirmed to Satti that the wretch was the constant butt of mockery. The twenty-seven-year-old furnace worker, Ottavio Farsini, had been present many times when the children were chanting, 'Baldy, Baldy' at Carlino. He threatened them in his turn saying, 'mind, you'll pay for this!' The twenty-nine-year-old policeman Piccioli and the eighteen-year-old scripture student Alessandro Daddi had heard the same. 'It's true that the children taunted Carlino to make him shout, and they used to go into his workshop and make him all confused.' There was also the testimony of Venanzio Ceccherini, a fifty-two-year-old landowner and a town councillor: 'Grandi was a target for the boys, who made him shout and rage'. During the last carnival festivities he had dressed up and gone around with a gang of the boys wearing a placard on his back on which he had written 'FROM BAD TO WORSE' in big letters. Was this a menacing warning, as was later said in retrospect, or simply a 'carnival buffoonery'? According to him, he was imitating a gesture which had remained proverbial in the town from when, twenty years earlier, his own father had exhibited the same words in protest against a disagreeable priest. Whatever the reason, once again on that occasion Carlino, with his large paper hat on his head, had drawn forth ridicule from the women and shrieks from the children. How many of the boys actually tormented him? Lots of them, answered Giulia, but then she added that she didn't remember the victims being among them. The boys who did the taunting were the bigger ones and so managed to escape from Carlino.

Arturo was not even four years old. He was the eldest, since an older boy had died three months after birth and Robertino was barely eighteen months old and soon fell fatally ill. So, after having had three sons, Odilone and Giuditta found themselves alone to mourn them. Degl'Innocenti, also called Diotisalvi, recalled before the magistrate how his son often went down to Grandi's workshop, which was right below their house. 'He went there to hold the tools and my child even had a little hammer which he used to play with.' 2 February was also a feast day and that morning his mother had left him there in the street while she went home to do the cooking. It was cold, but he was wearing 'his little boots and socks and he had a red beret on his head, a black cloth smock with a pale blue border and little white cloth trousers.' He remembered it well. When he went to call Arturo an hour later because the soup was almost ready, he couldn't find him. The father did not know what 'this child could ever have said to Carlino', nor did he know anything about him spilling paint on the cartwright's face (as Grandi had alleged) or anywhere else. All both he and his wife, who was questioned later, could say, was that they had never had any disagreements with Grandi and hadn't suspected anything.

Assunta Bonechi, a forty-year-old labourer, said the same. Some of the boys, the bigger ones, used to tease the cartwright, but her Luigi was too little, not yet four years old, he could 'never have done such a thing'. He was the smallest one. They had had six children in all and half of them were already buried. She took him with her whenever she could, when she wasn't working in the fields. He went with her when she did the cleaning for the tobacconist's wife, when she went to buy meat from the butcher or if she went out on some other errand. She held his hand in the road and sometimes bought him little sweets to keep him quiet, and then they would go back to the Francalanci house. If Luigino didn't want to come, as he hadn't that day – she had been pregnant then and very near her time – she would let him go to his aunt Agatina, who lived near Grandi's workshop. It was the Feast of Saint Joseph, and towards nine o'clock she left him in the square and watched him making his way alone towards the fair. She could still see him with his little blue and white striped cotton socks which she, his mother, had made him, and a pair of his uncle Giovanni's trousers 'made of black wool with the little waist which fastened at the back...the little jacket was of home-spun wool with small brown squares and yellow stripes.' Then the woman told the magistrate, 'and then I went into the Francalanci house, I put the meat in the oven, then I had a little coffee and only fifteen minutes after leaving my son I went out into the street again.' She went to her sister-in-law's, who had caught sight of Luigino 'for a moment round there on his own'. But then she had lost sight of him, at first not giving it a thought. It was normal for even quite small children to wander about and play around on their own.

Further testimony came from Maddalena Daviddi, Paladini's thirty-two-year-old wife and the mother of two young girls. Her only son had disappeared about ten days before 'as though the earth had swallowed him up'. Affortunato was nine years old, but he was not as strong as Amerigo and had not been able to put up a fight. 'Poor little thing, he was a bit delicate and sickly and to think that that wretch Grandi buried him alive,' the mother agonized, 'he trod on him with his feet.' Her child was timid and had never upset anyone. As for her, she had never done Carlino any harm and nor had her husband, who was away working 'over towards La Spezia'. He had not been home for a year and only sent her just enough to live on.

The motive

Why Carlo Grandi should have decided to kill those four children was still not at all clear. Amerigo didn't know, nor did he know why Carlino wanted to kill him too. His answer to the magistrate's next question was negative: 'No, sir, Carlino didn't unbutton my trousers nor did he strip me, he didn't touch my arse or my belly, he only made me lie down stretched out in the hole.'

'Carlino is not a lecherous man and does not chase women,' explained Rachele Turchi. According to her, it was unlikely that he had 'killed those children in order to abuse them', and the judge was mistaken in thinking it. Those people who had been present when the little corpses were dug up stated that they were neither naked nor half-clothed, although the evidence of the experts apparently stated that the two smallest corpses, which had deteriorated considerably with time, had been buried naked. It was only possible to make judgements relating to the most recent victims, however. The twenty-nine-year-old Francesco Somigli, married with children, did not think that Grandi 'had done filthy things with them', and the policeman Piccioli, also twenty-nine and married, confirmed that he had not done anything to the bodies.

At half past five in the afternoon of the following day, 1 September 1875, when the sky was cloudy and the Arno was swollen by the previous night's downpour, the medical experts Migliarini and Giaconi conducted the autopsy in the graveyard precinct of Incisa. They confirmed that the well-preserved bodies of Fortunato Paladini and Angelo Martelli bore no 'sign or trace of sexual violation'.[44]

Rachele Turchi was sure of it. Grandi had killed the children 'from pure malice and hatred'. When questioned, she added that she 'believed that his family . . . is innocent, they knew nothing and had no idea of anything at all and they are a good family.' Her husband, too, was inclined to believe that Carlino had acted from hatred 'because he harbours ill will towards those boys'. Giulia had often heard similar things going on in the house next door. She said she had heard Carlino quarrelling with his mother many times: 'he said he wanted to kill her and his mother said . . . actually she kept quiet, and Carlino also said his brother-in-law was not welcome in the house, and Carlino was wicked,' the little girl concluded.

His reputation in town was that of a wolf in sheep's clothing. According to Odilone Diotisalvi, 'he went to church' and 'he never swore and he went to confession.' He had seen him having several conversations with Father Brachetti when he had been alive. But then it was common knowledge that he bullied his family, who were all afraid of him. They were above suspicion, a fact agreed to by the witnesses Luti and Francalanci.

Most of the victims' parents said they could not understand why he should have killed their sons. 'He must have killed them for sheer wickedness,' said Maddalena Daviddi. Angelo Martelli's mother said, 'He is a scoundrel, but even so it doesn't seem possible that he is capable of such actions.' In fact her other son Alpinolo, who had been going to the cartwright's workshop since he was twelve to learn the trade, had never realized anything was going on. 'A rascal,' said one of the fathers, Anacleto Bonechi, although according to him, 'at first he seems simply to be a fool.' Clementina Martelli did not agree: 'he argues well, like a judge,' she assured the magistrate. Ottavio Farsini swore again that as far as Carlino's family were concerned, 'there is not a word to be said against them and the whole town is convinced that they are blameless.'

Cunning as well as resentful, so some people described him. He trapped the boys by trickery with the enticement of playing hide-and-seek, insisted Turchi and Degl'Innocenti. The mothers of Amerigo and Affortunato declared him to be a malicious liar who had pretended to look for the children when they had disappeared. They, the little Monsecchi girl and the municipal guard all recalled that Grandi had spread the story that he had met a bad man who would have killed him if he could.

The municipal usher had been one of the party who searched for the stranger in the woods and his interrogation brought forth new information. On 23 August, a day after Angiolo Martelli had disappeared, just as Ottavio Focardi's grandson Arturo, his daughter Giuditta's boy had done, Focardi found an anonymous note near Ernesto Nannoni's workshop. He thought it referred to the missing children. The note was now in the possession of the Public Security officer at Figline, and the magistrate therefore sent a written request for an explanation to the commissioner. The response was the very prompt delivery of the 'fragment of writing' received on the 27th of August.[45] Further enquiries were called for.

Meanwhile, on the basis of what they had learned from the witnesses, Satti and Melegari went back at six o'clock to question the accused again. Grandi confirmed that he kept the accounts for his house because he was the head of the household. He corrected certain details of his victims' names and the time of the crimes. He insisted that it was not true that he had wanted to kill any other boys, it was not true that he had made a list as was being rumoured in town.

He had already told the truth and he had nothing else to add. Why had he killed them? 'I repeat . . . because they mocked me and because they came into my workshop and played all sorts of tricks and sending them away was like trying to swat at flies.' The magistrate pressed him for details and this time the clerk finally wrote down the question: why had Grandi let two years elapse between the first and second crime? Grandi explained that after having buried the first child in March 1873, he had spent many months working on farms outside the town, and he was left in peace. But when he came back to his workshop the usual torment started again: 'those boys threw my cap on the ground to see my bald head, especially Martelli and Paladini, and they never left me in peace, not even in church.' The magistrate

'ought to know that I am a miserable man, that I have every deformity, that everyone in Incisa and Figline mocks me and I would have liked to be a thousand miles away, and when they saw my bald head they collapsed with laughter and I could feel myself eaten up with rage and I would have liked to have killed them all, even in church, so great was my bitterness.'

With these words the interrogation ended. Satti then requested the carabinieri at Pontassieve to allow Grandi to be transferred from the prison at Figline to the Murate prison in Florence.[46]

'It grieves us to have to relate a horrendous crime, one of those events which we fortunately witness very rarely.' On 31 August 1875 *La Nazione* announced that 'the child killer'[47] had been discovered in Incisa. In these first reports, the readers were given a fairly accurate picture of how the murderer was discovered, the nature of the 'horrendous sights' in the workshop and the condition of the 'poor little boy'. Further particulars were revealed the following day in an article which concentrated on two points: the brave Turchi child's account of events, and the intervention by the local authorities and the forces of law and order in the face of the angry crowd.

Celestino Bianchi's newspaper was not the only one to concentrate on the dark tale for many days. The *Gazzetta d'Italia* was his main rival, although it shared the same moderate right wing ideology. On 31 August the *Gazzetta* published a lengthy report written from Incisa two days earlier.[48] This, the readers were assured, would present 'every minute detail concerning the atrocious events'. Indeed, the author showed that he had followed the enquiries accurately and gave much praise to the officials involved, giving their full names, most especially 'our honoured friend, the lawyer Chelini', magistrate of Figline.

The report began with a description of the profound grief suffered by the 'warm-hearted populace' with the disappearance of the first two children and of the fruitless search in the town's four mill ponds. The author then moved on to the rumours which had begun to spread about 'gypsy kidnappers and witches who kill to make candles out of human fat'. He also dwelled on the more realistic hypothesis that 'an extraordinary malevolence' was involved. The account went on in considerable detail to the point at which the murderer was discovered, although it included many errors which show that the author cannot have been very familiar with the places and people of Incisa.

In *La Nazione*, on the other hand, the full report which was promised daily did not in fact appear until 4 September. When it did appear, it included an assessment of the probable motive explained in words and concepts similar to those used by the Public Security official in his report. Grandi's deformed and ridiculous appearance were described, his very irascible nature and his decision to take revenge on the boys for their insults. Three days earlier the same newspaper had reported that Grandi 'gave no one any cause for complaint; he was well thought of and had many friends and acquaintances.'

The *Gazzetta d'Italia*, however, had immediately reported that local people believed the cartwright's 'brutal tendency to murder' came from his hatred of the boys because of their constant mockery. But the person who interested the reporter more than anything or anyone else in the affair was the 'child killer' himself.

He presented a powerful portrait for his readers. He had seen Grandi in person, and had seen the 'repulsive look' of his head and face. He described certain details in almost phrenological terms, of which he had some knowledge. In the writer's opinion, the cartwright's physiognomy – which Grandi himself had apparently portrayed in carriage paint on the wall of his workshop in the form of a devil with a scythe and four severed heads – displayed some bestial instinct rather than a lack of intelligence. His intelligence appeared to be 'only slightly below average', and indeed the reporter mentioned Grandi's cunning in ordering the workmen to pave only half his floor and leave the other half bare earth. Moreover, the murderer had made calm, stubborn denials during the magistrate's interrogation. Part of his alibi was that if he had killed the suffocated children his clothes would have been bloodstained. Not only that, but when 'he was pressed with questions he said, "But do you take me for an idiot? I can read and write better than you and I have read such and such a book."' From all of this the anonymous reporter, who was clearly unaware of the inherent contradictions in Grandi's statements, deduced 'the reasonable intelligence of the accused'.

Readers of the more scanty report which first appeared in the *Opinione Nazionale* on 30 August learned on the contrary that 'the kidnapper and child murderer is a little, twisted, deformed man who is, moreover, mentally deficient.'[49] Who knows whether the examining magistrate had time to follow the newspapers' commentaries on his case. They all made several errors, including maintaining that Grandi had denied all the charges, whereas in fact he had confessed immediately.[50]

Satti was extremely busy throughout the whole day of Tuesday, 31 August, summoning the witnesses and nominating the draughtsman Lodovico Sarri of Figline, a bachelor of twenty-nine, to accompany him and Melegari to inspect Grandi's workshop. He then had to ensure that Sarri drew up a detailed description and plan of the place, 'with expertise and in good conscience'. He ordered various documents from the commune. He had to arrange for the grave digger, Giovanni Donnini, to bury the remains in Incisa cemetery at half past five the following morning after the doctors had performed the autopsy and the bodies had been identified by witnesses.[51] He also had to pass on several instructions to the Public Security officer and, together with the prosecutor, meet many of the country people, with whom it was often not easy to communicate.

From six in the morning until six in the evening, for twelve hours without stopping, they questioned fifteen people and the accused. Luckily the magistrate Agostino Satti was able, as prescribed, to call on the help of the local magistrate, who examined five of the witnesses that morning.

These five witnesses were not related to the victims, apart from Assunta Bonechi, a labourer, the mother of the first child to have been killed two years earlier. As far as it is possible to judge from the recorded answers, Raffaello Chelini adopted a line of questioning which was quite different from that being used by the examining magistrate and the prosecutor. He did not ask whether Grandi had been motivated by revenge, he did not look for proof that Grandi's hatred for the boys was ill-founded. He never asked how bad Grandi's reputation was nor when and how he displayed ill will and malicious cunning. It would seem superfluous for the witnesses to describe Grandi's physical appearance, since the officials were able to judge for themselves, nor did Satti ask them to do so. But the witnesses questioned by Chelini commented specifically on Grandi's appearance either at the beginning or the end of their testimony, and on another matter closely connected to it. Chelini asked about, or at least the answers provide the witnesses' opinion of, Grandi's mental state and whether, in their judgement, he behaved normally or not.

Giovacchino Francalanci, fifty-five years old and married with children, was certainly in a good position to know what was being generally said in town. He owned the tobacconists shop in the square where the Town Hall stood, and where the men usually met in the evenings to talk. The tobacconist was used to being at the heart of things and he liked to hold forth and pontificate on all subjects, possibly because he did not come from Incisa but from Regello, a larger town in the Valdarno. Francalanci was comfortably off, rich enough anyway to afford domestic help for his wife, and so the magistrate questioned him first, for at least an hour.[52]

Naturally the shopkeeper knew 'the young man Carlo Grandi . . . His appearance is fairly revolting since he has no hair and he is a rather repulsive and ridiculous figure.' Grandi never conversed with the other men in the square. Francalanci did not consider him to be cut out 'for conversation with serious, sensible men, as much by his manner as by his lack of intelligence'. On the previous Thursday and Friday evenings, however, he had appeared in front of the tobacconist's shop and started telling the story about the man he had met in the woods. He gave such incredible details, though, that the shopkeeper claimed not to have believed him. In fact, he became so fed up that when Grandi started to tell his story again on Saturday evening with his usual melodrama, 'I lost my patience and as I was in the shop I told Grandi, who was outside, "stop telling these fairy stories once and for all and go away."'

'"Oh, does it look like rain?" the shoemaker said, as though to show that Grandi was talking nonsense or was mad,' explained Francesco Luti, who worked in front of the cartwright's. He told the magistrate that he didn't think Grandi was 'really mad' because he had a trade and looked after his own interests and was even very keen on making money. 'But he certainly had moments and ways of behaving when he didn't seem quite as sane as other people.'

'He is physically deformed,' repeated Francalanci, 'he is certainly not highly intelligent but he has always been able to do his work though with no great skill.' It was true that he looked after his family's interests, in fact, 'he always wanted to be boss. His brutal ways and his constantly argumentative nature meant that his family always had to give way to him . . . for the sake of keeping peace.' The forty-eight-year-old Antonio Benucci, another shoemaker, had not believed Grandi's story either and remembered a certain strangeness about him: 'He was taciturn and thoughtful and when I asked him what the matter was he announced very abruptly "I'm alright, I'm always alright."' He was hard to fathom: 'Sometimes he showed cunning and astuteness and at other times he appeared to be half-witted.' He was certainly 'physically deformed and the boys often . . . made fun of him.' Flavio Masini, a nineteen-year-old cobbler, thought that Grandi 'felt his deformity deeply'. Masini agreed that 'in general Carlo Grandi reacted and was alert to his own interests and appeared to be aware and intelligent, but he sometimes gave signs of being mentally deficient.'

Argenta Monsecchi, the illiterate, forty-year-old house servant, had already said as much on 30 August at half past nine in the morning at the Town Hall. She was Giulia's mother and had been the first adult witness questioned in the early stages of gathering information about the accused and his motives for the crime. She had declared that 'Grandi sometimes did things that made you think he was a bit weak in the head.'

> It was I Domenico Lesio who put the
> Hat and at 10 was at the Fagiolo with a
> Stranger who had a bundle[53]

This was the sibylline message written in an unknown hand on the sheet of paper found by Ottavio Focardi. When he was questioned again Focardi explained that Fagiolo was a country hamlet about a mile and a half from Incisa. There was in fact a man called Lesio living there whose first name was Pandolfi and who was a sheep trader. Ceccherini recorded that the man had been the subject of official warnings and a supervision order. During his third interrogation on 4 September, Callisto Grandi said that the man Lesio was a 'quarrelsome rascal', but that he had never had anything against him. As for the hat mentioned in the message, it seems likely that this was the straw hat which Fortunato Paladini had worn and which had been found under the arches near the Arno. 'I threw it in there after I had killed him,' said the murderer, 'so that they would be able to find it again.'

Judge Satti sought help from Sebastiano Donnini, a forty-two-year-old Florentine expert in calligraphy, whom he asked to compare the mysterious note 'with a sample of Carlo Grandi's handwriting'. The expert made every effort to find similarities between the two hands, though they are not readily apparent from the originals in the archives. He claimed to discern consistently 'rough, unpleasant characteristics' in the broken links, uneven down-strokes and 'heavy pen strokes'. On the other hand, he had to admit that he could not swear to it. The few samples of Grandi's signature with which he was provided were meagre indeed on which to base a comparison, particularly in view of the fact that while in prison Grandi had already begun to exhibit a mania for writing. But nothing more was sent to Donnini, even though the magistrate had a legal duty to provide experts with everything 'necessary for the convenience and accomplishment of their task'.[54]

Grandi declared that the note, which was shown to him in his cell, had not been written by him. He continued to deny that he had written it even though the magistrate untruthfully told him and officially reported that the 'calligraphic expert states that the note was written by the accused'.[55] And at that point, on Saturday, 4 September 1875, the initial investigation was ended.

The charge

Agostino Satti's duties did not end there, however. He next had to provide a viva voce report on the Grandi case to the two members of the court in chambers, where he had to present all the evidence, enquiries, expert testimony and other elements which might be called on by either the defence or the prosecution in an eventual trial. Every element had to be given its proper balance for or against the accused, and the examining magistrate had a duty to be unbiased in his search for the truth.

This was all set out in the Penal Procedure Code of 1866, which was at that very time under discussion by the authorities because of the difficult and ambiguous role assigned to the examining magistrate. The magistrate was only supposed to assess the facts but in reality he could not help but be selective in some sense if the investigation were to advance at all. Thus it was inevitable that for reasons of personal inclination, intelligence or temperament the examining magistrate might give more weight to certain evidence and build 'onto this an overly narrow structure of proof, ignoring other elements which might be very important in the opinion of a good judge'.[56] Some critics of the system also pointed out that the examining magistrate all too often 'considered the accused a wily character who was out to deceive him', and that this attitude conflicted with his duty, which was to protect the accused and either prove his innocence or provide justification or mitigation if he were found to be guilty (Article 233).

The anomalies did not relate only to the particular character of a magistrate, but were also inherent in the very process of indictment. Some people believed that the contradictory nature of the role could only be remedied by removing the figure of the examining magistrate altogether. Among these was the lawyer Luigi Lucchini, who had founded in 1874 the very authoritative *Rivista Penale*, a publication devoted to improving existing legislation. Most people believed at least that the examining magistrate's functions should be reduced and that he should be given greater autonomy. So long as the examining magistrate remained an official of the Criminal Police

Department he would always be subjected to excessive influence from the ministry. The rights of the defence were consequently given less protection than had been afforded by the principles of the mixed system and the various amendments which had existed in the pre-unitarian code.[57]

It is important to be aware of these problems and controversies even while concentrating on the actual judicial procedures with which Agostino Satti, the Public Prosecutor Melegari and the other magistrates on the case were involved. The lawyers Agostino Bandini and Francesco Biancini, judges at the Correctional Court of Florence, had been appointed to court chambers at the beginning of the year by the president of the Court of Appeal (Article 198). There were in all three members of the chamber, of which Agostino Satti was the third. After having listened to Satti's report in the presence of the public prosecutor, Giovanni Melegari, the chamber would then assess Melegari's own deposition. All this was done so that the three members of the court chambers could fulfil their required tasks: to establish whether the investigation was complete, and then on the basis of their decision either to give orders for the accused to be released or to confirm the charge and set procedures in motion for a criminal trial. Even in this phase, which was strictly regulated by law, it was clear that the examining magistrate's role served to accentuate the defects of the system, because his dual function in court chambers meant that he sometimes acted as a simple reporter of facts and sometimes, along with the other two members, had to make decisions based on his own report.

The deputy prosecutor, Giovanni Melegari, did not lack a certain effective rhetorical style, nor was he slow to display this style when on 6 September 1875 he presented his deposition against Callisto Grandi on eight pages of paper headed 'Public Prosecutor's Office, Civil and Correctional Court of Florence'. The style was concise, the sentences very short, the phrases effective, albeit dry; the narrative of events was in the present tense. His judgements were put forward unclouded by any element of doubt and supported by arguments which were didactic rather than probing.

Melegari had been through the whole judicial process and had been alongside the examining magistrate throughout all the interrogations, expert testimony and other enquiries. It seemed to him now that charges of actual and attempted murder and the motive for the crimes were sufficiently justified by the murderer's confession of 30 August. Melegari declared that this confession alone provided 'full and sufficient proof – both objective and subjective'.

Grandi had admitted during interrogation his desperation because of his many physical handicaps and because everyone 'taunted him and split their sides laughing at him', and how he felt himself 'eaten up with bitterness'. Here alone lay the explanation for the crime: 'hatred and a passion for revenge' had been brewing in a malevolent spirit and the bitterness grew greater with every insult, however tiny. This was the prosecutor's theory, even though he himself said that the prisoner had at one time asserted that he had never 'been annoyed by the insults he suffered daily because of his deformities'. The deposition went on to state that the knowledge of his own weakness and deformity produced a great rage in Grandi, and his 'obsessive need for defence and great desire for retaliation' became stronger with each derisory taunt.

Melegari invited the judges to consider the murderer's psychology, which he, albeit with little knowledge of the subject, oulined as follows:

Grandi was *cowardly*. Unable to attack the strong, he was cruel to the weak, 'wreaking his revenge indirectly on them'. The ultimate proof of his cowardice was that he himself feared death.

He was *cunning*. He had spread false rumours about strangers, planted one of his victims' hats to be discovered, 'and pinned up the anonymous note', all to deflect suspicion away from himself.

He was *savage*. 'He enjoyed the thought of revenge.' This was demonstrated by the carnival episode remembered by two witnesses when Grandi walked through the streets wearing the placard saying 'FROM BAD TO WORSE' to warn or threaten his fellow townspeople. In his own words he preferred to make people 'suffer, suffer . . . and not kill immediately'.

He was *quarrelsome and bullying*. 'He is always threatening and cursing even his own family.'

Melegari pre-empted the possible objection that the motive ascribed was 'unjust and irrational' in the same way that the prosecutor in the court would do during the trial, by stating that it was indeed just in view of the accused's 'vicious nature'. On this point the prosecutor Melegari, the examining magistrate Satti and later the prosecutor Dini all agreed in their reports.

Raffaello Chelini held a different view. According to him, Grandi had simply been impelled by 'a brutal, malevolent impulse', with no particular reason[58] – not for revenge nor with premeditation –

contrary to the deposition, which stated that the crime was undoubtedly premeditated and showed all the marks of having been
conceived and planned thoroughly before the act was committed. As
further proof, the document quoted the 'pretence of friendship'
which Grandi adopted to attract his victims. This was evidence of
the most dangerous form of insidious behaviour and was recognized
as such by the entire Tuscan penal school, according to the teachings
of Francesco Carrara.[59]

On 7 September 1875[60] the court chambers decided that Grandi
had acted with 'deception, premeditation and from motives of hatred
and vengeance'. A few more facts were added to the public prosecutor's deposition: that Grandi had nursed 'the intention of continuing with this massacre of innocents', since some witnesses
confirmed that he had announced that other children would disappear; and that on 29 August he had 'offered the same enticements
to the ten-year-old Franco Brachetti to go into his workshop to
play "nocino"'. The boy himself had omitted this fact from his
statement.[61]

Finally the court chambers, represented in the persons of Bandini,
Bianchi and Satti, decided to accept 'the public prosecutor's deposition in every detail'. They therefore confirmed 'the legitimate arrest
of Carlo Grandi', at present in prison, and on the same day, 7
September, they ordered that the facts be passed on to the Attorney
General. This was a necessary stage in the proceedings prescribed
for the furtherance of the course of justice (Article 255) if the facts
of a case constituted a crime which came within the competence of
the Court of Assize.

Within ten days of receipt of the documents, the Public Prosecutor
was supposed to prepare his case for the Attorney General and
notify the accused of its contents (Article 422). Sante Dini did not
in fact complete this duty, as we have already noted, until 9 and 22
October, respectively. After the latter date, all the documents which
had up until then been subject to secrecy were lodged in chancery so
that the accused could, subject to a written request, allow his own
lawyer access to them (Article 423). In this way the defence not only
learned the precise motives attributed to the accused but could also
draw on the information gathered during the investigation to represent impartially the two conflicting interests of society on the
one hand and the accused on the other. The law also allowed the
defence to make use of those elements in the investigation which
had been rejected or interpreted differently by the prosecutor in
order to serve his own ends.

But Grandi, in his prison cell, did not think of choosing a lawyer for himself. The defence lawyers were appointed on his behalf by the Court of Appeal in Florence on 7 February 1876, more than five months after his arrest.[62]

2

Carlino and Public Opinion

Dramatic action

The doors were about to be opened. No sooner had the usher Pepi given the order than a flood of people poured in noisily, pushing, pulling and bumping into each other, and almost immediately the courtroom was crammed full.

By nine o'clock, apparently, the little square of San Pancrazio, on the corner of via della Spada and via della Vigna Nuova, was already crowded with about 1500 people – and this despite the fact that it was a working day and the weather was cold. No more than half of them would be able to get in but even so they all waited, squeezed and crushed together.[1] They all wanted to see in the flesh the murderer who was finally about to be judged, sixteen months after his arrest. And they wanted to see for themselves those poor women, the mothers of the five children, who had come to Florence to see justice done and who would find themselves face to face with that wretch after such a long time.

Thus at half past ten on 18 December 1876 began the trial against Callisto Grandi, 'charged with premeditated murder and attempted murder'. There were guards positioned in the corners of the court-room, and two others paced among the uneasy, fairly mixed crowd. The country people could be spotted immediately, just as they could on Fridays when they mingled with the city folk in the market in Piazza della Signoria. All Florentines prided themselves on recognizing the country bumpkins who never travelled by horse-drawn omnibus. You only needed to look at them, at their faces, hands and shoes, the very way they moved, and you only had to hear them speak. Now, however, in court, in these particular circumstances, things were different. This time the country people were looked upon with compassion and respect, especially the families of the dead children.

In the court-room dedicated to Saint Pancras, the avenger of all perjurors, most people had come out of curiosity. There were common people and distinguished men and even some ladies with their daughters. The most elegant of these had installed themselves in the gallery overlooking the dock, a prime position for which a ticket of invitation was required. There were ordinary working people, shopkeepers, some journalists, various students and university professors and colleagues of the lawyers and experts who had a specific or general interest in this highly topical case. That morning *La Nazione* had announced that 'both from the legal and the psychological point of view, the case cannot fail to carry great importance.'

Opposite the public sat the members of the court, presided over by Giorgio Mori Ubaldini, councillor at the Court of Appeal and holder of many titles. He had worked in the courts of the city of his birth since the days of the provisional government, and he was naturally a fairly well-known figure even though he lived quietly with his mother and two sisters. On either side of him sat the judges Filippo Petrucci and Agostino Bonini. The president himself announced their names at the opening of the hearing, while close by the clerk, Tommaso Grossi, leaned over large sheets of paper writing and writing as though nothing would escape him.[2]

Further along was Sante Dini, the public prosecutor, and on the defence benches the lawyers Carlo Galardi and Ernesto Papasogli. They were all dressed in black, but the details of their apparel differed somewhat. The public prosecutor's woollen robe was open, the long sleeves were gathered with white cuffs and there was no ribbon on his cap.[3] According to legal practice, he always stood bare-headed to speak. It was easy to distinguish him when he was speaking even from a distance because Dini was a man in his sixties, whereas the defence lawyers were both comparatively young.

The jury – fourteen men in all, including two supplementary members – sat opposite the accused. They would be presented with the numerous testimonies, including the accused man's confession. Nineteen witnesses had been called by the prosecution and another fourteen by the defence, a group which, according to *La Nazione*, included some very distinguished people. A bench had been placed in court for the five expert witnesses who had been charged with conducting a special study of Grandi and who would also contribute by giving evidence. Thus, in the temple of the law, everything was ready.

But at the last moment one member of the jury could not be found. Another had already been granted dispensation from official duty after sending in a written justification. So the court had to call again on the thirty jurors who were liable for duty in that particular session dating from 11 December, so that a new jury could be selected behind closed doors. The court was cleared with great difficulty amid much pushing, shoving, confusion and protest. What on earth was happening? Few people knew what was going on or indeed would have been able to understand the technicalities. Then the doors were reopened, the same crowd poured back in and the president went to great lengths to place everyone in the same seats so as to contain the general unrest. What were they waiting for? When would it start?

Suddenly, everyone's attention was riveted. The door behind the dock closed and the accused was led forward in chains by the carabinieri. 'Good day to all these gentlemen!' he exclaimed in a loud voice, courteously doffing his hat. Astonished whispers ran through the court-room.

> Callisto Grandi of Incisa is a small man . . . little more than a metre in height . . . his head is out of proportion to the rest of his body, he has a large, bald, shiny scalp covered at sparse intervals with a light down which, they say, grew while he was in prison. His forehead is low and receding, he has hardly any eyebrows and his eyes are small and shiny like two brown stripes slanting upwards towards his temples. He has sharp, high cheekbones, a pointed nose, his mouth is a lipless gash marked by a short, rudimentary, faded, yellowing moustache. He has a square chin and a strongly developed jaw.[4]

He had taken some care with his clothes: 'a fairly decent jacket and waistcoat' and a white cravat tied tightly at his neck.

The legal procedures continued. The president recited legal formulas and articles in a monotonous voice and complex language, the court clerk read out the usher's duties with regard to the missing jurors, the judges held a secret consultation then made a pronouncement read out by the same clerk, the lay assessors listened to the president reminding them of their duties, and other procedures must also have taken place which eluded even the keenest observer. While all this was going on there was plenty of time to study the looks and manner of the accused, at least for those few who were close enough, since once he had sat down Grandi was completely hidden by the dock. He seemed calm, if a little uncertain. He often turned to the tall, uniformed carabiniere standing beside him and gazed up at him as though the guard gave him a sense of protection.

'The accused will stand. Give your name and surname.'
'My name is Callisto Grandi, telegraph operator.'
'Are you married or single?'
'My wife is the Madonna ... I'm eighty years old ... I'm an artist in Incisa.'

Did he really say such nonsense? A few of those who were present and not likely to be disbelieved, such as Dr Enrico Morselli, said that he did.[5] The newspapers did not report the murderer's words, but then they were not allowed to do so. Once the trial had started the journalists were 'obliged to maintain silence in accordance with the famous Article 49', noted the well-known Yorick in the columns of *La Nazione*. A recent law of 8 June 1874 forbade the press from reporting on criminal trials before sentence had been passed under pain of a fine and sequestration. The law's intention was to leave the jury unbiased, but the effect not only reduced the freedom of the press but actually went against the 'principle of public information' which was supposed to pertain to trials. After numerous complaints, the extremely unpopular law was to be abolished on 7 May 1877. Meanwhile, however, and throughout the whole of Grandi's trial, journalists went through every contortion possible to get round the bare 'account' permissible by law and to wriggle out of the censor's straightjacket. Yorick in particular managed this brilliantly. Otherwise, they conformed to the regulations by omitting evidence, cross-examination and all or part of what was said during the hearings.

Nor were the accused's strange answers transcribed in the court records. The clerk was not obliged to do so – it was enough for him to confirm that the president had asked certain prescribed questions and to state what these related to. Once again this meant that the words of the witnesses and the accused were inevitably omitted or altered beyond recognition, built into an artificial coherence couched in technical language and jargon.

The terms of the code itself made it inevitable that the transcripts of the trial were meagre and inexact. Since the sentence of that particular court was not open to appeal there was no need to prepare precise records in readiness for possible use in the Appeal Court. The clerk was not obliged to transcribe the evidence of witnesses or experts. The 'spirit of the law', the principles of orality (the judges passed judgement based solely on what they heard and saw) and routine procedure all meant that many of the accused's answers went unrecorded. Nevertheless, if the answers he gave during the trial differed in any way from those recorded during the investigation, then every change or addition had to be recorded or the trial could be deemed invalid. This was the case, however, only if it were requested by the president or one of the barristers; once again, therefore, it depended largely on individual interpretation.[6]

Mori Ubaldini clearly did not consider that Callisto Grandi's statements contained any elements which were significantly different from those he had made to the examining magistrate Satti; nor, apparently, did the defence lawyers. But the fact that the accused declared himself to be a telegraph operator instead of a cartwright and married to the Madonna instead of single was not only new and false testimony, but showed a disrespect for the court which made the public even more indignant. It may have been an attempt to have himself declared insane and therefore unfit to plead – unless, of course, Grandi really was mad.

For the judges the question would have been a complicated one. There were methods of distinguishing simulated from real insanity in every legal and medical textbook and all of them recommended caution, since the mental state of one who had committed a crime changed the whole picture and made it impossible to judge the crime itself. The prosecution insinuated throughout the trial that the child killer was feigning insanity, without it ever being openly stated and neither, therefore, openly refuted.

None of the nineteen pages filled by the clerk Grossi during the first hearing, nor any of the subsequent ones, contained any reference to a word or manner on Grandi's part which could raise any doubt as to his mental state. All the same, two separate questions regarding his mental health were issued by the president himself and these were transcribed in full, as was legally required. It is not clear why or at what point in the judicial process these questions arose. The issue of insanity had not arisen in the investigation conducted by Agostino Satti, nor in the formal confirmation of the charge on which the trial was based. And yet according to the code, the question should have arisen at the initial stages if further enquiries in this direction were considered to be necessary.[7]

The initial investigation had been deemed complete and ready for trial on 7 September 1875. But on 18 December 1876, during the first public hearing, Mori Ubaldini posed the question 'whether Grandi committed the crimes in the full awareness of his actions and with freedom of choice'. It was as though the whole case were suddenly re-opened. The entire motivation had to be reconsidered, not just one particular aspect of it. This was the unexpected new element which marked the opening of the public trial.

What had happened between the end of the very hurried initial investigation and the beginning of the trial fifteen months later? Certainly there would have been bureaucratic holdups and various delays in the legal process due to the mass of paperwork involved. But how and at what point did the crucial question of the self-confessed murderer's mental health arise? The request for Grandi to be submitted to an expert psychiatric examination came from the defence lawyers who had been appointed on 7 February 1876, when the president of the court discovered that the accused had still not engaged a lawyer of his own,[8] five months after the arrest and barely a month from the proposed opening of the trial.

Carlo Galardi and Ernesto Papasogli had not lost any time. They were young, fresh from their studies and, to judge from their behaviour, fairly combative. Even though their client was not an important person but only a miserable country cartwright, and even though his crime was vile and horrible, the two lawyers put their hearts into their task. They knew they would be up against a public prosecutor who was much more experienced than they. Dini's reputation in Florence was that of 'a Cato, with a vigorous incisiveness not only against the accused but also against the defence lawyers'.[9] Galardi and Papasogli's first official action, even before attending to their list of witnesses, was to request clearly in writing that experts be engaged who, as they specified to the president, 'should be questioned during their due attendance at the trial and *according to the criteria of their own discipline* about the accused Grandi's mental state in general and with particular reference to the acts forming the substance of the charge'.[10]

Their request was received the following day, 2 March 1876, and the public prosecutor was notified. The medical experts chosen by the defence were due to present themselves at the opening hearing on 9 March. Two days before, on 7 March, the public prosecutor Dini, having read through the defence list of experts and witnesses (which had been presented on the 3rd and 4th of the month) and having deduced that the line of defence was likely to be that 'the accused was not responsible for his actions because his handicaps affected his judgement', decided to act accordingly. He requested that other expert witnesses, equal in number to those called by the defence, should attend the trial and speak for the prosecution. And he wanted them to be given time to assess Grandi's mental state before the opening of the trial.

This was a dramatic move. The trial was adjourned until a later session and the defence lawyers and accused were advised of the postponement. The witnesses were told not to present themselves before a date which was still to be decided. A jury was re-elected from the current session's list and the trial reconvened for the next quarterly session. All this was done so that the president, having accepted the public prosecutor's 'request, demand even', could nominate expert witnesses for the prosecution. He took some considerable time to do so, more than five months. On 23 August 1876 Mori Ubaldini finally elected two doctors to pronounce on the 'mental state of the accused', Callisto Grandi. The trial was then fixed for 15 September at nine o'clock.

But on 11 and 12 September the court usher, Ildebrando Lucchesi, had once again to go round to the homes and offices of all the lawyers, doctors and witnesses and even to the accused in prison at Murate, to tell them all of yet another setback. This time the problem concerned one of the experts who, due to an unspecified 'serious inconvenience', had been obliged to leave Florence. The lawyers explained the matter to the illustrious president and persuaded him 'that professor Morselli was an expert witness who was indispensable to the defence because his colleagues had put him in charge of all the study and research necessary to give a serious judgement at the trial and that without him the other experts would not be able to do so'.[11]

Another three months went by and the whole process involved in postponement was repeated. And so it was that the public trial of the child killer finally opened on 18 December 1876 in via dell' Arme 10, in the court of San Pancrazio.

Carlino 'the victim' and decent people

Why did the lawyers Galardi and Papasogli decide to call in expert witnesses? Did they mean to base their defence on the accused's absence of responsibility? They certainly would not have got this idea from the examining magistrate's report, nor from the written depositions of the two prosecutors – Giovanni Melegari in the first stage and Sante Dini in the second. If, however, they had examined the police reports closely, they would have come across some interesting clues, particularly in the enquiries conducted by Chelini.

Even before that they may have been alerted to the possibility in a much more direct manner during their visits to their client in prison. They met him, and learned from the prison staff of his strange behaviour and how certain people of standing, including doctors and professors, went to Murate prison to see and talk to him whenever possible. The two lawyers, who lived in the centre of town in the Santa Maria Nuova area, may have been personally acquainted with some of Grandi's visitors. Florence was a small city and people enjoyed chatting in the street where rich houses sat side by side with poor ones, or discussing affairs during the soirees which were held among intellectual and political circles. There had even been commentaries in the press which reflected various people's impressions and shades of opinion. Perhaps the two lawyers remembered them. They must certainly have read the newspapers and they clearly took account of public opinion in their dealings with their client.

He had barely been discovered in his workshop on the point of killing yet another child when the *Opinione Nazionale* gave a description of him: 'The mysterious kidnapper and child killer is a little, twisted, deformed man and moreover he is *of unsound mind.*' This had certainly been said about him in the town at the time, although that newspaper never referred to it again and from then on took the view that he was definitely responsible for his actions. The next day, on 31 August, in the *Gazzetta d'Italia*, the reporter from Incisa provided a detailed portrait which considerably impressed the readers. The cartwright Grandi

> has a definitely revolting appearance. He is very short, has no beard growth and is bald, but with an extremity of baldness which is unique, particularly in that age group. His skull is quite large but has several protruberances here and there and a furrow running across the top of the forehead which is neither high nor particularly low. His eyebrows are fair and partly conceal his small, deep-set, bluish eyes. He has a short face with certain bony protrusions which, together with his lashes and his expression, give him the look of an orang-utan. There is a mild prognathism in his upper jaw. His temperament is lymphatic and extremely cold.

The anonymous reporter stated that Carlino had a moderate intellect, only slightly below average. It seemed to him that the murderer's physiognomy indicated a bestial, primitive instinct rather than a lack of awareness. An interpretation so arbitrary and so uncomplimentary towards peasants in general was clearly unsatisfactory, but it certainly aroused the interest of anthropologists, doctors and psychiatrists as well as stimulating the imagination of the general reader – more so than the first report in *La Nazione*, which had confined itself to a physical description of Grandi as 'a short little man of twenty-four without . . . a hair on his head'.[12] The report in *La Nazione* referred to Grandi's ugliness mainly to explain why he had been taunted by the town children. Indeed, a debate was initiated in the newspaper on 22 September on that very subject, entitled 'Concerning the child killer'.

Under this heading was a letter to the editor about the events which had devastated Incisa, deploring once again the ferocity, cowardice and cruelty involved. The letter did not, however, refer only to the murderer. The writer said that he did not know whether the murderer had been 'more cretinous or cruel', but claimed that he had been 'driven to crime by the mockery' that the town boys subjected him to; 'they taunted him and mistreated him continually, even in church while he was praying.' And all because Grandi had the misfortune to be deformed. It was impossible to deny that the vice 'of ill-treating the handicapped is unfortunately common among us, particularly in small towns . . . the children take their lead from grown men.' The letter pointed out that the innumerable sayings and stories about the deformed and the feeble-minded reflected the popular attitude to human weakness which, in certain cases, is so vicious as to touch 'the hearts of all kindly people'.

Such wicked habits should be corrected, and the problem was deliberately addressed in the books especially written for children, the populace and for country people whose education was considered so important by the directors of *La Nazione*, Lambruschini, Ricasoli and Capponi; they decided to make it one of the main objectives for moderate Tuscans.[13] Even a witty writer like Carlo Lorenzini, already famous in the pages of *Fanfulla* under the pseudonym Collodi, dedicated a few pages to moralizing against the evils of mockery. He wrote, for example, about a sickly little boy who suffered greatly but in silent resignation from his companions who teased him for his weak appearance. He called the little boy Carlino. This was also the eponymous title of a story in the very timely children's book first published in 1875 in Florence, where the author of 'Pinocchio' lived, contributing to various newspapers and working as a theatrical censor in the prefecture. The appalling events in the Valdarno cannot have escaped his notice.

Teasing people and mocking them with rhymes and ridiculous nicknames is always bad; but then to humiliate unfortunate people and to humiliate them because of those very illnesses and physical defects which they cannot help at all is not only cruel but seems to me to be truly cowardly.[14]

Lorenzini makes the wise doctor Boccadoro deliver this moral at the end of Carlino's story, and this was more or less the same attitude adopted by those who publicly defended Carlo Grandi of Incisa. The first to do so was the Umbrian writer Luigi Morandi, a thirty-one-year-old teacher of Italian literature at the Technical Institute of Forlì, an ex-supporter of Garibaldi and a pioneer of circulating libraries in Italy.[15] In his previously quoted letter to *La Nazione* he recalled how the cartwright had constantly complained that they 'never left him in peace even for a moment' and that nobody took his side. Morandi did not find the appalling consequences so surprising: 'It is natural that this cowardly and pitiless taunting should drive the victim to fierce and desperate measures.' He drew certain conclusions which the newspaper defined as 'both opportune and just' and he made a vague proposal that everyone should do everything they could 'to eliminate this ugly habit wherever it exists', whether it be the public authorities by applying legal sanctions or simply by decent people using their good sense and good hearts.

From Figline came a reply from the magistrate Raffaello Chelini, who was pained and surprised at having been named by the author of the letter. It was absolutely untrue that 'the magistrate had laughed in Grandi's face when he appealed for help'. Grandi in fact had never appealed to the prefecture at all and the only time he had been there was when he was answering a summons for damages which had later been withdrawn. Chelini agreed with the main substance of the letter. The Umbrian professor was absolutely right, in fact after the murderer's arrest he himself had spoken to the few influential, cultured people in Incisa, asking them to 'teach the townspeople to correct their bad habit of mocking those unfortunate persons who suffered from physical defects or ugliness.'[16]

Specific support for Morandi's proposal appeared in *La Nazione* on Saturday, 25 September. As an example of a possible initiative which might be established to support the afflicted, the teacher had already mentioned the Society for the Protection of Animals, which had been started in Florence in 1873. From the same city, Professor Mario Manfroni added that the recent revival of compassion should not be confined to 'four-legged animals alone'. It would be more admirable to display 'concern for those unfortunate people whom nature, circumstance and misadventure have left deformed'. Not only that, but it would be a more genuine feeling than an excessive affection for dogs and cats, which could be considered a neurosis rather than genuine goodness of heart. Certainly animals should be protected but so should the most disadvantaged of men: a double analogy in which the only difference appeared to be among the protectors rather than the protected. Appealing to common sentiments of kindness, Manfroni professed to be convinced that the protectors of animals would be glad to extend their care to afflicted people. In both cases the enemy was the same: not the snare of the dog-catcher nor the vivisectionist so much as the anonymous hordes of 'insolent urchins'.

The idea of founding a new society – and there were already so many – whose aim would be 'to protect the unfortunate, the mentally deficient or the deformed against the torments of urchins' required a certain courage, admitted Professor Morandi. Perhaps he alone did not have the courage, but Manfroni did. They both agreed that it was up to all civilized Tuscans to set a good example and particularly to Incisa 'above all towns . . . and if I had a friend there,' suggested the optimistic teacher from Forlì, 'I would earnestly entreat him to take the matter to heart.' Everyone everywhere should denounce to the press such cases as the one he had just read 'with pleasure in the *Bacchiglione* of Padua'. This was a diatribe against some children who had mistreated a 'deformed and mentally deficient' match-seller.[17]

Following Morandi's second letter *La Nazione* answered the call by publishing a reader's letter describing an event which had taken place not long before on the Carraia bridge: 'six or seven great rascals tormented a poor, pitiful old woman.' Signor Basilio Bianchi told how he had first tried to intervene with reason and good manners and then, 'moral methods' proving insufficient, with a few persuasive clouts. He too proposed an idea: that the proposed Society for the Protection of Unfortunate People against Torments should join forces with the existing Association against Swearing and Foul Language, whose founding committee was composed of members from 'the venerable Gino Capponi . . . Monsignor Giovanni, down to the most modest shopkeepers'.

The editor, Celestino Bianchi, continued to invite his readers' disdain for the 'scoundrels and good-for-nothings who, purely from the cruel instinct to mock their fellows, think that it is witty to taunt and mistreat those poor people whom Mother Nature brought into the world deformed and ridiculous'. He also published a dialogue which had supposedly taken place in a city tavern between a certain Signor Antonio and a certain Beppe. Beppe told the story of a poor man who became enraged whenever he was called 'donkey thief'. Whenever he was down he was pushed and kicked so much that finally he couldn't take any more and burst into tears. 'Then the rabble felt really big and there were jeers and whistles and floods of insults and a thousand other unmentionable things.' Something similar had happened to another poor wretch they knew and to a hundred others. But what did the police do in such cases? They watched, they joined in the laughter and they carried on regardless, said Beppe. Signor Antonio thought that the police had put a stop to the hubbub by taking those two poor wretches they had talked about to jail. Thus the poor creatures were cut off from human contact 'because of other people's faults and without having done anything wrong themselves'. And so the proposed Society to Protect the Deformed and the Ridiculed was a good idea, exclaimed Beppe, 'the best idea in the world'. Such a thing would 'have prevented the carnage at Incisa' – Signor Antonio promised to join immediately.

At that point, concluded the anonymous chronicler, a young man, a servant 'who was hunch-backed, cross-eyed and bald', interrupted their conversation. He had been moved by what he had heard and he swore on his honour that if those blessed proposals came into being, he too would do something. He would raise 'a subscription from all his deformed and twisted brothers in Italy to build a bronze statue' representing Carlo Grandi of Incisa, with the dedication

> Let it be remembered
> that not all that looks evil
> comes to do harm.

Possibly all or most of this story was invented. At the very least the conversation did not take the precise form in which it was presented, nor had quite the edifying ardour as was reported by A. S., who described himself as an 'assiduous reader' of *La Nazione*, which was promoting those ideals. *La Nazione* drew the line, however, at the idea of a statue to Grandi, who was and who remained 'a horrific murderer'. This story concluded the debate so loaded with paternalistic concern for those most ill-favoured by man and nature. The recognition that these people, even including the wretched Incisan, deserved some respect, manifested the commonly accepted moral view on the need for kindness and good manners. It was only sensible to show respect to inferiors if they were to retain their propensity for endurance. In fact, behind seemingly enlightened attitudes it was clear that the presumed progressiveness of moderate, middle-class Tuscans was founded on other, more pragmatic considerations.[18]

Carlino and the urchins

One fundamental issue had been raised: that the murderer could himself be considered a victim of his own victims. The decent people in *La Nazione* and the murderer himself both agreed in condemning the children. They were 'badly brought up' by their mothers from a very early age, they were truly 'rascals', as the cartwright never tired of saying. Luigi, for example, 'if he had been allowed to grow up he would have created mayhem.' And Fortunato 'was a smooth-tongued boy but a rogue', a 'trickster'. It was the parents' fault. Parents were fools – all of them, even in his own family. Even Bibi, that is, Belluci, husband of his sister Ernesta who had already brought four girls into the world. They never left you alone, they all lived in the same house and Carlino told everyone what they were like. He even wrote it down on the day when he had been discovered with Amerigo: 'Oh, people of Incisa, send your children to the municipal school.'[19]

You learned so much at school. He had enjoyed it there. He could even remember the teacher: 'I counted him as one of the few who cared for me with love because he gave me hope', he told *La Nazione*.[20] Country people did not appreciate the joys of reading and writing, but he was passionate about them. So much so that when he was arrested and the crowd outside was threatening to lynch him, he 'sat himself down on a little table reading something or other'. He often went to look through his books, even between committing crimes. He planned to write his own memoirs and sometimes he went to see a neighbour who was fond of him, Rosa Grifoni, to read her his *Carlino's Book*, as he called it. This appears to have been a sort of story of 'a man who had comitted thirteen murders and had been rewarded'. 'It's a fine book, you know,' he would tell her; 'that man did well and was rewarded.'

At school he had heard about the actions of great men for whom he had enormous respect. He used to say he would like to model himself on them – 'Gino Capponi, Rosini, Manzoni, Strozzi, Niccolini, Francesco Pietrarca, Alfonso'; while he was in prison he made a list of them which included his own name. He had bought portraits of Mazzini and others and on his free days he would sit and look at them for hours, or read the life of Garibaldi. He was very fond of the novels of the Livornese author Guerazzi, which in Guerazzi's words were about 'crimes, the atrocious and cruel crimes which wicked men who hated nature and the Creator were capable of committing'.[21] The descriptions were violent and the images, which were horrifying, dwelled on deformed bodies and wretched, violated people. The reader's attention was morbidly attracted. On the other hand, the heroes' nobility redeemed everything and the inevitable punishment of the wicked appeared to justify all the gratuitous violence. The principle of revenge often triumphed, as in *Veronica Cybo*, which was being performed successfully as a play in Florence on the very night of 29 August 1875, when the murderer was arrested.

Who knows whether the cartwright knew when he ended up in prison at the Murate and then at Maschio di Volterra, that Guerazzi had also been in jail. The author died in 1873 after a life that was so strange it even attracted the notice of the criminal anthropologist, Lombroso. All his characters had to come to a bad end but not simply by sudden death, which involved too little suffering. It was always a case of 'stretching body and soul apart, minute by slow minute and shattering you into pieces like iron filings, prolonging the agony and denying you the release of death'. Sentences of this kind came under attack for being 'full of rage and powerful passions which could disturb the calm, gentle nature of the adolescent spirit'.[22]

Certainly the young Grandi was fairly impressionable. Some people said that all that reading did him no good. He only read the newspapers to follow the accounts of criminal trials. He had known all about the trial of Verzeni, 'the woman strangler', who had been condemned to life imprisonment in April 1873. Verzeni raped the women, then cut them up and smelt their entrails, which according to Carlino 'was a terrible thing – it hurt to read about it.'[23] He preferred the great works and 'always read' them: the Psalms and Graduals, the Bible and *The Book of Nature*. Who knows where he came across such books or how much of them he understood – everyone else in his household was illiterate. Perhaps he had found them during his frequent visits to the parish priest, Don Brachetti. The archdiocesan press in Florence had published an Italian translation of the Bible by Monsignor Martini in twenty-three volumes. There were copies of the work in many parishes, especially in Tuscany: it had been distributed as a gift by the translator, who came from Prato originally and was Archbishop of Florence for nearly thirty years until 1809. There were also several smaller editions in circulation, some even pocket-sized. From the end of the eighteenth century certain Florentine publishers had decided to strike out on their own and publish unauthorized versions, some of them considerably abridged, simply to make the Holy Word more accessible and widely spread. Possibly Carlino had no more than a compendium of the Old and New Testaments which were then in existence, printed with large letters and small illustrations and always including the story of Elisha. But this was enough for him to spend hours reading and so feel himself different, better than the others, to be able to say that he read the Bible. Not everyone could do that, in fact you needed the bishop's permission.[24]

Then there were also the readings set by the teacher, 'because he was in a school which made particular progress, moving slowly through Petrarch, Buonarotti and all the great works about kings', including *The Royal Families of France* by Andrea da Barberino, for example, which was published in thousands of popular editions and sold everywhere, even at fairground stalls.

Books written especially for elementary schools were not quite adventurous enough for him, but even they contained something of interest, such as the list of 'true virtues . . . knowledge and goodness; you can learn the former by study and the latter by containing your passions and loving your neighbour.' Even in this genre, however, Carlino may have come across ideas which were difficult or painful: true evil 'is to allow oneself to be ruled by hatred and vengeance'; true good lies in a healthy soul and 'strength of body'. Whole pages were dedicated to the human body in, for example, the reading passages for schools by Pietro Thouar and in 'the most popular book in Italy', praised by Gino Capponi and two aristocrats from Figline, the Marquis Corsini and Count dei Serristori. The book stated that man had the advantage of his height, for 'if he had been smaller he would not have been able to tame horses, bulls and other animals . . . he would not easily have been able to gather fruit from the trees.' His head is covered in 'very fine threads whose roots are hidden beneath the skin . . . hair protects the head from blows and bad weather, it helps to preserve the correct body temperature and it enhances man's appearance.' Man is planted on two feet which uphold him 'by moving forwards . . . and which end in the five toes which make his steps secure and facilitate his running'.[25] *Dwarf, Baldy, Twenty-one-toes* . . . How could he fail to feel ashamed?

The good thing was that so many little tales featured boys called Carlino, just like him. Carlino was the best character in Pietro

Thouar's stories. He was the wise and generous one who reformed thoughtless children who had become involved in the 'bad company' of the feckless and ignorant. Or he was the honest lad, the proverbial good boy. He was the one who was virtuous and happy while his older brother was a good-for-nothing. Carlino, the model whom others admired and loved: 'They would have given their lives for Carlino.'[26]

It must have been a pleasure to hear his own story. Carlino was a good scholar; so was he 'studious and intelligent'. He worked hard at his studies, not like those urchins who 'led each other into bad ways'. But the people of Incisa and Figline did not realize it. 'Oh, fathers and mothers you are obstinate; things will go from bad to worse – you were warned – Oh, fathers and mothers of children. Because your children are not wise and are very wicked.' They pulled his hat off and jeered at him. In *Readings from the Gradual*, which his teacher made him read in class, it was written: 'It is not lawful for anyone to vilify or mock any other person.' And what was more, they were 'half thieves, the Incisans, they stole from me too, the Incisans, the tools from my workshop'.[27]

In one book was written, 'When Franceschino stole your little book you should have told me, you should have told his parents and we would have made him give your things back, we would have punished' the guilty. But this one was a really hard case; he did not change his ways and a few pages later was in prison. But it was not true. He had told people that the boys wouldn't leave him alone and still no one helped him. And in one of his school books it was written: 'Know that it is not lawful for anyone to take their own revenge. If this were done all would be tumult and continual fighting and killing.' Well, he had killed them. Justice had been done. Did they know the story in the Bible of the prophet Elisha? Well, it had been like that, said Grandi. Elisha had been bald too and he was mocked. But 'God didn't send the bear to Carlino ... and Carlino did it himself.'[28]

The point which the defence needed to consider carefully was whether it would be advantageous at the trial to argue that the murderer was himself a victim and whether it would be useful to recount in public the torments inflicted on him by the urchins and others.

Moralists maintained that there were good children and bad children, but it was not always easy to adhere to such strict distinctions, not even in the books written by the Catholic Thouar, who had himself been an 'incorrigible rascal', expelled from the Piarist school and remanded to the workhouse at Monte Domini. Even Thouar's sententious proselytizing became weak and hedged with contradictions when he tackled the misadventures of the poorest and most wretched in society, whether they were adults or children. Moreover, as Idelfonso Nieri said, the popular opinion of very good children was that they were 'dull and vapid'. The idea of the child as an innocent creature was not a widely held one, and it was no accident that there was a Tuscan saying expressing this view:

> The disrespectful years or the disrespectful age. That is what they call it – and this is said in Florence too – the time around four, five and six years old when children lose many of their childish graces and become rude, impertinent, disrespectful in fact.[29]

It was only natural that it should be so, in fact it was a sign that the child was growing up healthy and alert. The fact that they disobeyed, quarrelled, fought and clamoured just had to be borne. Even the scientists confirmed that 'a passion for rudeness' was a typical manifestation of childhood. The anthropologist and popularizer Paolo Mantegazza, who was then in Florence, discussed the matter, even drawing on his personal memories. He analysed rudeness, the desire to humiliate someone and the rage and resentment which led to revenge. According to him, these were all psychological manifestations of a moral anguish which the child suffered more than adults because 'he is capable of experiencing many more unpleasant feelings than pleasant ones.' Poets proclaimed the smiles and innocence of childhood. Science, on the other hand, showed that children had a strong instinct towards evil, this according to Lino Ferriani, a magistrate and sociologist who studied the darker side of the juvenile world. Positivist studies of the child often tended to take the same view. It was an Italian anthropologist, a follower of Lombroso, who pre-empted the advent of psychoanalysis by perceiving that the child was not a little angel but rather a 'petit être presque pervers', an almost perverted little creature.[30]

During the course of a normal childhood the negative instincts would be suppressed and corrected, but while they lasted it was pointless being shocked by this natural phenomenon. Much depended on the child's education and the surroundings in which certain attitudes were accepted. The habit of mocking the weakness of others for example, was considered normal and typical of a country mentality and was very common. It was certainly a somewhat cruel habit but not always entirely negative. Some said it was character-building. Everybody had to go through the experience to some degree, and those who resented it were simply storing up trouble for themselves.

It would have been very risky to blame the behaviour of the cheeky boys and a peasant mentality for the events at Incisa. It might also have proved to be counter-productive, and this realization must have been behind the decision taken by the two lawyers, who elected to conduct the defence along different lines. There were many other elements in the press reports, however, which were equally inspiring to them in the line of defence which they did eventually choose to adopt.

Carlino and the scientists

Even before the debate in *La Nazione*, a very long article had appeared on 8 September 1875 in *Fanfulla*, a daily paper which had started in Florence in 1870, based in via Ricasoli, before moving to Rome. *Fanfulla* was successful both because of its innovative format and the quality of its writers, including Lorenzini and Ferrigni, who wrote under the names of Collodi and Yorick.[31] One of the contributors, Salvatore Vincenzo, whose pseudonym was 'Ego', had been to the Murate prison in via Ghibellina to see 'the child killer who is the talk of Florence', and he reported the following impressions:

> Anyone expecting to find the menacing, bloodthirsty looks which are the instant hallmarks of wickedness would be disappointed. Carlo Grandi ... is extremely short with enormous hands and feet, a squashed and slightly crooked nose and a very sinister eye. There is not a hair on his head ... it is so smooth, white and shiny that it looks like a billiard ball. He is very pale and a smile comes constantly to his lips, a smile which is vapid and devoid of ferocity. To see him, anyone who has ever been to Val d'Aosta cannot help being reminded of the cretins who abound there.

At that time the press reports all emphasized that Grandi had denied having committed the crimes, but it was not true. Not only had he confessed to the magistrate but he told everyone he met, including the disconcerted journalist and his companions. He had no regrets, or rather, he only had one. He was sorry that he hadn't killed the one woman he hated more than anyone else in Incisa (referring to his neighbour Argenta Monsecchi, who had raised the alarm). He had had it all planned. He was going to get her into the workshop on a pretext, then push her into a trap he would prepare: a hole he was going to dig in the floor and cover with sawdust. He demonstrated with great satisfaction how he had put the children to death. He said he had made each one put his head in a noose tied with a running knot, one end of which passed through a ring in the ceiling. Then he pulled the rope and tied it onto something and left the victims hanging until they were truly dead – a somewhat contrived method. He made the whole thing up as he was talking, and kept repeating that the children wouldn't 'leave him in peace'. Would he kill them again? 'Yessir, if they wouldn't leave me in peace.'

How did he spend his days in prison? – in isolation. Apparently he read the Bible much of the time and was very grateful to the governor for having given it to him, because the child killer, commented Ego, was devout. He was also given paper, pen and ink, and so he wrote. That very morning, Monday, 6 September, he had written a screed which the contributor to *Fanfulla* reproduced in full, with a few explanatory brackets, so that readers could 'form an idea of the man's character, a full account of which might be provided by phrenology'. Grandi's writing seemed to be a kind of proclamation backdated to the day when he had been discovered and taken away.

> 29 August 1875
>
> People of Incisa
>
> The young man Carlo Grandi aged 24 was in the hands of the law at the hour of half past eleven – the people wanted me in their hands – they wanted to kill me and set fire to me.
>
> People of Incisa, people of Incisa, perish perish.
> Long live the king and his soldiers
> Long live justice
> On the 18th March was the first son Luigi Buchi, the second...

There followed a list of his victims, their names misspelled and the dates mistaken. Then he continued:

> My family are good – I the young man am de-graced (disgraced) – and because I have merry defetts (many defects) I am mush (much) de-graced I poor young man was sorry not ago (to go) to church because the boys tucof (took off) my hat, because the parents don't look after them, because the children have no mother or father poor children are animals not christians poor parents heaven bring you Christ in Paradise.
>
> People of Incisa, people of Incisa long live the court and the King of heaven and long live Mary and the king of heaven.

'What can one possibly make of this man?' asked the journalist. There was no answer but to await the verdict of human justice. The disconcerted Ego confessed that he was 'even more anxious to hear the verdict of science, which would provide the definitive word in this case'.

The appeal to scientists who might be able to throw some light on this strange person was clear. All experts – anthropologists, psychologists, doctors, even the phrenologists – were called on, though there were few in Italy at the time who assessed the character and mental faculties of a person by touching and measuring the head in the assumption that the brain was the organ of the mind and that the shape of the skull perfectly reproduced it. Not even the psychiatrists in the Phreniatric Society gave much credence to the theories of Gall and Spurzheim. But the cranial approach was practised and discussed with different assumptions in Florence by the many members of the Italian Ethnological and Anthropological Society, under the direction of Paolo Mantegazza.[32] Among the many academics who studied the human sciences from various different perspectives, there must have been several who were aware of Ego's appeal and therefore of the Grandi case.

In fact, the prisoner in cell number 16 was visited by 'nearly all the most knowledgeable doctors in Florence', and others besides.[33] Among his visitors were two young doctors who were to gain considerable prestige among Italian psychiatrists: Augusto Tamburini, who was then assistant at the Reggio Emilia asylum, and Enrico Morselli, assistant at the medical clinic of the Istituto di Studi Superiori in Florence. On 23 September Grandi was also visited by Francesco Bini, who for years had been director of the Florentine lunatic asylums of Bonifazio and Castelpulci. Many other well-known academic figures were received at the Murate prison by the governor Alessandro Soffiutti, who authorized the visits. The examining magistrate Agostino Satti had the courtesy to accompany the superintendent of Siena's psychiatric asylum (later of Reggio Emilia) to the prison, and was thus able to hear his expert opinion for himself.

Meanwhile, the magistrates were proceeding with the bureaucratic course of justice. But a certain section of public opinion was concerned with the problem of assessing Grandi scientifically rather then legally.

Antonio Martinati and the Police Chief of Florence were old acquaintances. The latter had a file in his office growing ever thicker on the conspiratorial activities of the militant socialist Martinati, who was fifty-two years old in 1875, and whose main adherents were the followers of Mazzini, the anarchists and the internationalists. Personally, the founder (in 1870) of the International Democratic Society, a literature teacher by profession, believed in an evolutionary socialism which would resolve social divides by applying modern scientific principles in the belief that history moves in an 'infinite human progression'. He had great respect therefore for scientists, especially those in Florence who were openly progressive, such as Aleksandr Herzen, the Schiffs, the physiologist Moritz and the chemist Ugo; these were all challenging the traditional older generation represented by Capponi, Conti and Lambruschini. The new scientific spirit operated beyond the confines of academia. In fact, free-thinking organizations flourished in the democratic Freemasonry of the city and in 1872 the Union of Free Thinkers was established and presided over by Antonio Martinati[34] and the rationalist Luigi Stefanoni.

Martinati had to collect certain membership cards which had been 'confiscated among others in the confusion of the house searches' during the major trial of the Internationalists. He went to the Police Chief's office one day in September and the two men started to discuss matters – first, public security in Tuscany, and then Grandi. It seemed to the Police Chief that Grandi's case was relevant to ideas concerning the abolition of the death penalty which this respected acquaintance had expressed at a meeting in the Pagliano Theatre in via del Fosso (now the via Verdi). Parliament was at that time debating whether to follow the example of Tuscany and abolish it throughout the rest of Italy. Professor Livi, among others, had addressed the matter. Possibly Martinati might be interested to meet the child killer? The Police Chief kindly offered to take him to meet Grandi whenever he cared to go. Martinati gladly accepted the offer and decided to write an account afterwards for the *Gazzetta d'Italia*, a moderate newspaper with a respectable readership.

They visited the Murate on Tuesday, 21 September at one o'clock, staying for about an hour. Besides Martinati and the Police Chief, the prison governor was also present and Bernardi, dispenser at the San Marco pharmacy.

I confess that at first sight his features and small, twisted body gave me the feeling of being in the presence of an animal of an inferior species. This is not the case when he speaks, unless he is talking about the insults he has received because of his deformities, and then he is just like a bulldog or a tiger who has suddenly, magically, gained the power of speech. Whoever hears him can say that they have for the first time ever listened to the internal monologue of an animal.[35]

They asked him many questions, to which they received categorical replies. They had planned the questions 'mainly within a psychological framework, so that as far as possible they might understand the source of his ideas and feelings'. Not only that, but Martinati had noticed a congenital link between the man's deformities: he 'squinted with his left eye and it is his left foot also which is deformed and, as though in compensation, has six upturned toes shaped, as he himself says, like a fan'. The four visitors all formed the same judgement of Grandi. What that judgement was Martinati did not want to specify in public, maintaining that 'the explanation of both moral and physical phenomena' was necessarily the job of science to provide. There were, however, two facts which he stated clearly in the newspaper: that the case 'merited particular study and that Grandi ought to be visited and indeed would be visited by men of opposing ideas'.

It was to this end that the free-thinker who lived 'apart . . . from everything and everyone' on the outskirts of Florence had written to the editor of the *Gazzetta d'Italia*. This was Carlo Pancrazi, a Tuscan from Cortona, son of the engineer Nunzio who worked for the municipality of Florence, proprietor of many newspapers and a contributor to *La Stampa*. He was an influential man with distinguished friends like Ruggero Bonghi and others within the legal circles from which he himself came, having studied law at Siena and Pisa. Martinati had actually named certain academics of various opinions who might give their judgement of the case. On the one hand, for example, there was the aged Augusto Conti, an authority on moral, or rather Catholic, philosophy, and at the opposite end of the spectrum of opinion, the progressive scientists Mantegazza and Schiff.

In fact, none of the three professors answered the call. Not the teacher of metaphysics (who was also a colleague of Abbot Lambruschini), who was committed to teaching at the Istituto di Studi Superiori for the year, and whose subject matter was nothing less than 'the existence, origins, perfecting and end of the universe'.[36] Nor was there any response from the anthropologist Mantegazza, otherwise known as the 'senator of erotica' for having written *The Hygiene of Love* and *The Physiology of Love*, which he had dedicated 'to the daughters of Eve, so that they may teach men that love is not a luxury . . . but the joy of heaven on earth'. Mantegazza's constant curiosity would normally have induced him to become involved and the fact that he did not is perhaps partly because at that time he was 'subject to grave and prolonged bouts of Hypochondria', which temporarily hampered his prolific activities. As for the physiologist Schiff, he was at that very time spending his last tormented months in Florence. He had been accused and insulted by Gino Capponi and, far from becoming involved in other issues, was preparing to leave Florence; he left for Geneva in April 1876.[37]

The people whom Martinati suggested should interest themselves in the Grandi case would not in fact have been the most suitable, and there were other scholars in the city who could provide more relevant opinions. The rigorous study of man in both his physical and mental aspects had become so specialized that it demanded increasingly particular skills.

In 1871 Florence had suddenly been demoted from its role as capital of the kingdom. The mayor, Ubaldini Peruzzi, had let it be known that the financial damage alone amounted to debts of 17 million lire. Yet the city still retained its pride and in terms of culture still regarded itself as the 'scientific and moral mentor of Italy'.[38] The Istituto di Studi Superiori Pratici e di Perfezionamento, which had been founded by Ricasoli's provisional government in December 1859 and whose president from 1870 to 1880 was Peruzzi, established its importance. Not that there weren't ambiguities and muddles in the process of achieving its original aim as a model of teaching and post-graduate research. Nevertheless, despite the difficulties the Institute grew in strength throughout that decade of disappointments when the city was used as a provisional capital. In 1872 the government ratified an agreement about the Institute's finances, in 1876 the Natural Science Department followed the example of the departments of Philosophy and Philology and became a university faculty, and in 1875 the School of Social Sciences and Politics was established under the aegis of the Marquis Carlo Alfieri.

The Institute was housed in a series of buildings which were all very close to each other, mostly in the San Marco area near the School of Fine Arts and the main hospital of Santa Maria Nuova. It was easy for scholars to meet each other within the complex. Inter-disciplinary discussions took place and there was a deliberate fostering of exchanges between the historical and the scientific approach to problems. The whole spirit of that cultural climate and its 'positive philosophy' refuted the idea of 'studying man as an abstract entity outside the context of space and time and composed

only of empty formulas and categories'. This was declared by
Pasquale Villari during the Institute's inaugural lecture, which constituted the manifesto of Italian positivism. The object of study
was 'man, alive and real, mutable in multifarious guises, driven by
many passions, limited at every turn and yet full of aspirations to
infinity'.[39]

The spirit of research therefore was to be anthropological. But
anthropology itself contained complexities which were reflected by
the many topics discussed by the Italian Anthropological Society and
by the various leanings of those who attended the monthly meetings
in via Ricasoli. Lambruschini, who was dead by then, had in his
time declined to teach anthropology, admitting that he knew nothing
about it. By 1869 however, the first University chair and the first
museum in Italy devoted to the subject had been established in
Florence. In 1875 both chair and museum were transferred from the
Faculty of Philosophy to that of Natural Sciences, a significant move
for the scientific identity of the discipline. Professor Mantegazza
taught the subject for three hours a week in 1874/5 and his lectures
must have been experimental, science-based and linked to the course
in psychology. Mantegazza had studied medicine at Pisa and Pavia
then had travelled through Argentina where, instead of making his
fortune (he made bad investments), he found his first wife and his
passion for the study of man in his many varieties, which at that
time he applied to certain Latin American communities. Between
1870 and 1873 he was mainly interested in the 'modifying factors of
human nature and the laws governing the mutability of individuals
and species and in the effects of heredity and environment. He went
on to study 'the most important aspect of man ... sensations and
feelings – the passions'. He later wrote a psycho-physiological work
about love, hate, pleasure and pain.[40]

The general basis of the work of the Institute was a clear adherence
to Darwinism. At least it had been since 1868, when the physiologist
and free-thinker Aleksandr Herzen had given a public lecture at the
Natural History Museum, 'On the Kinship Between Man and
Monkeys', which was published in *La Nazione* together with an
aggrieved commentary by Lambruschini. He did not deny the
unflattering line of descent but requested that it should not be aired
in public. The publication of the lecture had in fact caused a sensation
without, however, calling down the disastrous moral consequences
predicted by the abbot. 'He's the one who said his dad was born
from a monkey,' was the whisper whenever the young Russian
scientist appeared: 'Supposing it's true?'[41]

The rich interaction between theoretical studies and techno-professional training promoted by the Institute had already led to the establishment of the medico-surgical school of Florence, which was copied in France and elsewhere. The masters were Francesco Puccinotti and Maurizio Bufalini, who had inspired the initial conception of the Institute as a whole. Both were proponents of the experimental, clinical approach and both were opposed to all forms of reductionism, whether it be the Brownian inclination to dualize illness into debility and diathesis caused by external factors, or the excessive reliance placed by phrenology on pathological anatomy and organicism. In order to teach young doctors to recognize the periodic emergence in their science of abstract theories which over-simplified the living being, Puccinotti had taught and written the *History of Medicine* (1850–66). Bufalini stressed that the science of pathology, of disorder, could not be deduced from physiology, nor could a theory of randomness be derived from one of order – even less so when the anomalies concerned mental functions, in which case the doctor needed to specialize in that particular area of research.[42]

Carlo Livi and Francesco Bini followed this teaching and had devoted themselves to psychiatry. They had both been directors of the major Tuscan lunatic asylums at Siena and Florence, where the legendary Vincenzo Chiarugi had worked. Anyone following their courses on mental illness would have been instructed to 'look at the whole man' in order to pinpoint his anomalies. The most disturbing of these, obviously, were manifested by madness, but it was important to recognize the wide variety of differences – of sex, age, temperament, habits etc., which existed even within the range of normal groups and individuals. Anthropology addressed this variety.

At least Professor Mantegazza's brand of anthropology did. From the pages of his *Archivio* he condemned his French colleagues from Broca to Topinard and their followers for claiming to gain an understanding of intellectual and moral character from the shape of the human skull. He said that since 'the brain is still too little understood and the comparative psychology of man is a far more complex matter than ... the measurement of angles and circumferences', the craniologists tried to over-simplify matters but remained embroiled in complexities and ran the risk of demeaning the ancient metaphysics of the discipline. The Italian Anthropological Society was seeking to move in more fruitful directions. In March 1873, at a meeting held in Florence, a committee presented the '*Instructions for the Study of Comparative Psychology'*, which included a section on mental pathology edited by Cesare Lombroso.

> Although anthropology is the youngest of the biologica! sciences...it should now take a step forward. Without ceasing to measure skulls, without abandoning the scales and compasses and without neglecting man's morphology, anthropology must now seek to reveal man as a thinking, living creature. In other words, it must now move from the static to the dynamic phase, because anthropologists will not wish to limit themselves indefinitely to classifying man as a botanist classifies the plants in his garden.[43]

There was certainly a great deal to be learned from those scholars in Florence by a young man attracted to science but unsure of his own direction and wanting to gain some experience. Enrico Morselli was very happy to be living there. In July 1874 he had graduated in medicine at the age of twenty-two from the University of Modena where, thanks to the teaching of the zoologist Giovanni Canestrini, 'the most Darwinian of the Italian Darwinians', he had been converted to positivism and had shaken off the spiritualistic, anti-materialistic education he had received in college.[44] Morselli would have ended up in the unenviable position of a country doctor somewhere if he hadn't been rescued by Carlo Livi, who had taught him medical jurisprudence. The professor had advised him to take up psychiatry and join the asylum at Reggio Emilia. The place did not attract him particularly – the few times he had attended lectures there had left Morselli feeling rather disturbed. But the advantages were that he would have an authoritative and paternal figure under whom to work and free board and lodging, which he needed. Moreover, Livi had offered to use his friendship with Mantegazza to secure a position for Morselli to study anthropology at the famous Institute which, he said, would be useful if he were to become a good psychiatrist.

To be in Florence, that beautiful city! How could he not accept? He would meet important people, he would be in contact with the pioneers of anthropology and he would certainly make himself noticed since he lacked neither brains nor ambition. Within a few months he was settled. He had a welcoming room at 49 via dei Servi, parallel with the via Ricasoli. He had intelligent companionship and had made a friend of Mantegazza's assistant, the eccentric palaeontologist Ettore Regalia. He had even become engaged to Maria Pia, Ettore's sister. Moreover, he had found a real job. He became Professor

Carlo Ghinozzi's medical assistant at the main hospital and started to give lectures in neuropathology at the Institute. He also began to contribute to the *Archivio per l'antropologia e l'etnografia* and to *Sperimentale*, edited by Bufalini (who died in March 1875 and was commemorated by the mayor with full, solemn funeral celebrations). Besides all this activity, Morselli attended all the meetings of the Anthropological Society, of which Mantegazza was president.

The young doctor related to his teacher Livi, who had thirty years more experience, what was being said and done in Florence. They would often discuss matters with Augusto Tamburini, who had chosen to remain at Reggio to take care of the lunatics at San Lazzaro and the 'Rivista sperimentale di freniatria e medicina legale', which had been founded by all three of them in the autumn of 1874.

They were naturally interested in the Grandi case. The newspapers were saying that the murderer was quite physically deformed and had no conscience or sense of guilt, that he had probably acted on animal instinct and that he was a cretin. *Fanfulla* and *Opinione Nazionale* were calling for scientists to offer their opinions, to examine the accused's skull and body and make a judgement, and the three of them were experts.

Livi had seen all types of lunatics during his career. From 1858 he had spent sixteen years in the Siennese asylum of San Nicolò and then had travelled all over the country preparing his *Scientific journey to the asylums of Italy*. He had ended up at San Lazzaro, which under his direction had gained fame throughout Europe. He was an expert and he knew well how to recognize a real lunatic from a pretender. From 1860 he had taught forensic medicine, first at Siena then at Modena. He had examined many criminals and lunatics for the courts and had written the first Italian text on *Forensic phrenology – Forms of insanity considered within the criminal context.*[45] Naturally Tamburini, who was still under thirty, did not have the same experience, but as Livi's assistant and lecturer in clinical psychology at Pavia, he had a thorough grounding. He had already provided expert evidence on occasion and would continue to do so since he too was convinced that psychiatrists should demonstrate the social usefulness of their work outside the narrow confines of the asylums whenever and wherever possible.[46]

The twenty-three-year-old Morselli had the least knowledge of the three men, but he kept himself up to date in the field, including reading foreign publications. He had reviewed the works of Claude Bernard, Paul Broca and Henry Maudsley, whose *Responsibility in mental diseases* was published in translation in 1875 by the positivist Dumolard. The young man was keen to learn, and in his discussions with Paolo Mantegazza he had formulated his thoughts on the major questions of evolutionism, atavism and neo-genesis – in other words, on the re-emergence of certain ancient characteristics of the human species in certain individuals. Morselli practised experimental and clinical work among the mentally ill at Reggio. During those months he was writing something about idiots from the animalistic aspect and also, together with Tamburini, something on physical and mental degeneration. All this experience would have helped him to discern what really lay behind Grandi's doltish physiognomy and abnormal body. Moreover, he knew about the anthropological characteristics of Tuscans. Two summers previously he had foregone his holiday to help Cesare Lombroso in his research into the population of Lunigiani and Garfagnana. The two men had visited very remote villages where they stayed, observed the inhabitants and held many discussions together, and the young man had thus learned about the anthropological study of abnormality which Lombroso was pursuing.

At Pavia, Tamburini had also heard of the study. Several preliminary essays had appeared and the work itself was on sale in the spring of 1876 as *L'Uomo delinquente studiato in rapporto all'- antropologia, alla medicina legale e alle discipline carcere.** Among other topics in the book, Lombroso sought to distinguish the born criminal from the insane.[47] Young men like Morselli and Tamburini were inspired by Lombroso's work, which gave them hope for a new perspective in the field of psychiatry which was still then dominated in Italy by the over-revered figures of Andrea Verga and Serafino Biffi. It was time for change. Even Livi thought so, though he was far from convinced by Lombroso's ideas; and as for Lombroso's methodology, 'neither profound nor precise', he was almost as scathing as Mantegazza, who had openly quarrelled with his colleague while working at Pavia as a pathologist and had spoken little good of him since then.[48] If positivist criminology was to bear the mark of Lombroso then it would be better to hold dialogue with Francesco Carrara, founder of criminal science. Livi preferred to see Carrara's name on the frontispiece of the *Rivista sperimentale di freniatria e medicina legale*, rather than the anthropologist whom the two younger editors supported.[49]

---

* *A Study of the Criminal with Reference to Anthropology, Forensic Medicine and Prison Discipline* [trans].

The two of them were therefore warned, and as Morselli was to point out, they could see the defects inherent in Lombroso's impressionist theory for themselves. Nevertheless, Morselli was attracted to criminal anthropology, to the promise of finally conferring meaning on the meticulous collection of detailed figures, reports and statistics which more or less all positivist researchers thought necessary at the time. They pursued their minute and tedious research with infinite patience in an effort to apply the rigours of mathematics and natural sciences to the study of man. By observing, examining and measuring a body in the correct areas with the appropriate instruments and controls, it seemed possible to define an individual's characteristics and state whether he might be a criminal and if so, of what type. One might be a genius or a fool, another might be a moral degenerate or a decent person. It seemed as though science might be able to resolve the uncertainties and differences of the instinctive moralistic judgements made by the general public.[50]

Such results would have been particularly important for craniological studies, which up until then had been accumulating in great quantities but with no clear sense of direction. Morselli knew something of this, for since he had aspired to become an anthropologist he had automatically become a craniologist. According to his teacher Paolo Gaddi, this was the way it had to be. Craniology was said to be the most scientific branch of anthropology because of its objectivity and the rigorous methodology of the measuring. At the age of twenty Morselli, ever more confused, found himself at the professor's instigation handling and cataloguing dusty skulls in the anatomincal museum at Modena. He was even comitted to writing about his morbid work, desperately looking for a spark of interest to motivate him. The anomaly of a particular bone as proof of atavism had been discussed by Luigi Calori, Giovanni Canestrini, Rudolf Virchow and even Charles Darwin. Morselli tried to do the same in 1872 and turned for help to Mantegazza. They agreed that craniology and skull classifications had proved of little use to the study of man and to insist blindly that it was useful was either a delusion or deceit – this despite the fact that the famous Societé d'Antropologie de Paris in 1875 issued *Instruction craniologiques et craniométriques*.[51]

Certainly measuring the head of a live, flesh-and-blood person whose history one knew was better than dealing with skulls. If Grandi had such extraordinary deformities, Morselli may have thought that his boring studies might prove to be of some use. Few people knew as much as he did about cephalic indicators, Camper's

angle, bifrontal diameters, bizigomatic diameters etc.... He knew
more than his friends Tamburini and Livi; maybe his studies would
prove to have been worthwhile. The brilliant young doctor decided
to satisfy his curiosity, considered a vice in a woman but surely a
virtue in a scientist!

Carlino the degenerate

They waited in the room to which, with the prison governor Soffietti's
kind consent, a guard had led them. The day was 13 September
1875. They felt a certain anticipation: 'we were expecting to see one
of those anomalies of human nature which are so interesting to
students of psychology.' But, admitted Morselli, they could never
have believed that they would see 'such a great physical and moral
degeneracy as was actually manifested'.[52]
For Callisto Grandi, when he stood before them, was 'extraordinarily ugly'. He evoked disgust and horror, and Morselli was
instinctively revolted. Livi and Tamburini were also appalled as he
entered, laughing and saying 'now I'm for death.' He may have
mistaken them for magistrates, and so started to confess to them all
over again in a monotonous, childlike, often falsetto voice, and
between grimaces his lips and chin were seized with twitches. He
told again how he had been persecuted by everyone in town and
how he ought to have killed them all. He took the cap from his
head as though to show off his bald scalp. Often he smoothed
his hand almost thoughtfully over his head and turned with an
affectionate smile to look at the guard before taking up his story,
radiant whenever he glorified his own actions or writings.
It took a little while before the three psychiatrists were able to
observe him dispassionately with a clinical eye. First they made him
undress. He smiled, 'looking at us and then suddenly becoming
serious: "I've always been wretched, me . . . poor thing, poor thing
with all these defects."' They described his physiognomy in minute
detail: he was a dwarf with a weak constitution, flaccid muscles,
extremely pallid complexion, squint-eyed and nystagmic. He did not
have a hair on his body, not even under his armpits nor in the pubic
area. He had a scoliotic spinal column which twisted to the left in
the lumbar region, a deformed pelvis, his right buttock protruded
above his left, his right knee was higher than the left and he limped.
His torso was too long in proportion to his lower limbs, his costal

arches were asymmetrical, his left foot was turned inwards and had a sixth toe which was almost the same size as the big toe and was complete with toenail. They were particularly interested by the fact that the deformities were all on the same side of the body. His genitals were almost atrophied: the penis was small and completely covered by the foreskin, the testicles too were small and the scrotum contracted. In fact, he was 'at the stage of development of a twelve year old boy'.

They then questioned him. They asked if he had 'in conscience ... ever regretted the atrocious deeds he had committed and felt remorse in the middle of the night'. 'My conscience?' he asked, and they realized that he felt no remorse. Wouldn't he be ashamed to find himself in court with all eyes upon him? 'Yes, I will be ashamed because my trousers are torn,' he answered. They found that he had 'an inflated self-esteem, an obsessive sense of self'. Was it true that the whole of Italy was interested in him? he asked the doctors. Did they know that he kept portraits of famous men in his chest of drawers, that he had read all the important books including the Bible? He told them the story of the prophet Elisha and the bear. 'I am going to study a great, great deal ... I want to be better than a magistrate, because there's nothing wrong with my memory and ... I have a good brain. I study, but really a lot.' He was perfectly satisfied with his present situation. He was fond of the carabinieri and of the magistrate (Agostino Satti, who was also present during this visit) and he was also very attached to the King's soldiers because they had carried him away in triumph from Incisa, where he would have been killed, and now he too, long live the King of Italy, was part of the government. He had even written it down in black and white. They could see for themselves:

> Gentlemen of the government, on 5 September 1875 Callisto Grandi of Incisa arrived at Murate at the hour of six o'clock with the Figline carabinieri. Callisto Grandi is still grateful to the King's carabinieri. Long live the King of Kings! Sky overcast at Moncalieri and Genova: cloudy as far as Livorno ... almost perfectly calm over land and sea: barometer fallen to 4 millimetres.

They managed to decipher this from one of the scrawled sheets of paper of which Grandi was so proud. He showed them other sheets, which included the draft of a play dedicated to the 'bad men of Incisa'.

Carlino open, Carlino open
O people no. Carlino open
No, no, o pepepeeople of Incisa, no, no, no pen o people
Incisan no no pen no
Antonio. Carlino open
no ansa
Bastiano. Carlino open
no, Bastiano no ansa
Rachele . . . Carlino open. No no
Carlino is def [deaf] and laughs
Orestes I'm dying of pain. Carlino open: no and Carlino laughs no no.
Farewell people I'm dying of pain my Antonio farewell I'm dying.
Rachele is dying of pain . . . ansas Bastiano
And my wife is dead of pain, Antonio
Antonio cries and then laughs. Away Antonio laughs and cries with pain.
Father and son . . .

This was the scene when he had been discovered, and included the voices of his brother-in-law Antonio and the child Amerigo's parents. Again, on another page:

1. Florence, Florences is a flower
2. Incisa is a place of wicked women Figline is a place for dogs . . . for wicked men, thieves
3. Callisto Grandi is not a thief
4. People of Figline and Incisa
5. Sky great light.
6. October 1873 September
7. Long live the King Carabidio
8. Callisto thanks
9. The carabinieri for
10. His bad from Incisa

What did it mean? The scientists thought that these were perhaps chapter headings for the *Beautiful Romance* which Grandi declared that he himself had written, he 'Marianos Tommasos Carlinos Grandis and 3 sons . . . praise us who for the third time come to light for the good of Italy and I give thanks. 15, 83, 80.'

That was enough for the first visit. They watched him as, flanked by the guard, he returned with dragging footsteps to the cell. One can only guess at the strength of his impression on them, particularly on Dr Morselli.

The young psychiatrist thought about the dwarf cartwright all day. He had killed four children. He had a horrendously deformed body. Born in 1851, he was twenty-four years old – only a year older than the doctor himself.

The next morning, 14 September, Morselli was at the gates of Murate prison. He wanted to see Grandi again – alone. He had brought his instruments with him this time: tape measures, compasses, goniometer, craniometer and dynamometer. This would make his visit more fruitful, as he would be able to measure Grandi's head and face:[53]

total skull diameter	179 mm
biparietal diameter	145
bifrontal diameter	130
chin to lambda	208
occipital lobe to bregma	215
height of forehead	140
curve of forehead	300
length of face	130
length of nose	52
horizontal circumference	540
ante-posterior circumference	320
bisauricular curve	310
anterior part of circumference	270
posterior part of circumference	270

He then calculated the cephalic indicator – the relation between the length and width of the skull in relation to certain angles. The results were not particularly abnormal, though he did discover a depression at the meeting point between the frontal lobe and the sagittal, and a raised section running along the parietals. He wrote everything down: protruding occipital lobe, right anterior plagiocephalic, the irregular shape of the skull and the many lesions.

To judge from his eyes – the windows of the soul – the 'little monster' seemed incapable of concentration. His breathing was regular, however, and so was his heart beat. Tests with the Mathieu dynamometer proved he was strong; he could lift forty kilos with his right hand and thirty with his left. Other tests followed. Could he feel exactly where the pressure was applied on his hand, forearm and neck? Could he determine the exact distance between the points of Weber's compass placed at his throat and tongue? There appeared to be a certain degree of hypersensitivity, but the figures did not vary greatly from the average:

	Grandi's measurements in mm	Average measurements
Right hand		
digits	3	2.7
palm	4	10
Left hand		
digits	2	2.7
palm	6	10
Forehead	10	27
throat	5	13.5
tongue	narrow	–
back of neck	20	–
right upper limb	20	–
left forearm	10	–

Morselli concluded, however, that the figures were not really reliable. He overcame his repugnance and felt the six-toed left foot. He asked Grandi if he slept well, and about his moods. Sometimes he was melancholy and sometimes excited. Anything else?

Morselli was helped with these answers by the Murate prison doctor, Chiarino Chiarini, and his friend, Dr Andrea Ceccherelli, who lived on the corner of Via dei Macci in Via Ghibellina, next door to the prison. Together the two men provided much useful information about the prisoner's nervous state, and Morselli learned even more from the guards. During the first days of his imprisonment Grandi had been very calm, reading and writing a lot and spending a great deal of time singing. It was not clear what he sang – often just monologues, something about how he had wanted to enrol with the Bersaglieri but the grenadiers couldn't take him because he was too short. Or how he had wanted to be a mounted carabiniere. He held forth against the thieves and bad men of Incisa and eulogized the philosophers and poets among whom he included himself. He asked Morselli if it was true that a statue of him was to be erected. Once, on 27 November, at two o'clock in the morning, he started raving so loudly that the other prisoners were woken and began throwing insults at him, including the hated 'Baldy', 'Twenty-one-toes' and even 'child killer'. Serious disorder was threatened as Grandi, in his solitary cell, made as much noise as he could. He threatened the guards, who had come running, with his bunk bed and rambled on that 'I want revenge against the poisoners, I want revenge.' The governor ordered him to be put into a straightjacket for a few nights. Garnieri, the guard who tied him into the jacket, was told happily by Grandi that 'this would make him taller and make his hair grow.' He remained in this state for ten days. He didn't sleep, he shouted out all the usual things, he refused to eat because he said the food was poisoned. Then, finally, he calmed down.

Morselli continued to visit Grandi from time to time and noticed towards the end of the following January that he was displaying more strange behaviour. He moulded a big doll out of bread which he had been secretly collecting and dressed it up in his own clothes. It was his memorial – he had made it himself and no one was allowed to touch it, even though the figure began to grow mouldy and smelly after a few days. Using a plank from his bed, he lifted some of the flagstones, dug a hole and buried the doll, for which he was punished with six days' bread and water. Within the prison, general opinion was increasing that Grandi was more of 'an idiot child than a terrible murderer', according to one guard. Apart from his occasional wild excesses he was usually happy, loquacious and always ready to welcome any visitors, especially the doctors.

And then a change manifested itself in his body and mind. Morselli noted on 17 February 1876 that Grandi had reached the state of puberty. Feeble rudiments of beard growth had appeared on his chin, a fine down was growing on his head and hairs had appeared in his armpits and groin. He noted 'a considerable development of the genital organs and the complete descent of the testicles into the scrotum'. Above all, he noted a mental change to match the physical one. Grandi's carelessness and wild hilarity was replaced by anxiety for the future and some traces of pain and remorse. His quantities of writing no longer concentrated on blowing his own horn and cursing the people of Incisa. He seemed, finally, to have acquired a measure of conscience.

The Life of Callisto Grandi of Incisa

My destiny is full of pain and sweated labour. Let it be known in writing that the poor wretch was hairless and I am 24 years old and I was born without hair the poor Carlino suffered passion and severe pain that he was aged 9 since he worked in his cartwright's workshop he worked willingly since he was a little thing. His disgrace his head suffers with grave pain and travail that Carlino suffered nervous pain that he did not feel the evil the bad pain in the head never stops the pain in the head like an angry dog . . .

Carlino has put on hair. On 6 October 1876 he thanks the honourable professors of Italy. Name of painter and poet and philosopher with fine brain . . . Carlino's pain is over.[54]

Apart from the physical and psychological examination it was necessary, as with every patient, to establish a case history. Morselli went to Incisa himself and asked various questions about what people thought or knew of Callisto Grandi – with little success, however. The townspeople were unforthcoming and the doctor complained that Grandi's relatives refused to show him his writings and drawings. Nevertheless, he was not discouraged. The murderer had had a paternal grandfather who was a drunkard and a father who was an eccentric' and kept a skull in his bedroom, calling himself an artist though he was a simple cartwright. The mother was 'half-cretinous, daughter of another notorious drunkard . . . she was irritable, short-tempered and seems to have mistreated her children.' These were all his own opinions, drawn from information which was frequently inaccurate.

When questioned, the neighbours had spoken nothing but good of Grandi's family. The doctor, however, was obviously looking for signs of bad ancestry: the history of drinking through the grandfathers for example, the physical and mental retardation manifested in the second-born Callisto (in fact he was the third child after two girls); apparently, the sister who had died aged seven was also bald and mentally deficient. It seemed that even his older (in fact younger) brother was of low intelligence. The young doctor reached this conclusion from the fact that when Grandi's father disappeared in 1861, the house and workshop were taken over by Bellacci, the eldest sister's husband, rather than by the two sons (who were still children at the time).[55]

It was easier to find out from people what Carlino's reputation had been. It was significant that everyone considered him 'a fool, a retard', especially when he vaunted himself as a philosopher and learned man – when he took it into his head, for example, to teach that the earth went round the sun rather than the opposite. Morselli did not attempt to establish how his relations with family and friends might have affected Grandi, with his weak, confused, sick mind so obsessed with the thought of appearing ridiculous or worse in the eyes of the world. The doctor considered the stories of Grandi as a laughing stock in order to see how widely his imbecility was acknowledged, as though this were sufficient proof that he really was mentally defective. In fact, the two are of course unconnected; the prevalence of general opinion is no proof of scientific fact. Morselli certainly knew this in theory, but in this particular case he chose to ignore it.

The popular refrains of 'they say' and 'everyone knows' were not enough; justice required a scientific verdict. When the lawyers Galardi and Papasogli decided to call in experts they turned to Livi and Morselli, who willingly accepted the duty. But three experts would carry more weight in court than two, particularly since the esteemed and authoritative Livi of Reggio Emilia could not follow the case as directly and closely as his young pupil who, however worthy, did not carry the same weight. Livi and Morselli agreed to collaborate with another psychiatrist who was well known to everyone in the city, and whose name even appeared in the *Dizionario del vernacolo fiorentino*:* Bini. 'To go to Bini' meant to go out of your head, to go mad, because Francesco Bini, born in Pontedera in 1815, had been governor of the asylum in Via San Gallo since 1844; the governors of the Lucca and Pistoia asylums were his pupils.[56] He had been a fellow student of the younger Carlo Livi at Pisa. In Florence he had worked as a doctor since 1837, had been an assistant of Bufalini's in 1840, and had then become professor of the first university faculty of psychiatry in Italy.

At that point the prosecution clearly lost some advantage. How would they find similarly authoritative experts who would hold different views from the defence experts and would be prepared to contradict them? According to Morselli there were no other comparable figures in the Florentine medical world. Everyone agreed with himself, Bini or Livi – or almost everyone. After many months of searching the prosecution finally turned to the sixty-four-year-old professor, Giuseppe Lazzaretti. Lazzaretti was a single man from the province of Siena, where he had studied medicine and forensic science; he had held an important position in Florence for twenty years, beginning in 1843, but had been a citizen of Padua since 1864, when he was appointed to the chair of forensic science and police medicine there.[57] He had been educated by the Piarist fathers in the philosophy of Rosmini, and although there was no question that he had taken an experimental direction in the area of his expertise, which was physical deformity, the same could not be said of his attitude to mental pathology. He was nominated as an expert witness together with Carlo Morelli, born in Campiglia in 1816, an ex-deputy of the Right in 1866, who with his philanthropic spirit was very involved in popular education. Morelli was a doctor of course, trained at Pisa; but he was not, as it transpired during the trial, a teacher of forensic science in Florence (as the toxicologist

* *Dictionary of Florentine Vernacular*

Ramieri Bellini was), although he had taught the history of medicine since 1861, when he succeeded Puccinotti. Thirty years earlier he had edited the Italian edition of *Des maladies mentales* by Esquirol, but did not appear to have taken a great interest in psychiatry after that.[58] Presumably it was Morelli, who lived in Florence, who gathered material for the prosecution. As the younger man, Morselli was in charge of doing for the defence.

3

The Trial

Yorick and the celebrated trials

How best to describe a trial? Not a political trial nor one involving mundane minor offences but a trial about a bloody crime. People wanted to read blood-curdling stories and to hear about ferocious, almost abnormal criminals. Better still if the murderer was someone who had seemed to be above suspicion – a decent citizen or one who appeared to be incapable of violence against weak, innocent victims. Stories of bandits were also popular but for quite different reasons. The protagonist of such stories was certainly violent but only against his peers and he was basically brave – admired for his devil-may-care actions. During the second half of the nineteenth century a new literary genre based on the exploits of bandits and criminals was gaining great success. Originally French, it quickly took hold in Italy, finding fertile ground in the credulity of the populace and the already existing ballad tradition.

In Florence there were some who were making a fortune from publishing such material. They produced booklets at minimal cost, with few pages and sparse illustrations, which were quickly sold for a song by pedlars. Adriano Salani took his inspiration from the crime press reports and from his publishing house in the Via San Niccolò produced a mass of these booklets to meet the public taste – which happened to coincide with his own. Salani was a Florentine, son of a greengrocer, who had reached the top class in elementary school and had been learning his trade since childhood. First he had been with the publishing house of Niccolai, then Le Monnier, and finally in 1862, at the age of twenty-eight, he had started his own press. He was good at the work and knew how to choose authors, not often for their literary style but because they were trained to produce work which satisfied the demands of the ingenuous reader; the formulae and ingredients were always the same.[1]

Pietro Franceso Leopoldo Coccoluto Ferrigni could certainly not be bracketed with the 'penny dreadful' writers. In all his activities as a writer and tireless lecturer, where he was learned without being boring, he displayed an affection for the popular Tuscan character, especially his humour – though he always maintained the detachment of one looking on from his own entrenched social position. He held firm convictions and was politically very moderate: 'pro-government and the monarchy'.

In his accounts of trials he often used the pseudonym, 'Yorick son of Yorick'. He had been trained as a lawyer and had studied jurisprudence at the Grand Duchy's universities in Florence, Siena and Pisa, where he had first enrolled in 1851 as a fifteen-year-old prodigy.[2] This meant that in his accounts of trials, readers were presented not only with the lively style and perception for which he was famous but were also offered the informed opinion of one who knew the world he wrote about from the inside. It is easy to see why it was natural for his childhood friend Celestino Bianchi to entrust the usually boring judicial reports to Ferrigni whenever a particularly interesting trial was underway.

In December 1876 there were two trials being conducted in Florence on which Ferrigni was commissioned to report. One was the libel action brought by Giovanni Nicotera against Sebastiano Visconti, the editor of *Gazzetta d'Italia*; the other was the case of actual and attempted murder against Callisto Grandi. In the Civil Court, therefore, the argument concerned a baron who was a Minister of the Interior, and the imputation that he had been a spy for the Bourbons rather than a heroic liberal who had fallen prisoner to them. The trial was clearly political, following the inauguration of Depretis's government after the so-called parliamentary uprising and collapse of the Right brought about by the problems of the railways and the opposition of the moderate Tuscan group led by Peruzzi, mayor of Florence.

On the other hand, the Court of Assize was sitting in judgement on a cartwright, a miserable peasant, the protagonist of a horrendous tale which stood outside any specificity of time or place. Events were being recounted which had shaken the timeless existence of ordinary people in a town which lay not many miles from the ex-capital and yet was a world apart.

To pass from one court-room to the other, as Pietro Ferrigni had to do for his job, was like moving between separate worlds which bore no relation to each other – from the official world of politics, with its importance for the nation's history and destiny, to the obscure world of a daily existence where the great national events left no trace and where what was really important were the needs and habits of a small community and the values and prejudices of individuals.

Very few people went to the Nicotera trial. The public galleries were deserted apart from the odd journalist and even the defence benches were fairly empty. Yorick wrote in his notebook that while high-flown depositions were proclaimed praising the Minister's great patriotism, 'one by one the lawyers gather their papers together and go for a stroll.' In San Pancrazio, it was a different story: 'All the corridors, all the hallways, all the rooms are packed.' There was always a huge crowd, and people stayed for the length of the trial, from before the court sat down at about half past nine until after it adjourned at sunset.

Even Ferrigni, who was involved in political life himself, always escaped from the soporific Nicotera trial as soon as he could to hurry to the trial of the child killer. He wanted to observe the accused, to know what the judges were discussing and the lawyers and the expert witnesses, to watch the reactions of the heterogeneous public and to hear the comments passed around the 'room of lost direction'. His reports of the trial were brilliant; they gripped the attention of the daily readers, enthusing them with his own interest.[3]

Why was there so much interest in this trial – interest which varied with the diversity of spectators and readers? Why, for example, did all those ladies and bonneted girls never miss a single hearing? The lawyer Ferrigni would have preferred them to have stayed decently at home, like his own wife. Especially the young girls, he wrote, who would have been better employed practising the piano than attending the trial. From his disapproving male standpoint he could not understand why they came.

It was a taste for sensationalism which attracted the women, as the young lady from Voghera understood very well. She lived in Florence and from 1877 her novels were published by Salani, who discovered her inexhaustible ability to produce them.[4] Newspaper reports provided ample material to satisfy the collective need 'for the fantastic, the incredible, the amazing', which seemed to be a real 'passion among women'. Who knows whether Carolina Invernizio, with her predilection for crime and feathered bonnets, ever attended the trial of the Incisan cartwright who had been born in the same year as herself.

Even if she wasn't there, some of her future readers must certainly have been among those women who followed the trial with under-standable emotion. They were moved by the sight of the victims' poor mothers, alarmed by the threatening cries from the public; they shuddered with horror at the details of the crimes and above all vied with each other to pet the child who had escaped from the murderer by a miracle (and by his own wits).

Amerigo now found himself 'lovingly enfolded in the arms of the most elegant and noble ladies of Florence, smothered with caresses, sweets and kisses, invited to lunch every day and sent home in the evening with his pockets full of sweetmeats and . . . tender notes'. The poor thing was not used to such attentions and Yorick considered the boy in danger of being spoiled. But the 'pretty ladies are always right.' Naturally, they sided with the victim and since in this case the victim was a young boy, it was understandable that their pity should be manifested by a kind of maternal feeling as a reaction to the horror which everyone must feel at the killing of innocent creatures.

Only up to a certain point, however. No one could deny that some children raised on the streets were, so to speak, a little too lively. Newspapers had written about badly-brought-up ragamuffins who took pleasure in being cruel to unfortunate creatures who were deformed or mentally deficient. It was clear that this was exactly what had happened to Grandi. And many people believed that he had reasons for his ghastly acts, though this in no sense justified his acts; nor was there any support for his pet project of erecting a statue to the victim of street urchins' taunts.

It had to be admitted that the accused did not have the menacing look of a criminal, nor did he have the too-respectable look which some criminals donned like a mask to hide their true natures. The prison guards said that he seemed more like a boy, and they were certainly in a position to judge, being used to criminals. Various other people said the same and Yorick reported it. Grandi was generally seen as a miserable creature who gave himself so many airs because he didn't really understand what was going on, not even when the judges addressed him. He had no idea of the trouble he was in.

Basically, therefore, the trial of the child killer lacked the essential ingredients for a really sensational trial: harsh passions, a devilish intelligence and intense personal relationships which resulted in the spilling of blood. The general opinion was that the protagonists did not display the proper stereotypical appearance of murderer and victim. They did not fit perfectly into those roles which aficionados of dark deeds expected, and which involved clear distinctions between good and evil. The whole reason for the trial failed to evoke those natural sentiments which inclined people to support the principles of law.

It was the person of Grandi himself which aroused the greatest curiosity. In San Pancrazio people squeezed themselves 'into a corner for hours on end just to get to a tiny space where they could better see the pale, sullen face of the accused'. The newspapers had already described how extraordinarily ugly, even deformed, he was. Such physical characteristics were usually telling; for example, 'Poca barba e niun colore, sotto il ciel non vi a peggiore' (little beard and colour wan, there is no worse under the sun) everyone knew that. They may be only proverbs, manners of speaking, but still they meant something. Even the scientists, after all, could tell something about a person's character, feelings and intellect from their physical deformities; at least they were able to tell if a person was normal or not.

It was said that he was a cretin. That was the opinion in his home town, where the boys treated him as an idiot. Granted he could read and write, but even if he had read all those books he boasted about, that was no proof that he was right in the head. The 'first stage of madness is to think yourself wise', as the proverb says. But he was not mad. Or perhaps he was? It was important to be clear about the meaning of 'mad'. He was certainly dangerous. Nobody had expected him to react in such a way to the mockery of children. There were plenty of people like him around – was there anyone who hadn't come across them? Such people often played with children because they were not really grown men themselves, not even at thirty years old. You had to be careful. But how on earth could you spot the danger?

The doctors would explain everything. It had been announced. Those doctors and scientists who had been present in court since the very first day provided the other main focus of interest at the trial. In fact, during the hearing in which the defence experts were due to give evidence, an even greater number of people than usual appeared in the public galleries, and this time they were a rather specialized group: 'students of medical science, future psychiatrists, budding physiologists and psychologists who invade the spaces reserved for invited guests and even spill over onto the judges' bench. The common people, who don't understand any of the scientific language, sit listening attentively in the great chamber and the less they understand the more filled they are with admiration.' For the ordinary observer, it was a spectacle. Yorick commented that even the ubiquitous ladies and girls seemed to enjoy the 'pastime of a fairly appetizing psychological study'.

There was less interest later on, when it came to the prosecutor's summing up, because it was easy to predict what he would say. Those who were aware of the fact may have found it interesting that the deputy prosecutor, born in 1817, was also a native of the Valdarno – like the murderer and his victims. Sante Dini came from the Arezzo district, however, (his wife was from Arezzo itself), from Terranova, which was a bigger and more prosperous town than Incisa. He also came from a good family: his brother Luigi was a friend of the baron. In fact, it was thanks to Bettino Ricasoli's recommendation that Dini had been transferred to Florence from Ancona in 1873. There at the Court of Appeal he had quickly become known and feared for his moral rigour and untiring energy in criminal trials.[5]

Faced with such an adversary, what could the defence lawyers, both young and brilliant according to Yorick, come up with? They had put so much effort into defending the accused, even though he had confessed, that they must have had something good up their sleeves.

Thus it was that a trial which seemed at the outset to be quite clear cut was gradually becoming more complicated. Not that there were camps drawn up for and against the accused, who clearly was and remained a murderer. But some people changed their minds about the crime from one hearing to the next, including the lawyer Pietro Ferrigni, whose authoritative words could, as he was well aware, have a great influence on public opinion.

How did Yorick report the trial of the child killer, the trial which eventually became almost a 'cause célèbre'? Along with the stories of the famous brigand Musolino and the strangler Vincenzo Verzeni there appeared in 1878 a booklet in the popular series published by Adriano Salani entitled *Carlo Grandi* – number twenty-one in the collection of illustrated booklets.[6]

Yorick began with a knowledgeable description of the scene, of the crowd's restless anticipation and the procession of witnesses, 'all of them moved and shaken by terror, compassion or scorn … which made a great impression on the spectators'. He dwelled on Grandi's looks, on his 'harsh, strident, arrogant' voice and his strangely 'calm' demeanour. He drew readers' attention to the fact that the

presiding judge often had to recall the attention of the accused –
perhaps Grandi was hard of hearing.

Since he was prevented by Article 49 from reporting the evidence
heard in court, Yorick devised ingenious strategies to avoid restricting
himself to the meagre, boring accounts which was all that the other
journalists could produce.[7] If he wanted to explain in detail what
the schoolmaster Scoti had to say about his ex-pupil Grandi and the
other Incisans, then he produced someone who had a cousin who
was a good friend of a friend of Scoti. Thus he was able to write a
piece for *La Nazione* indirectly including the schoolmaster's evidence,
which he could then compare with the different opinion of another
teacher from the same school, Simoni. Or, since even the highly
qualified scientific experts were 'men who eat, drink, wear clothes
and often frequent eating houses, theatres and social gatherings',
Yorick swore that he had heard Professor Morselli's opinion in a
café one evening and not in the courtroom at San Pancrazio. He
devoted two articles to Morselli, which, though faintly ironic about
the young man's pomposity, were nevertheless full of praise. He
wrote that Morselli's arguments and examples were so well expressed
that they would be, if not convincing, at least clearly understood by
everyone.

But Yorick did not just want to present a package of facts which
were already known, however rich it might be. From the very
beginning he noted that there were two distinct and incompatible
points of view and he made it clear that the evidence took on a
different significance according to which point of view was adopted.
For whoever

> aspires to apply the law and to protect society, a murderer who waits
> with feline cunning for the time, method and opportunity to kill and then
> does so quickly and surely, who then hides the bodies for long days and
> months, who has a clear notion of life and death and who for himself
> loves the first and fears the second while being prepared lightly to inflict
> death on others . . . is indisputably wicked.

Grandi was not a madman, explained Yorick to his readers. In his
professional legal capacity he knew well that the examining magistrate
had proceeded on the basis of a conviction that Grandi was sane.
The psychiatric experts, however, completely disagreed. The 'illustrious professors who are determined to enlighten the lawyers and
prevent the punishment of one who is not responsible for his actions'
maintained that Grandi should be confined for life in an asylum.
Everyone had already learned from the newspapers that Grandi

displayed 'physical signs of degeneracy and that there were many who attested to the feebleness of his brain'. But both Yorick and the anonymous journalist in the *Opinione Nazionale* used identical words on 20 December 1876, when they noted that this same brain had been capable not only of planning and committing the crimes but also of cunningly laying the blame on others.

Grandi's was a strange case, therefore. In the two newspapers it was defined in the following inaccurate but suggestive words: 'the abnormal case of a hardworking, honest, quiet, studious man who commits a series of atrocious murders as though it were the most natural thing in the world'.

According to Yorick, the central issue was that

> between science and the application of criminal justice ... there is a complete opposition of ideas; it is almost that the one side suspects the other of having too great an attachment to scientific problems and being consequently indifferent to the rationale of justice, while the other side sees the principles of science being undermined because of an excessive adherence to the injunctions of the law.

If a final verdict was to be reached, this conflict would have to be resolved – but in which direction? Instead of siding firmly with the typical magistrate's mentality, Ferrigni the lawyer became daily more open to the opposite view expressed by the psychiatrists. Possibly he was attracted by their desire to expose errors and prejudices which were not only inherent to the common people but persisted even in more cultured circles.

> The error lies in believing that a madman is incapable of thinking, of reflecting, of considering an idea up to a point, whereas the truth is that madmen think and reflect with often singular tenacity. The prejudice lies in believing that madmen lose all awareness of themselves and that they are not inspired by certain passions, whereas, on the contrary, such passions are most powerful in those who lack the rationality to restrain them. The emotions are not absent in the insane nor is their intellect always atrophied or destroyed.

Ferrigni had learned this from Professor Carlo Livi, who had honoured him with his friendship. In the court-room, Livi's expert evidence had impressed everyone: 'a truly great display of oratory and science, a feast for the ears and the mind'.

The journalist also heaped praise on Francesco Bini, the last expert witness to speak for the defence. Indeed, his eulogies were sometimes excessive. He was a 'most knowledgeable man ... univer-

sally known as one of the most illustrious and justly famous psychiatrists in Italy'. The lawyer Ferrigni had gone to shake Bini's
hand after the hearing and he wished his readers to know this. The
impassioned defence evidence of all three psychiatrists had truly
provided a 'useful lesson'.

In contrast, he demolished the evidence of the prosecution experts
in three short paragraphs published a day after the hearing. He had
not a word of praise for Carlo Morelli, and Giuseppe Lazzaretti was
merely 'well versed . . . in forensic medicine'. Yorick stated that their
arguments, of which he gave no summary, would have 'in any case
had no interest for the reader', and was couched in such refinements
as to bore rigid the jurors who were constrained to listen. He was
left with a strong sense of unease by the fact that although 'taking
the same starting point and pursuing more or less the same paths',
the scientists – one lot called by the defence lawyers and the others
by the King's Deputy Prosecutor – reached such different conclusions.

According to Sante Dini, the evidence produced by the defence
was not sufficient to convince serious people that the murderer
was a lunatic who should be confined to an asylum. The so-called
biographical novel by the Incisan cartwright, which the court had
first accepted as material evidence and then rejected, counted for
nothing. And yet the lawyers and experts for the defence had regarded
that document, which now lay on Yorick's table, as crucial. 'Oh . . .
gentle readers! If only I might be allowed to place Grandi's novel
before your eyes!' The novel, rejected by the judges and removed
from the jurors' scrutiny, was published in *La Nazione* in a full-page
reproduction on Saturday, 30 December, after delivery of the final
sentence – with which the accused, at least, declared himself 'very
satisfied'.

Yorick fulfilled his duty as a chronicler in every particular in his
account of the final court hearing, apart from the fact that he made
no reference to the curses launched at Grandi by the enormous
crowd at the exit. The trial was over and there was no possibility of
an appeal. Pietro Ferrigni solemnly affirmed that from then on there
would remain in the public conscience 'the great unresolved problem
of [the man's] state of mind'. It was for this reason, to 'throw a little
light on the shadows of that feeble brain', that he had decided to
publish the pages written in prison by the murderer. He launched an
appeal to 'psychiatrists, students of psychic problems, physiologists
and scientists' to assess the writing, drawing, content and thence the
sick personality of the author.

The lawyer-journalist did not write a word about the judges.

During his whole account he left them very much in the shadow of the other personalities, including the general public. This omission was suitable for the men who were not in court to represent themselves or the litigants, but the principle of justice itself – values which ranked above their own feelings and opinions. The judges' duty was to uphold respect for the due process of law. The trial should appear to unfold itself according to the process dictated by the code and applied by the court. What the procedures were and how they were applied in a particular trial remained mysteries to the public and difficult to explain. Even when the reporter was an expert on legal matters like Yorick, *La Nazione* readers would certainly have been put off by an excess of boring legal details.

The judges in court

To understand the internal functioning of a trial in the light of the current Penal Procedure Code and the most important principles of jurisprudence and even by knowing something of the real flesh and blood judges conducting it, it is necessary to have some knowledge of the threads which had been drawn together to form the seemingly inevitable process. Was there any point at which things might have gone differently?

The question is worth asking not only when anomalies appear which would be of no great significance in comparison to the normal procedure. Even assuming that everything ran true to norm, it is worth questioning whether and how, within pre-established structures, a trial could have taken a different direction – and why it did not do so. Which interpretations, informed choices, prejudices or habits were the predominant influences? It is particularly relevant to pose these questions if the problems met with in the course of the trial did not have any firm legal precedent or if the system was undergoing a radical reassessment which had not yet reached any conclusions. This was the case regarding the question of imputability which was central to the case against Carlo Grandi.

The *La Nazione* reports, with their suggestion of a certain direction which might influence not only the public but also the judges, make one think that up until the very last moment the outcome of the trial was far from predictable. Occasionally Yorick would write that if he were the presiding judge he would have said this or that, done this or that. The real judge, Giorgio Mori Ubaldini, was probably less than delighted to read in the newspaper what the enterprising journalist would have done in his shoes and how he himself ought to be behaving.

The two men certainly knew each other: the judge had been working at the Court of Appeal in Florence since 1862, the place where in 1864 Pietro Ferrigni had failed his advocacy examinations – a fact which did not prevent him from being promoted when he applied directly to the minister.[8] But quite apart from any personal friction, Yorick's little game of 'if-I-were-the-presiding-judge' made one thing clear: that the judge did in fact have a variety of choices. He could conduct himself as he was in fact doing in the trial, or as Ferrigni would have done, or as another person might have chosen to do in his place.

This scope was acknowledged in the Penal Procedure Code, as the regulations allowed for different ways of conducting a trial. The role of presiding judge carried widely discretionary powers in comparison with other jobs within the legal profession. The judge could order whatever action he deemed useful for the discovery of the truth; he could accept or reject requests from the litigants; he could question the accused, witnesses and experts. He directed the whole trial and the jury in particular as he formulated the questions they should address, summarized the arguments and decided when the trial was concluded.[9] Some legal experts argued that the presiding judge's powers were too wide, even granted that he did not have total freedom. What he enjoyed was the power of self-determination within a context structured by a few rules, the same power in fact which the law recognized as the right of every reasonable person; as such he also had the choice to behave in other ways. So how did the presiding judge conduct the trial against Grandi? It is not only murderers who leave clues behind them, but judges as well.

Born in Florence at the end of March 1816, single and with no personal wealth, Giorgio Mori Ubaldini lived with his aged mother and two older sisters. His service record reveals few facts about him and none of any great interest. He took up advocacy in 1839 and followed that career until 1846, when he became a magistrate at the court of Portoferraio on the island of Elba. From there he was transferred to other centres in the Grand Duchy of Volterra and Grosseto. During the provisional government he became prosecutor at the Court of Appeal in Florence, where he pursued a slow but steady career until he became councillor of the Court of Cassation* in 1877, a few months after Grandi's trial.[10]

* The Court of Cassation (Corte di Cassazione) was the highest decision-making body in both civil and criminal law. Its function was to ensure strict observation of the law, to make decisions related to it and to ensure uniformity of interpretation.

When the child killer's trial was passed to him on 12 November 1875, Mori Ubaldini had been a councillor at the Court of Appeal for thirteen years and was presiding judge of one of the two Assize circuits. As such he had a prime duty to go and question the accused 'twenty-four hours at most after his arrival in the city where he is to be tried' according to Article 456 of the Penal Procedure Code. Nevertheless, for unknown reasons he delayed until 7 February the visit to Murate prison where Grandi had been incarcerated since 1 September. The presiding judge can certainly not have been a curious man. Many ordinary citizens, having heard that he was an astonishing person, had already visited Grandi in prison, but Mori Ubaldini felt no pressing need to become acquainted with the man on whom he was to sit in judgement. When he did go, his questioning was completed in a few minutes and consisted of only five officially recorded sentences.

The judge also had a duty to gather any other information which seemed to him useful or relevant, but Mori Ubaldini made no use of these liberal powers. He limited himself to accepting the requests from the defence and then the prosecution to call expert witnesses. It would appear that he judged any further information to be unnecessary and, to the chagrin of some commentators, Articles 464 and 465 of the Penal Procedure Code deemed that his was the final word on that question.[11]

In fact, as soon as a case reached the courts the authority of the investigating stage diminished; moreover, the judges worked within criteria which were in direct opposition to those which operated during the investigation. Hearings were no longer secret but open, vociferous and adversarial, and the rights of the defence were fully aired whereas they had been completely ignored during the examining stage. To this end the presence of the accused was always required during criminal trials. If this was not possible, for example if the accused became mentally ill and could not defend himself, the trial had to be postponed until his normal health was restored.

Mori Ubaldini prepared for the trial without pause. In court he was flanked by the fifty-six-year-old Filippo Petrucci and by Agostino Bonini, forty-eight. They were both merely court judges and so ranked below the presiding judge. This meant that they tended to give way to their superior to such an extent that it was feared that the collegiate consensus which was supposed to operate was undermined.[12] This was especially true if a judge lacked experience, as was certainly the case with the Florentine Bonini, who had only been in the Tuscan capital since 1873 and had only been on the bench thirteen times in twenty years. His speciality was not criminal but civil cases and he displayed no particular merit. 'A mediocre mind ... adequate competence, average industry, indifferent moral and political conduct'. This was the assessment of him in 1875 by his superiors at the Court of Appeal in Florence, one of whom was Mori Ubaldini.

Bonini had completed his studies at Pisa. He had gained his diploma in philosophy in 1845, in jurisprudence two years later, and in 1849 gained his degree with a thesis on civil and canonical law. Of the latter his colleague also had some knowledge. Petrucci had gained his degree in Rome, his birthplace. He had been a lawyer at the Curia for nine years then held a position on the Holy See's legal circuit, travelling to various parts of the Papal States as a judge until in 1869 he found a rather different position in Florence. There, even in the liberal Tuscan courts, he brought with him the methods and theory which had been his first training, based on an inquisitorial system and the most reactionary penal code in existence, the *Regolamenti sui delitti e delle pene** passed by Gregory XVI and still in force until 1871.

Apart from Perrucci, all the judges in court or in the committal section who were involved in the Grandi case were born and had studied in Tuscany.[13] They had all been educated within the Grand Duchy, at the University of Siena or at La Sapienza in Pisa, where Carrara had graduated in 1827, where his tutor Giovanni Carmignani taught criminal law and the philosophy of law, and where Girolamo Poggi and Francesco Forti waged war on formalism with their civilized passion and European culture. In Florence, however, apart from the ancient jurisprudence of 1472, there were only two schools; these were integrated into the school founded by Leopold II (later to become the Dante School) in 1859. One dealt with civil institutions and was badly taught. The other concerned itself with criminal law and until 1860 had been directed by the Sienese Giuseppe Puccioni, champion of pure oratory and author of the excellent *Codice Penale Toscano Illustrato*.[14] These faculties were established to train future civil service bureaucrats and were therefore more geared towards the practical whereas in Pisa and Siena the emphasis was on theory, giving rise to complaints about scholasticism and detachment from social problems in those institutions. When the Istituto di Studi Superiori was established in 1859 the intention had been to set up a department of legal studies. But this came to nothing and the provision for the study of law in the capital remained fairly bleak from the academic point of view.

* Rules on Crimes and Penalties

And yet there were several major figures in Florence. Among both the old and the new groups whose spirit was anti-academic, the study of law was not only welcomed but actively promoted in conjunction with various social disciplines which addressed labour problems such as the 'urbanization of peasants'. In 1875 the Carlo Alfieri School of Social Research hosted the jurisprudence faculty, funded by the local authority thanks to the interest of the mayor, Ubaldino Peruzzi. The ancient Accademia dei Georgofili had for some time put law students, whether they were well-known or not, in contact with agrarian economists in particular but also with natural scientists, historians and doctors whose post-graduate studies were organized by Maurizio Bufalini – who was also in charge of law students.[15] The Gabinetto Scientifico Letterario di Vieuseux involved in its work and in the *Nuova Antologia* and other journals those who returned to Florence to take up a legal career or advocacy. A group of young people had organized themselves to practise legal debates, simulating situations of litigation, first judgement and judgement on appeal. Their 'Accademia dei Nomofoli' was opened in 1839, the same year that Mori Ubaldini became a lawyer, and it is quite plausible to suppose that he may have taken part, as might Carlo Migliorini, who had qualified four years previously, Leopoldo Puccioni, a lawyer in Florence from 1848 to 1855, or possibly even Bonini, who enrolled in 1853.[16] Whoever wanted to lay the foundations of the profession went along to that hall of oratory in the Camera di Disciplina. The cultural level, however, left something to be desired, and there was no substantial methodology. Similar problems were highlighted by the 1859 commission to reorganize further education. After they had gained their qualifications, people were left more or less to fend for themselves.

Despite all this, it was still a matter of pride to belong to the famous Tuscan school whose reputation had grown with the incumbency of Francesco Carrara, tutor in penal law at Pisa from 1859. It was also a source of pride to be working autonomously according to the Tuscan penal code, which had been promulgated in 1853 along with police regulations and had resisted 'colonization' from Piedmont. In comparison, the Sardinian code practised everywhere else throughout the Kingdom seemed to lack scientific basis, was short on theoretic rigour and was still marked with the death penalty, which Leopold had abolished in 1786.[17]

The authoritative legislature and the reforms of Mori were always referred to in the continuous attempts to establish a unified code. They were particularly scrutinized whenever a new proposal reached parliament. Such a proposal was put forward by Mancini in 1864 just before Florence was made the capital, then ten years later by Chancellor Vigliani and again when his proposal was later taken up by Mancini in a left-wing government. In 1876, at the time of the Grandi trial, the question was being discussed by everyone: the magistrature, forensic associations, university legal faculties and even the medical profession, which the Minister, who was chairing a commission which included Carrara and two Florentine jurists, asked to address. The abolition of the death penalty, the role of a jury of peers (strongly supported by liberal Tuscans), the requirements for imputability which in the Sardo-Italian code rested on artificial and antiquated criteria: these were the main questions to be resolved. These were the questions which judges constantly came up against during trials without being able to rely on certainties established by precedent.

This then, briefly outlined, was the situation in which the judges in charge of the public trial of Carlo Grandi the child killer had to work. And there was one other interesting detail about them: none of the judges had any children – all three of them were and remained bachelors.

The investigation challenged

The procedure which the trial was to follow was strictly laid out in the Penal Procedure Code. First the judge questioned the accused on the facts of the prosecution case and then the court clerk read out the documentary evidence relevant to the case. Presumably this order of events was followed in Grandi's case.[18]

The first hearing, as we have seen, was on 18 December 1876. The accused was asked for his general personal details, the jury and expert witnesses were sworn in, the experts were presented with the questions they would have to answer, the presiding judge urged Grandi to pay close attention to what he was about to hear, and the clerk read aloud both the committal to trial issued on 12 November 1875 and the indictment of 24 November.[19]

The first document was twelve pages long and the second, nine. The jury and public heard the astonishing events recalled, from the mysterious disappearance of the children to the discovery of the murderer *in flagrante delicto*. The account was naturally not unbiased. It was presented by the prosecution, who emphasized the aggravating features of the case: how cunning Grandi had been to spread rumours of a kidnapper in town, the hatred he felt towards children in general, not just the victims in particular, the domineering way he behaved to his own family, how he had laid the flagstone floor in the workshop so he could bury the little bodies and how, therefore, the crimes were premeditated. This was all presented as fact, although in terms of the legal code it was merely 'presumed opinion', and unproven.

Then followed the even more suggestive report of Sante Dini, in court in his capacity as public prosecutor. He dwelled on the agony of the town and the anxious maternal hearts. He reported the dialogue between the last victim and his attacker, and the desperate cries of Amerigo's mother, as though he had heard them himself. He evoked again the revulsion of the populace and the murderer's confession. He even went so far as to make the claim, which even the calligraphic expert felt unable to do later in the hearing, that it was Grandi who had placed 'a placard in the streets of Incisa' (in fact, a small note that can be seen in the archives) to lay the blame on another suspect. *That's not my writing; my letters are more elegant, more beautiful*, Grandi protested in court when shown the paper. *My letters are better, much better. Some idiot must have written this.*[20]

After the reading, which made a strong impression on those who could hear it, the presiding judge gave instructions regarding all the lengthy procedures concerned with witnesses, jurors and experts. Only after that – on page sixteen, the penultimate page of the records – did Mori Ubaldini finally turn to the questioning of Grandi. He admitted having killed the four children and the circumstances surrounding their deaths. Thus the clerk summarized in two lines all that the accused had said during the investigation when, among other things, he had tried in his own way to explain why he resented the boys so much, how the whole of Incisa gave him nicknames and called him *dwarf, twenty-one-toes, monster, squint-eye*, and threw his hat on the ground to make fun of him. *I . . . got all angry and inflamed and I could not stay. I went to many people, even the priest*, but they would not stop. He threatened them with a broom but they still would not stop. Since it was all useless, he thought to himself, I will kill them, *I'll set a good example*. Those he had killed *were all wicked people.*

---

* Henceforth in this chapter all quotations taken directly from the court records are in inverted commas, while quotations from other sources are in italics, illustrating the significance of what was omitted from the records.

There followed the untranscribed 'observations and questions arising from the public prosecutor, the defence, the experts, the jurors and the court clerk'. From everyone in fact, except the presiding judge, who instead ordered the clerk to read out the three interrogations of the cartwright conducted by the prosecutor and examining magistrate. After this he intended to close the hearing. There were no objections to this, but in doing so Mori Ubaldini contravened two established rules of the Leopoldine legal reforms, namely the principle of orality and, more specifically, the direct injunction against reading out in court previous statements of anyone who was present and could be directly questioned in the presence of lawyers and the public. This deviation from the code of practice which was adopted by Ubaldini was allowed only if contradictions appeared between oral and written evidence or if clarification was required – but this was not the case in the Grandi trial.[21]

Something, therefore, was not right, either in the records compiled by the clerk Grossi or in the procedure adopted by Mori Ubaldini. There was something wrong with the means by which an artificially coherent account had been formulated by the judge and examining magistrate from the accused's admission of guilt and how his manner of expression had been formalized in the records and altered in the very process of being written down. This despite the fact that meanwhile, in court, Grandi was producing strange, incoherent, incongruous answers even when he was admitting to his deeds.

> *I ... did wrong, and I wanted to kill myself: I wanted to do the massacre on the 29th ... if I find the means to skewer them, I would make many other pairs of wrens fall ... and the mums stayed below: the dads stayed, and the mums who had come to see and there was a massacre of innocents.*

This, for example, he said with lively pleasure. But he became very confused in any long speech. He would start off vigorously: *Now I'll draw a parallel, a fine story and ... be quiet ... the bailiff at the palace said that the cartwright and the carpenter got on well together*, but then lose the thread.

The presiding judge was obliged to ask him only *restricted and limited questions*.[22] If he hadn't restricted the questioning people might have asked themselves if Grandi weren't perhaps truly mad – a hypothesis which neither the court judge nor his investigating colleagues wished to entertain. The judges in the committal session had written something which Mori Ubaldini ordered to be read out in court:

There is no doubt about the accused's mental state, which we know to be sufficient to take care of his own interests, and he is very able to pretend and dissemble . . . proud and domineering within his family, where . . . he succeeded in dominating everyone and being absolute master.

There was to be no doubt on this point, which may be why the report was read out. No doubt – despite what appeared in the newspapers, what was being said generally, what the defence experts and witnesses maintained and above all what was manifested by Grandi himself. His abnormal appearance, his bizarre demeanour, and his equally outlandish sentences and ideas – all could be seen and heard by everyone in court.

The question of sanity concerned not only the accused and the verdict against him. It was, above all, to do with the legitimacy of the methods adopted by the magistrates, who had effectively ignored the question of madness and allowed no doubts to appear in the investigating enquiry. The further the trial progressed, the more difficult it became to admit that the accused was mentally deficient and therefore unfit to plead, at least within the definition at the time. Once an individual had got as far as being committed for trial there were only two possibilities: either he was of sound mind and in full possession of his faculties or the examining magistrate had been negligent or mistaken, since it was technically impossible for a madman to stand trial. Chancellor Mancini was to say as much to Parliament in April 1877.[23]

Any doubts as to the accused's mental faculties should have been addressed immediately in the initial investigation. The code stated that the examining magistrate should appoint appropriate experts for the purpose and abide by their judgement. It was his duty, if necessary, to cancel the trial and commit the accused to an asylum. If, however, the investigation was completed, either because no doubt existed or all doubts had been dispelled, then the question could not be raised again. It was the council chamber's duty to verify that a trial was feasible and to note any circumstances indicating that the accused was not responsible for his actions. After that it was the duty of the committal session to make the final pronouncement, and then all was set in motion for the trial.

Once in court, as we have seen, the presiding judge had discretionary power to order further enquiries and even to stop the trial if the accused appeared to be unfit to plead. Not only that, but the question posed in respect to the past could also be valid for the present. The accused's mental state was relevant at two distinct points: at the time of trial it was the judge's duty to decide, but if the question referred to his mental state at the time of the crime, it was the jury who decided.[24]

In the case of Carlo Grandi, once the public trial had begun, though there was still some doubt on the part of the experts that the murderer was of sound mind, there was only one possibility left: that if the Incisan cartwright ever had been mad (which was the jury's duty to decide) then he may have been insane when he killed, either continuously or intermittently, from February 1873 to 29 August 1875, but completely sane a day later when questioned by Satti and sane again months later when the public trial began. In order to support the examining magistrate's decision therefore, it was imperative to eliminate all doubts as to Grandi's mental state.

The first witnesses to be called were the public prosecutor, Giovanni Melegari, and the examining magistrate, Agostino Satti. The choice was significant. They had not originally been called by the deputy prosecutor, Dini, on 24 November 1875, when he nominated all his prosecution witnesses, but later, on 8 September 1876, a week before the proposed opening of the trial, which was then postponed.[25] It was a last-minute nomination and one which was made, perhaps not entirely coincidentally, on the very day when the press called on scientists as well as magistrates to give their verdict on the Grandi case.

The decision, approved by Mori Ubaldini, to question the two magistrates 'on the impression they had formed of the accused's mental state from their many official contacts with him' must have caused some perplexity. They had already completed their duties, and the results were on record. Why then was the examining magistrate, who by definition should be impartial, being called as a witness for the prosecution? Satti and Melegari's presence in court pointed to a continuity of accusation between the examining stage and the trial. It was a defiant gesture in the face of questions from the public and attacks from psychiatrists about the whole process of establishing whether an accused person was fit to plead.

The Mantuan Giovanni Melegari, the King's deputy prosecutor, public prosecutor at Brescia and, since August 1870, in Florence, had already received many testimonials of praise for his work from his superiors. As recently as July 1875 a report from Florence praised his 'competence, great knowledge of the civil and penal codes, hard work and excellent political conduct'. Melegari declared that he always preferred taking the prosecuting role. His only regret seems to have been to find himself alone, far from his family and place of birth.[26]

He tried to go home to Medole whenever he could, whenever his work allowed – and sometimes more often than that. On 31 October 1876 he had taken forty-five days' leave to go to his parents' house, even though he knew he was due to appear in court as a witness. He sent a doctor's certificate to justify his absence. Whether he truly had lumbago or not, Melegari did not appear at San Pancrazio.

Instead, the celebrated examining magistrate, Agostino Satti, appeared on 19 December 1876 as the first witness. His evidence was clearly considered to be important, since some of it was recorded:

> I can say in all conscience, having had many meetings with Grandi in my official capacity and having questioned him often, that he always was and still is in full possession of his mental faculties; that I have not had any reason during the course of the trial to believe that his faculties have altered, and that the parish priest of Incisa, whom I questioned on the subject, never gave me any indication that Grandi was in any way mentally deficient.

Was he really convinced of this? Possibly not, because the last assertion was later corrected. Either because of his own change of mind or for some other reason, Satti stated that in fact he had talked about the case in only general terms with the priest and doctor. From the records of the investigation there is no sign that he ever questioned them at all. This is somewhat surprising, since they were both certainly well-informed about life in the town; he could also have ensured that they would act as his own witnesses instead of allowing them to be called by the defence.

When they did appear, two hearings later, one after the other and each forbidden to hear the other's evidence (according to the regulations relating to witnesses), Dr Migliarini and Don Fabio Somigli gave evidence which the court clerk failed to record at all. But *La Nazione* reported part of it, as the defence lawyers had anticipated they would. The fifty-four-year-old doctor, who had lived in Incisa with his wife and children for twenty-four years, gave the following evidence:

> *that he had sometimes been asked by the accused's family about how to go about committing him to an asylum. That the accused had very little skill in his work, although he claimed to be a clever man; that the*

father . . . was an unpredictable character and one of the sisters had the
same characteristics

as Callisto. Not only that, but when he learned that Grandi was
responsible for the crimes, Dr Migliarini swore in court that he
suspected a congenital mania and that he had told the examining
magistrate as much, but he did not want to know. For his part, the
sixty-year-old priest, who had been incumbent in the town for thirty
years, gave evidence that he had often seen Grandi

in an extraordinarily excitable state, that every change of season was
marked in him by physical signs, that he read books and claimed to be a
man of knowledge, although he was useless at everything, that the father
of the accused had an unpredictable nature and tendencies.

He kept *a skull on his table,* and according to the priest, Carlino's
mother had been frightened by this when pregnant, which is why
she had *given birth to a deformed, hairless boy.*[27]

After this evidence had been given, the examining magistrate was
recalled – rightly, according to Yorick – to clarify certain questions
which should have been recorded but were not. Satti was certainly
not one to pay attention to external characteristics, which may
explain why he had failed to complete the section on physical details
on the investigation form: 'age, height, hair, forehead, lashes, brows,
eyes, nose, mouth, beard, chin, colouring, physique and identifying
marks'. If he had completed the form, the magistrate might have
drawn a strange anthropological portrait – but he paid no attention
whatsoever to Grandi's appearance.

Professor Carlo Livi, who had listened attentively to Satti, wanted
to ask him some questions. He could not understand – again this
was reported by Yorick and omitted by the court clerk – how the
examining magistrate *had not realized from his enquiries that the*
prisoner was . . . a dangerous lunatic. He could not understand
how it was that Satti had never suspected it. Had Satti forgotten
accompanying him to the Murate prison to visit the child killer after
his arrest?

Yes, Satti remembered perfectly well, but he had believed *that the*
worthy professor, the illustrious psychiatrist, was convinced like
himself that Grandi was fully responsible for his actions. He swore
on oath to this, and no matter how astonishing his words may have
been he continued to justify them, explaining *that it is natural and*
easy to tell a madman at first sight – and the murderer of Incisa was

no madman. If he had been he would at least have attempted suicide (a clearly insane action); he would have been unmoved by the thought of his own death, whereas Grandi feared death, which was why he had thanked him and the carabinieri for saving him from the people of Incisa. Moreover, he had become very distressed when he thought his crimes were punishable by death and very relieved when he learned that the death penalty had been abolished in Tuscany.

These, according to Satti, were incontrovertible proofs of Grandi's sanity. 'Proofs' which, in fact, demonstrated nothing so clearly as the magistrate's own views on sanity and insanity, responsibility and guilt. To understand his attitude it is helpful to understand his perception of his own role, which was formed not only by his unpleasant nature but above all because he had studied law in the Duchy of Modena. The Duchy had one of the most restrictive codes of pre-unified Italy, giving enormous powers to examining magistrates and ascribing no duties towards the person, much less the rights, of the accused.[28]

Madness: fact and judgement

They had come to the crux of the matter. Ignored during the investigation, denied in the committal session, refuted by the public prosecutor and the presiding judge, the question could no longer be avoided.

Central to the Grandi case was not the usual question of whether the accused was guilty or not. There were very few doubts remaining about the circumstances of the crime and none at all about the perpetrator. Yet justice could not be done before the main questions were addressed regarding Grandi's mental illness and his imputability.

Given that the two issues were not the same, who would raise the questions and how? And who could provide the answers? In principle, only the court could decide on his fitness to plead and they had to translate the legalities into 'matters of fact' for the jurors, then back into legal terms when it came to the verdict and sentence. The problem involved the metaphysics of free will and theories of self-determination, compared with other theoretical concepts of responsibility, possibility and choice, which in their turn involved endless speculative interpretations.

In the actual practice of law, however, it was necessary to use prescribed formulas which were easily applied to real cases. The penal code forbore to speculate on what imputability actually meant and limited itself to stating how it was verifiable by listing the conditions necessary. In Tuscan law these were 'awareness of his own actions and freedom of choice' on the part of the criminal.[29] These criteria exercised not only the legal skills of the judges but also the non-specialized determination of the jury, who were restricted to addressing questions of fact and not allowed to discuss abstract points of law.

The question of imputability was dealt with differently in the Italian penal code, and the same case tried in another court in the kingdom would have raised different questions. Article 94 of the Italian code included in the definitions of unimputability 'complete imbecility, madness or morbid rage'. The jury would have had to base its decision on those three criteria, whose rigidity was inherited from Roman law with additions from the extremely adversarial French code, and whose premises were entirely antiquated from a clinical point of view.

The Tuscan code was much more up to date and was often cited for the scientific soundness of its Article 34. The code frequently floundered in the practical application of the law, however, even in 'the courts of cultured Tuscany' as the *Rivista Penale*[30] disappointedly admitted. The failure was apparently due to the inherent difficulties of the code. It was hard for jurors to have the necessary depth of understanding, since concepts of 'awareness' and 'freedom' have a complex range of meanings in human beings. It was also difficult for the judges, and the presiding judge in particular, to explain and mediate the different meanings that the terms might assume not only in common and legal language, but also in the medical and psychiatric language which was almost completely foreign to him.

That is why neither the Vigliani proposal of 1874 nor the latest Mancini one of 1876 copied the Tuscan code exactly on the question of imputability (though Zanardelli later did so in 1889). The magistrates who were used to working within the code knew its inadequacies and were in a sense forced to question it and become familiar with its merits as well as its defects. On the other hand, they were required to express an opinion on the alternatives, to be officially presented to the Minister before 20 November 1876. They had to be open to the seemingly inevitable need for a closer link with scientific principles. The proposals were still unsatisfactory, however, and it was to be almost thirty years before Italy had a single, unified penal code.

According to the authority Luigi Lucchini in 1874, the article in the penal code concerning imputability, which had just been considered by senatorial commission, should be rejected because it was 'incapable of meeting the requirements of science'. The Court of Appeal in Florence, among others, had also come out against it, recognizing a dangerous reduction in the conditions which qualified a defendant as unfit to plead; no account was taken of 'lunatics . . . who show awareness of their actions', for example. Rather than talking of moral or intellectual awareness or knowledge legal or otherwise, it would be better to concentrate on the question of individual freedom (and not only freedom from external factors). This was the view taken by the most advanced jurists and various medical men including Livi, Bini and even Lazzaretti, who all agreed that questions of mental illness went far beyond the limits of intellectual capacity to which, for example, forensic medicine and the Anglo-Saxon code adhered. The jurist Luigi Lucchini reminded everyone that a responsible man was the man who determined his actions on the basis of his own intelligence and will and not on external factors such as habits, passions and environment. Even in Parliament it was said that legislators should be more ready to listen to men such as doctors and psychiatrists, who were in contact with and made a study of mental illness. Others argued that they had no faith in certain tenets of modern science such as the concept of rational madness 'which are employed in the defence of the most wicked characters'.[31]

Certainly no one proposed replacing the old criteria of imputability with the very latest nosographic categories; the list would have been endless, incomplete and inexact. The doctors themselves admitted that their knowledge of mental pathology was new and continually developing. And a good legislator should no more provide a list of psycho-moral specifications than a good magistrate should ask an expert for a medical definition simply to determine whether it fell within the code and was therefore acceptable by the court. It was better to adopt less constrictive formulas (which is how the Tuscan procedure was perceived at the time) so that medical science could then provide precise definitions of symptoms and causes in each individual case and the judge could weigh his decision according to the expert information.[32]

That was the way things should have proceeded, at least according to Giuseppe Lazzaretti in his proposed modifications to the Vigliani proposal. In reality, however, matters were often conducted very differently, even in places where the most advanced codes were in operation, often prompting bitter comments in the legal press reports. Some considered that 'neither science nor the law could provide safe, solid criteria' for deciding whether the suspected madness of a defendant were real or simulated. This was the opinion of most magistrates, yet they had to continue with their work regardless. Besides, no particular scientific or legal knowledge was required from the jury. They were citizens chosen at random to be temporary representatives of popular justice and they had to state in court whether they found that any factual circumstance rendered the accused unfit to plead. According to Baldassare Paoli of the Court of Appeal in Florence in 1875, all the fourteen members of the jury needed in order to answer that question was a simple knowledge of the 'factors preceding, concomitant and subsequent to the crime to understand the criminal's state of mind'.[33]

They were to make this judgement with the help of experts and by taking account of all the information provided by the witnesses.[34] The witnesses themselves were expected to provide 'an exposition of the facts which chance has led them to witness'. The scientists were required to provide 'a detailed examination of the person or object . . . requiring specialist knowledge'. It could not be expected that doctors or handwriting experts or engineers should understand points of law such as the question of imputability. The experts were merely required to provide a narrowly defined 'declaration of technical truth', though the value ascribed to their evidence was at the court's discretion. The Turin Court of Appeal decreed in 1868 that expert evidence did not constitute 'a true and definitive judgement which restricts the judges' own assessment'. The other courts in the kingdom, including Florence, stated that 'the judges are not bound to agree with the experts' opinion,' and again in 1878 that 'the expert, though appointed by the court, cannot overrule the judges' opinion with his own.'[35]

When they asked for the assistance of three experts, the lawyers Galardi and Papasogli made one important stipulation: that the psychiatrists should be questioned 'according to the criteria of their own discipline'.[36] But Mori Ubaldini established from the very first hearing that the experts were expected to give an opinion on the following questions: 1) whether or not Grandi was aware of his own actions and had freedom of choice, and 2) whether, instead, he was acting in a state of mind close to that of one who is unaware or deprived of freedom.

The questions were formulated directly from the penal code. They were addressed to doctors but came from the legal discipline which was thus imposed on the medical. The questions considered the hypothesis of partial responsibility which many psychiatrists found unacceptable, as Livi and Bini pointed out.[37] They limited decisions about the illness to the times when the crimes were committed – a procedure which was in line with legal thinking but went against the anatomical-pathological diagnosis of the defence experts.

It was obviously difficult for specialists with different functions and disciplines to understand one another. It was no less difficult for them to discuss their opinions with the witnesses, especially if these were uneducated country men and women. But the code prescribed that witnesses should be allowed to express themselves in their own manner in whatever way was most natural and appropriate to them, without interference or the imposition of conditions. Only when a witness had finished giving evidence could he be questioned by the prosecutor, the experts and the judges, including the presiding judge, who could also ask questions on behalf of the defence and the accused; these were not allowed to ask questions directly except at the discretion of the presiding judge himself.

How were the questions formulated? How comprehensible were they and how comprehensible were the replies to the jury? How were they summarized by the presiding judge and invariably altered in the light of psychiatric or legal considerations? None of these questions is clarified by the official records, but there is no doubt that the language and mentalities of those who were to throw light on the case – the country people on the one hand and the medical professors on the other – were very different. And there were differences also in the language used by those who were prosecuting, defending and judging. The language of the judges was not the language of the jurors. So the same question should have been articulated in several different versions according to who was asking and who was answering, and the two could never tally exactly. Otherwise, answers given to the same question might relate to various unexpressed perceptions which, to be properly understood, required further questions.

Was Carlo Grandi imputable? That is, was he aware of his actions and did he have freedom of choice? Was he in full possession of his faculties or was he mad? Did the witness think Grandi was mad? What did the witness mean by mad? Did the jury know what the witness meant? What did the expert mean by mad? Did the jury know what the expert meant? Did the judges understand?

If imputability was a category defined by law then the cause of mental deficiency should also, in the legal mind, be presented as a fact. Many agreed with Carrara in denying that it was effectively possible to separate 'questions of fact' and 'questions of law'. It was on that point that the judges' competence divided. It was the presiding judge alone who always had to mediate and decide between one version or the other, between witnesses and experts, for the sake of the jury.[38] The jury had to reach its verdict on the basis of proven facts. This remained as true for a question of madness as it did for a gunshot or a forced lock. There was no acknowledgement that even the discussion of that particular fact involved some degree of interpretation. The existence of mental illness and its recognition have different but inseparable meanings.

What exactly was the imbecility about which the psychiatrists spoke? And what did it mean to the presiding judge who questioned everyone? And what meaning did it have for the listening members of the jury?

The village idiot and the schoolmaster

Giorgio Mori Ubaldini warned each witness of the moral import of his evidence and the religious duty which the believer owed before God. He reminded them of the legal penalties for perjury and refusal to give evidence as set out in Articles 365, 366, 367 and 369 of the code. It was no longer a requirement to place their right hands on the Bible, but the witnesses stood and swore to tell 'the truth and nothing but the truth'.[39] After each witness had been questioned, time was allotted to Carlo Grandi if he wanted to add anything.

Argenta Monsecchi and her daughter Giulia separately told of how they had raised the alarm upon hearing Amerigo's cries coming from the cartwright's workshop. Grandi had this to add: *We must all tell the truth or else we will go to the depths of hell.* The child's mother *stole more than eighty-six pounds of oil from me* was what he said about her having run and called for help. The boy also told what he remembered of those terrible moments and Grandi added, *I hit him with the wheel not the sand*:

> *And Carlino was discovered and the whole mess was discovered. I want to do forced labour, forced labour . . . they are not telling the truth: they came running with their hoops and they threw my sand on the ground, he . . . stole a nut from me and threw stones at my knee . . . I thank the carabinieri and I want to send a telegram to the whole universe.*

On the following day it was the turn of the victims' parents to speak, and they provided the most moving evidence. Did the accused have anything to add? Certainly. Referring, for example, to Bonechi's mother: *If they discovered the whole mess she would go to prison for ten years. I met her husband once carrying a basket of grapes ... I give thanks to Victor Emmanuel and the carabinieri.* And what about the poor victims? *But those boys caused more damage than a flood!* But he had a headache now, it was surely going to rain. *I am in the hands of the government: look it's written up there, The Law is Equal for All: therefore I confess, I will send a telegram and I will thank everyone, the judges, the carabinieri and the King.*

The court clerk did not record either Grandi's words or the preceding evidence, apart from a few additions which pointed to the accused's wickedness and cunning. Grandi's other neighbours in the town expressed the usual contempt for him: the cobblers Luti and Bannucci, the furnace worker Farsini, the guard Piccioli and the municipal officials Focardi and Daddi – even the town councillor Ceccherini and the tobacconist Francalanci, who was recalled to provide clarifications. Precisely what these were the court clerk did not specify, although he was supposed to. He also failed to record anything even when witnesses gave evidence which contradicted what they had said months earlier.

It was inevitable. It seems astonishing that they were called as prosecution witnesses at all, given the impressions of Grandi's mental faculties which they had expressed in the initial investigation. Once in court, they changed their minds perhaps or, like Francalanci, changed their stories. The tobacconist now swore that he had 'never heard that Grandi or any of his family were mentally deficient'. He also volunteered that in Incisa, of which he was not a native himself, 'many other men have the same level of intelligence' as the accused – a depressing statement, but one which served to give the impression that the cartwright's peculiarities were not his own idiosyncrasies but part of a social and cultural backwardness inherent to the whole community.

After all this, Giorgio Mori Ubaldini closed the hearing on 20 December 1876 at six p.m. He first declared that if there were no objections, the expert witnesses could be released from their duties. He made this announcement, observed Yorick in *La Nazione*, at the very moment when the defence experts wanted to ask the witnesses questions about the accused's normal behaviour in comparison with his present manner. Grandi's family was not allowed to give evidence, as they were considered to be biased and therefore not reliable as witnesses.[40] This despite the fact that it was presumably they – his mother, two sisters, brother-in-law and two brothers – who knew Grandi's character better than anyone and would have been able to spot the changes in mood which others would not have suspected.

Poor Don Brachetti, at least, was well aware of something strange in Carlino, *changes of behaviour*. Moreover, he had suggested to Grandi's mother that he should be put under observation or directly *into an asylum, because with that lad in the house there was no feeling safe*. This was told to the judges by Maddalena Benucci, forty-seven years old, married, and the sister of the former priest of Incisa. We have already seen what the current priest, Somigli, and the town doctor thought. They declared that at the time of the second murder Grandi seemed *out of his mind and in a state of high excitement, he didn't pay attention to anyone, he didn't want to eat*. The housewife Rosa Pignotti recalled that at that very time she had found *Carlino's mother in tears* because her *abortion* of a son was doing all sorts of crazy things and she had *made him go to the doctor's, who had said 'have him committed; I can't do anything; it must be a nervous illness!'* She swore on oath that the cartwright's family considered him to be *mentally deficient*. The upholsterer Giuseppe Martelli, fifty years old and married, stated that this was the general opinion in town. Grandi boasted a lot, but *there was nothing in his conversation, he spoke nonsense and acted like an idiot*. He was considered a fool in Incisa, stated the builder Simone Pellegrini. When questioned by Ceccherini, however, he said that his boss told him not to pave the whole floor, not Carlino. The carpenter Narciso Galanti, thirty-three and married with children, stated in court that Grandi had sometimes shown *external signs* of mental trouble, especially once when Galanti thought Carlino was *going mad and he went to the doctor who told him to give him a purgative*. Rosa and Luigi Griffoni, a husband and wife in their sixties, she a dressmaker and he a labourer, said that Grandi had been *almost constantly ill* since childhood and complained all the time of pains and of not feeling well. Grandi used to go and read them his *Libro di Carlino*, which involved the murders of about ten boys and two girls, but the couple seemed basically fond of him. Carlino *was useless at doing anything and read many books*. He did not have *the awareness* (of his actions) *which a sane man ought to have*, and Signora Griffoni told the court how she used to tell him, *You're a donkey!*[41]

And that was all. The lawyers had not found anyone else from Incisa who was inclined to speak up in defence of the child killer, but there were witnesses who had nothing to do with the town, who were prepared to give evidence about the *mental and physical* condition of the accused. There were the prison guards Michelangelo Garnieri and Vincenzo Ceccaglini, both under thirty years old, and the authoritative Alessandro Soffietti, nearly seventy, the governor of the Murate prison. They had first received the prisoner Grandi as a criminal, but over the months they had become more and more convinced that he was a physically deformed madman, or rather, an *imbecile with dangerous instincts*. He used to go through extra-ordinarily agitated periods, especially when the weather changed. He had made a figure out of bread and boasted that it was his statue, he had dug a hole half a metre deep in his cell to put the figure in and had generally done all the strange things which Dr Morselli and his colleagues had recorded.

Two more people appeared in court to confirm the *unsound mind* theory: the fifty-five-year-old Chiarino Chiarini, who had been a most respected prison doctor for almost thirty years, and the younger doctor, Andrea Ceccherelli, whose job was to assess prisoners for transfer to asylums.[42] Chiarini stated that he had recognized in Grandi symptoms typical of *cerebral lesions*. Both doctors described his *sitophobic insomnia, the rambling, crazy songs and monologues, his mad claims . . . his indifference to everything . . . and the necessity for a straightjacket* which they sometimes had to use because he was *imbecilic, imperfect, with manifestations of real mental alienation*.

Yorick commented that the doctors' opinions seemed almost a ploy by the defence, and as they came so unexpectedly, both doctors were admonished by the court for not having come forward sooner. The presiding judge called for certain clarifications from other defence witnesses, which had the effect of ridiculing or at least casting doubt on the intelligence of the witnesses themselves, let alone Grandi. That, at least, is how it appeared to *La Nazione*.

The nominated witnesses had all given evidence, though nothing was in any way clear at that point. Far from it – the picture was more confused now than it had been at the beginning. The oral evidence was contradictory and also contradicted the earlier written testimony, since all the Incisans who appeared in court were called by the prosecution, and since the question was not simply a subjec-tive opinion of whether Grandi was mad or not but whether he was considered to be so in his home town. What had been said and thought about him before it was known that he was the murderer was one factor to be considered; it was quite another matter what the same people said or thought after he had been discovered and the authorities had intervened and the whole horrendous affair was known beyond the town and had even reached the newspapers and the city. In court, the evidence for or against the theory that he was mentally deficient and irresponsible was not simply a question of whether the witnesses agreed with the defence or the prosecution.

The investigation and public trial had led to a re-thinking in Incisa about the town fool. Not only was the cartwright's character reassessed but also people's relations with him. Those who knew him now had to readjust their ideas about their own ability or lack of it to make judgements and to predict events which, though unimaginable, had actually happened.

The presiding judge must have thought that what was needed to settle the uncertainty and the contradictory accounts of the country people and to break the impasse was one last piece of evidence.

When the court hearing opened on 22 December, Giorgio Mori Ubaldini availed himself of his discretionary powers and called for Paolo Scoti 'to ascertain Grandi's level of intelligence and education since early youth'. Scoti soon appeared and was questioned. Unusually, his evidence was recorded (although in the third, not the first person) 'by order of the public prosecutor and by order of the presiding judge'.

A qualified teacher, Scoti taught at the charity workhouse in Florence, which was ruled with iron discipline by Carlo Peri, the director of Tuscan prisons. But before that, until June 1872, Scoti had worked at the elementary school in Incisa. The school inspector, Dazzi, said of Scoti that he was 'an honourable man, which is rare in these hard times', although he was 'inclined to be too strict with his pupils'. Scoti was forty-two years old, with 'a severe face . . . loud deep voice, didactic tone, poor eyesight' and above all, an acute memory.[43]

There had been over a hundred pupils enrolled in the school, but Scoti remembered many details about the one who was now on trial. On 3 December 1868 Grandi had been able to recognize syllables and to write a bit, and he knew addition. The teacher had not been aware that Grandi was then 18 years old, rather than seven or eight. As a pupil he had made more or less average progress during the three or four months of that year and two of the following when he was in class. He moved on to the evening sessions when he had reached the stage of being able to take dictation. He improved his handwriting, learned multiplication and possibly even division. By the end he could read well and was able to compose informal letters which were clear and well expressed, though full of spelling mistakes.

The judges and gentlemen of the jury sought his opinion on the accused's intellect. 'As to his knowledge (it was) better than that of some of the other scholars.' During his long career the teacher had come across many less able pupils than Grandi, who at least applied himself to his work. The master swore on oath

> that he had never seen any signs of deficiencies in his mental faculties; that he had never fallen behind the average standard, which was very low; and that when the teacher left Incisa he had the impression that Grandi was an average youth like many others and that if he had continued his studies he would have gained much more knowledge... in regard to moral maturity.

Scoti stated that Grandi 'was an excitable and touchy character and that during his first year at the school he would not tolerate any remarks or jokes from his companions and that he was very easily upset.' So much so that at one point Scoti had once given him 'a friendly warning not to be so touchy' when he was threatening the other pupils with a chisel for annoying him. In reply, Grandi threatened to hurt him as well, but he had not made an issue of it since 'no one paid any attention to him.' His character, therefore, had been the same then as it was now, but Scoti affirmed that there was 'no question at all of his mental abilities', which were the same or better than those of his peers.

Scoti, in fact, had no complaints about Grandi, at least not in comparison with the other Incisan pupils. He had plenty to say on that score about the boys who had tormented him with 'absolutely intolerable behaviour'. He also had something to say about the parents who 'always refused to listen to the teacher'. In fact, he had complained of it to the mayor and asked him to intervene in person but had been humiliated in that quarter. Some of the wretched mothers did nothing but 'encourage their own sons' disobedience' to him. He had also been accused of many things, of having 'secret teacher's pets' among his pupils, of being unfair and even of having made the school 'the worst among all the schools in Tuscany'.[44] That was why he had left the town where he had spent four nightmare years because his wife was Incisan, although he himself was a Florentine.

The judges and the public in the courtroom knew nothing of Scoti's personal trials and had no way of knowing that he spoke of Incisa and its people with personal resentment. In a sense, Scoti's evidence seriously damaged the defence by his very praise of Grandi. But there was another teacher who gave completely different evidence, which Mori Ubaldini did not order to be recorded. Scoti's predecessor, Luigi Simoni, had taught at Incisa for three or four years since Carlino was six years old. He had not seen signs that the boy was *mad or an imbecile*, but everything had to be *gone over again and again* with him. He was slow; he had to make far more effort than the others and was therefore constantly behind.

After hearing the two teachers' evidence, it might have been useful to examine the writings which Grandi had composed in the Murate prison. The lawyer Galardi asked that they be shown to the witness Scoti. Did they seem to him, apart from the mistakes, to be clear and well expressed? Products of a normal mind? The prosecutor Dini objected to this and to any use of the documents in court. The defence insisted that they were most important, not least to the expert's evidence. The disagreement turned into an issue which could only be resolved by the judges in secret session. Mori Ubaldini declared that since the lawyers had only presented the papers in question at the first hearing, and given the fact that either side had the right to refuse to accept evidence which had not been presented at least three days before the opening of the trial, the court rejected the defence request and returned Grandi's writings to them. This was a decision based strictly on the letter of the law rather than on the value of the evidence itself. The judge had the power to either reject the evidence as valueless or to accept it as he had done six days before when the papers had first been presented and there had been no objection either from him or from Dini.

The defence protested. The psychiatrists saw themselves deprived of the chance to use material which they judged essential to support their expert evidence. Even the accused became very upset when the 'novel' he was so proud of was rejected: *Ah! Ah. . . . the papers . . . why aren't they showing the papers? . . . That is not good! Here I am in pain . . . from here to here, which means God is not pleased, it will rain, fire, water, streaks and lightning.*[45]

But there was nothing to be done apart from the little which the lawyer Pietro Ferrigni could achieve in *La Nazione* by publishing a facsimile of the documents. In articles published on Christmas and Boxing Day he also gave the defence experts' opinions of Scoti's evidence.

That schoolmaster, who was so foolishly wrong about Grandi's age showed himself to be completely ignorant of mental illness, stated Dr Morselli firmly. He had made deductions about his pupil based solely on the facility with which Carlino learned to read and write (a facility which was anyway only a presumption and one denied by others). But the ability to read and write was no proof of mental stability, as anyone visiting a lunatic asylum would realize. Nor, thankfully, was the reverse true, and a lack of education was not a sign of madness or imbecility. Only a pedantic schoolteacher could make such an error.

The psychiatric experts

The presiding judge called the defence expert witnesses on 23 December. The first to speak was Enrico Morselli, then Carlo Livi, and finally Francesco Bini. The scientists' words, which they themselves published the following year, were reported by Yorick in *La Nazione* in two long articles. The clerk of court, on the other hand, was completely silent on the matter since there was no statutory requirement to record expert evidence. The court records are consequently scanty and uninformative.

> Gentlemen, the case for calling scientific evidence in this trial is most serious and the question of Carlino Grandi's responsibility is of the utmost importance both to medical science and to the law ... the revulsion which all benevolent souls must feel in the face of such atrocious deeds ... is in stark contrast to the calm and serenity needed (to consider the question).

Luckily, science was at hand, and *with the noble voice* of science itself the young, self-assured Dr Morselli set out to display his expertise to the judges, the jury and the crowded public, including the many distinguished professors and students who had come to that particular hearing.[46]

There was not the slightest doubt. The child killer was sick, not criminal and his sickness was *imbecility*. His brain and nervous centres must certainly bear lesions, but since it was impossible to identify internal lesions on a living subject it was necessary to study the external manifestations of his nervous system. The medical expert set out to show that *the external aspect of Grandi alone is enough to justify our diagnosis*. Naturally he began with the *cranium since this vessel models itself on that noble organ*, the brain. He told how the appropriate tests, which were not specified, had revealed certain *abnormal configurations, asymmetries and arrested development.* Furthermore, *concerning his body – the dwarfism, the vacuous face, the completely hairless skin, the bare skull, the hunched spine, the lameness, the deformed foot* – these physical deformities could be clearly seen by everyone, and it was the expert's contention that they were *linked to a brain deformity.* The same was true of the crossed eyes and nystagmus and the *sinister look . . . which was always due to a defective connection between the musculature of the eyes* joining the cranial nerves, which indicated an aberration of the brain. And since the cranium is to the encephalon as the spinal column is to the medulla, so the scoliosis and muscular imbalance of the lumbar-sacral region seen in Grandi were proof of a compressed medulla and interrupted nervous system. The twisted foot signified a *corresponding lesion in the peripheral nerves of the lower limb closely linked to the trophic medullan centre.* The extra toe on the same foot was an atavistic deviation sometimes also found among *Negroes . . . among Hindus, Arabs and the Polynesians of Chatam's island.* The expert quoted Darwin, Prichard and Dieffenbach in his support. Running through the list of species, such anomalies had been found not in mammals, birds or reptiles but only in prehistoric fish. *From this . . . we must recognize that in Grandi nature has manifested itself below the scale of the human species to reproduce characteristics which have been extinct for millions of centuries* before the supremacy of the vertebrates.

The fact that the cartwright was underdeveloped was also attested by his lack of hair and the state of his reproductive organs. Grandi had never felt the *mysterious influence of the organs of love . . . the powerful sex instinct* which other young men of his age did. His body had stopped short *at the threshold of virility, just as his poor mind had been arrested beyond the first confines of reason.* When he killed he was still pre-pubescent and therefore not responsible for his actions, which the law itself admitted. Yorick confirmed the fact to his readers in *La Nazione*: the law treated minors differently to adults. Individuals such as Grandi did not procreate and they tended to die young because of hereditary degeneration. Morselli had seen, in the accused's family, a notoriously alcoholic grandfather, a father who was *eccentric and original with strange ideas, a self-proclaimed artist dead of consumption,* a mother who was half-cretinous, *nervous, irritable, of extremely low intelligence,* one sister dead for many years who had been a hairless imbecile like Carlino, one brother *of whom we only know that he was lazy at work, quick with his fists and short of brains*, as was the other sister. Despite the fact that their neighbours called them good people, the family were all degenerates, and the famous murderer was the worst of them all.

The physical abnormalities were obvious and so was the heredity factor. No one could doubt that there were parallel psychological defects, the psychiatrist stated; all the enquiries by the defence experts had confirmed them. This despite the fact, he did not fail to protest, that the court had obstructed their work. It had refused to allow the accused's body to be exhibited with all his deformities, for example, and had imposed silence on him instead of allowing everyone to hear his incoherent ravings.

Despite all this the fact was clear. Grandi was a congenital idiot and moreover, he was a lunatic by virtue of the aberrations risen from his organic substrata. Yes, he could read and write, but still not fluently after a dozen years of schooling; and even lunatics in asylums did well at school, sometimes even better than their nurses. Conversely, Massimo D'Azeglio could not add up, and he was no idiot. In short, the educational criterion was not a valid indicator of sanity. The cartwright had his work, but it was work of a *crude, manual, automatic* type requiring no intelligence, which even a child could have done. And then again, even people in psychiatric hospitals had tasks and jobs to perform, even the animals themselves did. As to his relationships with people, Carlino was misanthropic, friendless and spent his time in the company of children. According to Morselli, the fact that Grandi had killed four of those children was proof of his minimal capacity for affection towards them. He lacked any good influence to develop the powers of affection, and because of that his primary intellectual imbecility had become an even greater, moral imbecility. And what was a moral imbecile? Morselli explained: *for the slightest reason they scratch, bite, throw themselves onto the ground, insult other people and if there is no other victim they bite their own flesh furiously, they tear themselves to pieces without showing the slightest pain, they bang their heads against the wall.*

Morselli had seen them in the asylum (though Carlino was not like that). They were frightening and capable of committing the most terrible deeds, which couldn't be explained *without admitting* (that they had) *a horrendous perversion of moral sense, a complete lack of the affectionate senses.* Morselli concluded that Grandi's crimes came into this category, committed as they were for *inane and crazy motives.* He had his own peculiar concept of morality: he detested theft and wanted to kill all thieves; he believed he had a right to revenge, and when he killed, *at the bottom of his poor mind he had no awareness of doing wrong.* Because of that *it is necessary to conclude that allied to the lack of intelligence, that deformed brain lacked the organs of a moral sense.* The fact that Carlino often went to church meant nothing. All imbeciles were deeply religious, declared the expert. He went on to assert that in the lower classes religious sentiment did not prevent *the most knavish and criminal deeds (and) it has a decidedly negative value.*

It was true that normal criminals also lacked a sense of morality, but the child killer, who was a sick man, did not have the criminal's characteristic cunning – a fact which was also affirmed by the other witnesses, even those for the prosecution. In science, the concept of premeditation had no value whatsoever. It was a *very coarse concept which all psychiatrists rejected*, and Morselli did so at length. In certain lunatics the reasoning was false in the initial premise but extremely logical in consequence. Moreover, Grandi was not very quick at providing an alibi for hiding the victims' corpses. He had behaved more like a child bursting to tell his own story. *He did everything possible to be discovered and the fact that he wasn't was no thanks to him.* It was the Incisan people's fault and the fault of their *ignorance, apathy and credulity.*

The Incisans were right in one particular, namely that the affair was inexplicable; it was inconceivable how Carlino could have killed those four children. The motives ascribed to him were so *futile, crazy and infantile.* The psychiatrist asserted that *that monstrous creature in the dock . . . had no motive, not a single one which justified such blind vengeance.* But it was important not to forget the damaging influence of his physical deformities on his moral sense. According to Morselli, and he repeated it more than once, there was even some doubt that the boys had committed those minor injuries at all. Even if they had, the result – murder – was vastly out of proportion to the cause. But the imbecile was touchy, and self-important to the point of megalomania and delusions of grandeur. The elements which defined criminal behaviour were therefore absent from the lunatic: cunning and motivation and awareness of committing the crime.

The judge and the King's prosecutor believed the opposite and adhered to the old juridical concept. Morselli lost his patience:

But why is it that we psychiatrists always have to . . . repeat the same thing in these courts? To convince themselves of the truth of what we are saying why don't the men of law and all the scoffers and unbelievers come and lock themselves into the asylums with us to study the insane with the same care and devotion as we doctors?

He was outraged and offended by the doubt cast on their words – the words of science – and it seemed deplorable to him that the court had rejected the evidence of Grandi's autobiographical writings, which were proof of madness and which the jury had not been allowed to examine... at that point in his impassioned speech, reported Yorick, the young psychiatrist was interrupted by the presiding judge, Mori Ubaldini, who reminded him that it was not permitted for anyone *to criticize, much less blame, the decisions of the court.*

It was simply not permitted to discuss Grandi's so-called novel. It was as though the document did not exist, although, as usual, the journalist lawyer Ferrigni immediately gave some indication of its contents to the readers because it was an interesting document which confirmed the opinion of the defence psychiatrists. Morselli would have liked to have exhibited those pages – the childish, ungrammatical script, the megalomaniacal drawings – and discuss them in the light of Lombroso's studies, as he had done in his written evidence.[47] But he was not allowed to do so, and he fell back on repeating what had already been said. Ultimately, his diagnosis was

> imbecility mainly of the emotional faculties, but not less in the intellectual ones. Delusions of grandeur not fully established but sufficient to mark the subject as a real lunatic with dangerous instincts. Lack of awareness of his own actions and lack of freedom of choice, which the Tuscan code deems to be necessary attributes of a sane mind.

Professor Carlo Livi then stood to speak: 'a fine figure... eyes alight with intelligence... a voice which is harmonious, deep and pleasant... elegant, rich, truly learned words'. Everyone in court was quiet, reported Yorick. His was not a long speech. He said he had nothing to add to the analysis presented by *the worthy young man whom it was my honour to have as a pupil and whom today I have the satisfaction of naming a colleague.*

He stated that as expert witnesses they were able to decide whether or not the individual was responsible, but they had not the means to ascertain the semi-responsibility provided for in law – in other words, a half-illness or fraction of culpability in a sick mind. Grandi was completely irresponsible, and it was specious to deny it. Denial of the fact could only come from ignorance as to what an imbecile was. One objection put forward was that the murderer had acted for revenge. This was so, but the difference between the sane and the insane was not that the former were subject to passions which the latter were not. Even *the mad can love, hate, become enraged or jealous and take most terrible revenge!* But the normal individual *is restrained by a duty not to allow himself to become overwhelmed by passion but to master it*, whereas the madman knows no discipline or restraints; he is ruled by his passionate impulses and is therefore not answerable for his actions.

How and why did the idea of revenge take root in the cartwright's sick mind? Livi was convinced that if he had lived anywhere else Grandi would have remained a harmless simpleton like so many other wretches of his type. Instead, what happened?

> This poor imbecile is molested, insulted, offended and harried about his peaceful labours, in his own house, in the streets and in church when praying. He turns to his parents, he turns to the priest . . . he tries everything to no avail. So in his feeble mind, where instinct and not reason dominates, he begins to feel the instinctive need to rid himself of his tormentors.

He had to do it. It became an overwhelming compulsion, and the same would have been true for anyone in his condition.

Another argument put forward was that he had planned the murders with cunning, not like a madman. But madmen showed themselves to be very cunning indeed when they have a fixation, a single idea which their brain turns over tenaciously and single-mindedly without respite or distraction. As director of asylums he had seen many examples of such wretched single-mindedness, with suicides, for example. He had had one inmate at Siena who had managed, after several vain attempts, to trick his guards and hang himself from the railings before their very eyes. Or there had been the monomaniac who had spent two years building a portable guillotine in secret, with which he had finally killed himself. These were strange, impressive stories which Yorick took pleasure in reporting in detail in *La Nazione*. They served to explain that madness and a certain tenacity, even at work, were not incompatible.

Having explained this and removed all doubt that Grandi was of unsound mind, Professor Livi wanted to ensure that although he was not fit for punishment, the dangerous lunatic should not be set free at the risk of strangling, murdering and burying other victims. Grandi should, therefore, *leave all human intercourse behind, he should see none but people who care for and guard him. Thus and only thus will the rights of science, humanity and justice be served.*

It was then the turn of Professor Bini, who because he had been director of the asylum for decades was very well known in the city. Like Livi, he concluded that the only place to lock Grandi up was in his asylum, even though the law did not provide for such an outcome to the case. Like Morselli, he began by listing – though less exhaustively – the external signs of the mental and cerebral abnormalities with which Grandi had been born. He drew particular attention to the language Grandi used. He read out in court the words with which he had been greeted on his first visit to Grandi in prison.

> I'm not afraid of anything – let them try – everyone calls me Baldy, twenty-one-toes, dwarf, squint-eye – I went to the priest and he said be patient – I went to the Town Hall and nothing – If you knew what they were like at the Town Hall! Even one of those boys' mums told me 'Kill him', and I killed him – but I wanted to kill another two and a woman – O yes, that one was a wretch – she stole so much oil from me – And then I wanted to kill a miller – do you know how much flour he stole from one sack? A kilo!

The written report of the examination, which the experts had presented on 7 March, stated that the prisoner did not always understand the questions, gave fragmented answers and digressed into frivolities. Far from being anxious he seemed proud of himself. *Carlino sharp brain* he repeated. *What, will they kill me?* he asked laughing and then, seriously, *will they put up a statue to me?*

The public had already heard and even laughed at the crazy things Grandi had said in court until the presiding judge imposed silence on him. They had also heard the pertinent evidence of the witnesses from Incisa, the doctors and the guards (not the contrary opinions offered by the *families of the victims and the rough, common people*). Bini refreshed the jury's memory with extracts. If Grandi appeared to some people less mad than he really was, Bini thought this was due to two factors: the common people nurtured false conceptions about madness, and the magistrates appealed to these very misconceptions.

Bini summarized the conflict going on in the court in these terms: the prosecution posited that the accused had been motivated by revenge and that his actions were premeditated, whereas the defence considered him to be an imbecile and that therefore he had acted irrationally. This was also Bini's point of view, and he further considered *the lack of motive for the crime . . . to be a strong indication of insanity.* Yes, the murderer of Incisa had stated his reasons, but these simply came down to the fact that he had been annoyed. An imbecile behaves like a child and all children complain in the same way if they are scolded for doing the slightest harm to others. In any case, Carlino had exaggerated the extent of his sufferings, and the prosecution witnesses had in fact denied them altogether. Furthermore, the psychiatrist asked himself how hatred and revenge could reasonably have driven the cartwright against those children when *he only sought their company and enjoyed . . . playing childish games with them? . . . No one could explain, no one could understand,* not even the forensic psychiatrist. He recalled that within his field one often met with wicked deeds committed for inexplicable reasons, as when the idiot orphan killed the old woman who had mothered him because she scolded him for drinking too much. Morel and Maudsley had written about many such cases. All the murderers held the common conviction that they could not have acted in any other way. They had been gripped by a morbid impulse to do evil. The same thing was probably true of Grandi, who was not only underdeveloped morally and intellectually but also suffered periodic attacks of manic excitement. Some of the witnesses had confirmed the fact and Bini himself had seen it when he visited the prisoner at the Murate prison, where Grandi was always in a different mood, veering between *melancholic anxiety and homicidal impulses.*

The specific psychopathic diagnosis was possibly of no interest to their honours, but Bini reminded them that imbecility was recognized even in the most ancient penal codes. The principle that awareness of having committed a crime did not necessarily imply responsibility was accepted by the best specialists. *What a mistake it would be if the jury delivered a verdict of guilty simply because the accused showed awareness and discernment in committing the crime while science declared him to be mad and lacking free will.* Bini pointed out that this had recently been written by the prosecution expert Giuseppe Lazzaretti, who was present in court.[48] He and Morelli had plenty of time to prepare their speeches after listening to the defence experts.

That afternoon Giorgio Mori Ubaldini closed the hearing a few hours earlier than expected and adjourned the case until three days later. When it was reopened on 26 December it was the turn of the prosecution experts. Whether it was by order of the presiding judge or due to the court clerk's initiative, their evidence is better re-corded, albeit still sketchily.

> Carlo Morelli, after stating certain scientific considerations, concluded his expert evidence in the following manner: 'I maintain that although Callisto Grandi is weak of intellect and moral sense, he is capable of understanding the import of his criminal deeds and is therefore responsible for them, since they were committed with awareness and free will.'

He did not deny the existence of the physical anomalies demonstrated by Morselli, but he did not agree that mental aberrations could be deduced from these. Especially since such aberrations were related to the higher nervous system, whereas Grandi's problems lay in the lower region only. He admitted the existence of abnormal psychiatric symptoms but did not think they were serious, and besides, he suspected a certain degree of dissimulation. He believed that the accused was cunning and vengeful. Among all the evidence, that given by the schoolteacher Scoti seemed to him the most convincing. Finally, what impressed him least was the defence experts' theoretical foundation. Modern theories on criminality, craniometry and even anthropology seemed to him to be fairly unstable disciplines which were *still at a rudimentary stage*.

Lazzaretti, who taught medicine to the police, drew conclusions which were more fully recorded:

> 1) That when Grandi committed the murders of the children ... he had intellectual development, moral sense, discernment and education at least to the normal levels expected of a manual labourer such as himself. 2) That he knew moral values, that is, he *was aware* of the murders he had willingly committed and repeated in the *full knowledge* of his guilt in the eyes of the law. 3) That, yes, he had been impelled to commit these murders by passion, but that he had descended to motives of revenge. 4) That he was therefore responsible for the murders within the terms of the indictment.

The expert stated that he had seen many cases during his practice as police doctor and was therefore able to distinguish *a sane, calculating mind* even when, as in this case, the accused was intent on deceiving the judges.

The two experts, therefore, agreed on the legal aspect, if not on the medical analysis. Lazzaretti's opinion was more authoritative and respected. He alluded to requirements not prescribed in the Tuscan penal code. He referred to the concept of 'knowledge' and emphasized its legal aspect (the knowledge of committing a crime) as had been included in Mancini's last proposal, which had not been adopted. He stated that passion was not involved, given that when passion signified an irresistible force it excluded the possibility of guilt according to Article 94 of the current Italian code.[49] It was doubly strange that he referred to the Italian rather than the Tuscan code: first, the Tuscan code was in operation at the trial, and second, Lazzaretti was known to be a solid supporter of the rules of imputability set forth in that code. He favoured it because unlike other penal codes or proposals, it did not rely on the concept of 'awareness', but rather 'free will', which according to him made 'awareness' redundant.[50] But despite this, the expert particularly forbore to discuss the murderer's freedom of choice, referring instead to definitions which he himself normally claimed were too restrictive to allow an understanding of the various physical and psychological modes which implied responsibility.

The professor's most important point, however, was to ascribe the accused's mental and moral characteristics entirely to socio-cultural factors, as the prosecution had consistently maintained throughout the trial. There was no need to deny the patient's mental deficiency, as argued by the defence; it was enough simply to refuse to recognize that these defects were personal and individual. Carlo Grandi was as he was because labourers were like that – no better, no worse. Let that be enough. Apart from the fact that Carlino was an artisan, this line of thought was insulting to a whole class in general and to the people of Incisa in particular, although it served their desire to see the murderer condemned. Such an argument might well appeal to the jury, who were all drawn from higher levels of civic life.

In the end the prosecution experts reaffirmed the conclusions that the prosecution had reached before even calling on scientific expertise. Perhaps the experts were not even necessary. But there were signs of agitation on the defence benches. The lawyers requested that two witnesses be recalled, not ignorant peasants but persons with a certain status and sophistication: the prison governor and the Incisan doctor. The doctor repeated that he had 'always considered Grandi to be an adolescent, a boy'. He added that Grandi could not do his work, that he always spent his time with the children and never with the men and that, in short, he was not like the other townspeople. The experts Morselli and Bini asked to speak, Morelli and Lazzaretti replied, and each side insisted on their own opinions. But the hearing had already gone on too long and the presiding judge was obliged to adjourn the proceedings.

That evening, presumably, the defence discussed the matter and reached their decisions.

The jurors and the verdict

When the court hearing reopened on the morning of 28 December, the defence lawyer Galardi asked for the trial to be adjourned. He stated that Grandi should be placed under observation to verify whether he 'had been mentally affected by the time he had spent locked up in the Murate prison'. It was a ploy, a last attempt permissible within the law to prevent the only verdict possible. It would be inadmissible to pass sentence on the accused if he had become mentally deficient during the trial, even though the defence maintained that he had always been so.

Naturally Dini, the deputy prosecutor, opposed the request. Galardi objected. The judges therefore had to withdraw to resolve the problem in secret session. They very quickly did so: the request was refused 'in view of the fact that . . . the court has seen no reason to doubt that the accused, Callisto Grandi's, state of mind was established at the outset of the trial and does not consent to him even now continuing to be present at the trial which concerns him'. The judges Giorgio Mori Ubaldini, Filippo Petrucci and Agostino Bonini signed this in the name of His Majesty Victor Emmanuel.[51]

However incredible their lack of doubt may seem in a trial which had been constantly hedged by doubts, their response was predictable. It was only from a radical self-criticism that an opposite response could have come, going against everything the court always stood for. There was nothing surprising in the decree except that it went so far as to prescribe the judgement of members of the jury, who had to address the question in retrospect.

And if, to the judges, Grandi's behaviour in the courtroom and in prison seemed normal – albeit wicked, like all criminals and stupid and immoral, like all peasants – why should this not have been equally true three years earlier? Nobody, not even the defence experts, maintained that he had gone mad for one period and then become sane again.

In his summing up, the public prosecutor Dini asked the jury to return a verdict of guilty of the original charge 'in the assumption that Grandi, at the time of committing the crimes, was in full possession of his mental faculties'.

Ernesto Papasogli's address to the jury requested the exact opposite. The accused could not be found guilty, since at the time of the murders 'he was not of sound mind'. Carlo Galardi requested the same verdict but provided the court with a fuller polemical reasoning – that his client was not 'responsible for the criminal actions he had committed because at the time of the deeds, as now, he had not been and was still not in a normal state of mind'.

Apart from the summaries and conclusions of these addresses to the jury, nothing else was recorded nor was anything added to the records later. The jury had nothing to ask and neither side had anything to add. If the accused did indeed have the right to 'the last word', which was the standard formula written by the court clerk, he did not use his right, at least no words of his were entered in the records.

Giorgio Mori Ubaldini then spoke. He clarified the questions which the twelve members of the jury were called upon to consider, then declared the debate concluded and finally released the witnesses and experts. After that he gave his summing up to the jury. He explained the questions, underlined the main arguments for and against the accused, and reminded them of their official duties and the penalties they would incur if they failed to meet them, all according to the statutes of Article 47 of the law of 8 June 1874.

There were many ways in which a presiding judge, unconsciously or otherwise, was able to influence the jury. In order to bias the verdict in favour of the prosecution he might employ two particular strategies throughout the trial. One was at the beginning, when he set out the prosecutor's arguments. Mori Ubaldini had done this by his reading of the decision of the committal session and of the prosecutor's case. He also exercised his bias at the end, in his summing up after the trial was concluded and so no longer subject to interventions from either side, as was set out in the amendment to the law of 8 June 1874, ratified by the Right.[52]

At that time Parliament was discussing the role of the presiding judge and his relationship with the jury. Many were opposed to the principle of the 'summing up', but the Justice Minister, Vigliani, wanted to include it in the bill, saying that he trusted the good judgement of Italian judges. The purpose of the summing up was supposedly to interpret the legislation at the level of understanding of the jurors, who did not seem to be held in great esteem. The law submitted jurors to the judicial summing up 'like children on leading reins', said Francesco Carrara, who always defended the absolute freedom of the jury as opposed to the restrictions laid on the magistrature.

It was not impossible for the judge's summing up to propose a new bill of indictment, despite his supposedly neutral role. We cannot be sure that this happened when Mori Ubaldini concluded the case against Grandi. It is true, however, that he had not disguised his own bias. It must have been hard for the jury not to be influenced by him, not only because both he and the position he held were dignified and authoritative but also because he could refer to the 'truth' of the documents relating to the initial investigation, which he alone had access to and which no one else had the right to consult without his permission. In this case the relevant documents included the prosecution case, the interrogation and confession of Grandi and all the papers relating to the victims, including the autopsy reports.

At that point and on the basis of what they had seen and heard, the jury had to retire 'to reflect collectedly and silently and . . . examine in good conscience what impressions had been made on their reason by the proofs presented against the accused and the arguments in his defence'. Mori Ubaldini advised them that this was prescribed by the law but that they would not be called upon to give an account of 'the means by which they reached their conclusions'.

Their task was grave and difficult, and no matter how much 'conscience and reason' were deemed to be 'faculties universal to man', there was no denying that these qualities varied among individuals according to nature, character, education and social status. The recently approved system of jury selection took account of this factor, since from 1 January 1875 it was no longer sufficient merely to be on the electoral role to be a juror. Besides being a male between the ages of twenty-five and sixty-five with full civil and political rights, jurors were also required to have a certain level of competence, clearly described in twenty-one categories related to professions and educational qualifications. The last category was an exception, in that it included citizens of no particular ability but who simply paid a 300-lire subscription to the state (inclusion on the electoral register cost only forty lire). This ensured the availability of the 'illiterate rich', whom it was considered necessary to include lest there not be enough potential jurors.[53]

Three of the jurors on the Grandi case came into this category, being men of property and subscribers. One was Signor Emilio

Bettarini of Sesto Fiorentino, who was spokesman because he had
been called first. There were also five government employees, two
town councillors (one of whom came from Reggello, very near
Incisa), a teacher, a lecturer, an engineer and an accountant for the
Roman railways. There were no doctors, scientists or lawyers.
Including the two reserves, five of the jurors came from the province
and nine were from Florence itself.[54] Theoretically, each of them
should have displayed the qualities of 'the cultured man, the educated
man, the affluent man', which Minister Vigliani hoped to entrust
with the representation of the people. He hoped to avoid criminal
sentences being passed by 'the uncouth, ignorant man, with no
education'.[55]

On 28 December 1876, twelve citizens had been called to the
Florentine court on the basis of the superiority of their class and
culture to judge a murderer whose social and cultural inferiority,
like that of the victims and country witnesses, was obvious and
accurately reflected the balance of the world they lived in. Moreover,
the jury had to decide whether the accused was pathologically mentally deficient. From their relatively elevated social level how could
they distinguish between the two forms of handicap? Did they succeed
in distinguishing the individual's deficiencies from the general deprivations of his class?

According to the prosecution, the whole question lay in the
undefined inferiority of the populace, whose poverty extended to
their intelligence and emotional faculties. There was no room within
that to allow for a mental disorder which still had some logic, even
if it was a logic of revenge. Everyone had heard of 'moral insanity',
'rational folly', 'insanity of doubt' and various other labels which
most often appeared in foreign publications. It was well known that
many people suffered from these afflictions (and there were many
examples in the literature), to the point at which they were no
longer responsible for their actions. Such sophisticated disorders
were more appropriate to a certain level of patient, however: men
under pressure of work, youths overburdened with studies or lone-
liness like the melancholic neurasthenics in Britain, or lovesick young
girls with feverish imaginations. These were the stereotypical victims of mental illness which some murderers standing trial might
resemble.[56]

But this was not the case among the common people. The type
of mental disorder manifested among the lower classes was true
insanity – suffered by those who were incapable of looking after
themselves or performing the most basic functions, who were cared

for by local authorities and put into asylums.[57] Otherwise, they were good-natured idiots, the dim-wits whom you teased and sent your children to play with, although you were always watchful in case they did anything 'filthy'.

But the dwarf of Incisa seemed to be a different case. He demanded respect, he took offence, he would not put up with being mocked despite his ridiculous appearance. He was domineering, he worked, he wanted to study and improve himself. He was more knowledgeable than many of his country neighbours, who could not even read or write, and yet he talked nonsense. Maybe he was pretending. He was right to object to being mocked by the street urchins who really tormented him. Those women should have watched over their children better. You couldn't help but pity him. But what a way to react! He thought he could get away with it. What was it those experts had said? The professors. Which ones? The prosecution ones or the defence? Luckily the presiding judge had laid the whole thing out clearly for them. They, the jurors, only had to say yes or no.

After nearly two hours they returned to court. Emilio Bettarini rose to his feet, placed his right hand on his heart and said: 'On my honour and on my conscience the decision of the jury is this.' The majority had answered the first question in the affirmative: they were convinced that the accused had caused the violent death of the first child and they confirmed the verdict a further three times, once for each child. The answers were affirmative but only by a majority, so it was clear that someone did not believe that Grandi's responsibility had been proven despite his own confession, nor that he had committed the murders.

There remained the question of responsibility according to the conditions set out in Article 34 of the Tuscan penal code. Had the accused acted 'in a state of one who has no awareness of his own actions'? or 'in the state of one without freedom of choice'? These were the questions already addressed by the experts. Like them, the jury was not unanimous, but the majority answered 'no' to both questions.

It is interesting to note that Mori Ubaldini had not combined the last two questions – awareness or freedom – in the way he normally favoured. Instead, he had separated the concepts, as he was legally entitled to do. But the jury's votes could not be similarly broken down.[58] A university colleague of Professor Lazaretti had spotted the anomaly in the Tuscan system. If there were separate jury majority votes on the issues of lack of awareness and lack of choice, nevertheless the two votes were to count as a single decision on the question of imputability. It was important, therefore, to verify whether the sum of the separate minorities equalled the overall majority. Francesco Carrara had written in the *Rivista penale* in January 1876 that 'no Tuscan presiding judge' could persist in the absurd system of separating the votes regarding the total or partial mental deficiency of the accused.[59] Mori Ubaldini did precisely this in the Grandi trial, and he decided the outcome of imputability. The defence lawyers on their part failed to raise any objection.

The fourth question concerned premeditation and intent. The categories were confused in the Italian code, but the Tuscan school prided itself on keeping the two separate.[60] Every deliberate murder implied some degree of intent before the act, but as Carmignani and Carrara had explained, premeditation required intellect which sustained cold and firm reflection on the proposed deed. In both their written case and during the court hearings the prosecution had emphasized the cartwright's premeditation as a sign of his cunning and wickedness and presented it as proof that he was in full possession of his mental faculties. This was contrary to the decision of Italian jurisprudence and the Court of Cassation in Florence a few months previously, that the concept of premeditation did not necessarily imply a fully developed intellect and will, and was therefore not incompatible with a degree of mental deficiency.[61]

By answering 'yes' to this, as the majority of the jury did, they left open the question of the circumstances which reduced the accused's imputability, that is, if Grandi had acted when in a state 'close to one who is unaware of his actions' or, separately considered, 'close to one who has no freedom of choice'. The answer to both was a majority affirmative. They answered six identical questions for each of the four murders and the attempted murder: thirty questions, plus an additional one regarding whether the crimes were liable to penal sanction.

The verdict was pronounced. The jury were not supposed to take into account any eventual sentence. In fact, it was impossible for them not to do so, but it was strictly prohibited lest their verdict be affected by such considerations. Nevertheless, they could imagine the outcome for themselves. If they found Grandi fully responsible he would be sentenced to life imprisonment, the maximum penalty under Tuscan law. His sentence would be somewhat less if they found that there were factors indicating diminished responsibility.

It was not clear what would become of him if the verdict was one of mental deficiency. If he carried no blame and no sentence was passed, what was to be done with a dangerous lunatic? Parliament had made no provision for such cases, although it had been exhorted to do so by many, including psychiatrists. Given such a legal loophole, the terrifying prospect that the criminal lunatic might be entrusted to the care of his family or even set free did not seem at all impossible. In Parliament, Righi observed that this uncertainty often led judges to lean towards a verdict which carried specific penalties and which were consequently reassuring for society.[62]

The prosecution and defence both had to propose a sentence. The public prosecutor Sante Dini agreed with the verdict because, contrary to what he had said in his summing up, he conceded that the guilty man had been in a state of semi-responsibility. He requested a twenty-two-year prison sentence. The defence requested the minimum sentence. The court clerk conscientiously recorded that Grandi 'declared that he had nothing to say and therefore had the last word'.

The judges had to make the final decision and withdrew to consider. To decide the sentence on the basis of a verdict requiring consideration of Article 64, concerning diminished responsibility, was not merely a mechanical process of matching the offence and the prescribed sentence. In the case of diminished responsibility the sentence could be reduced, but the amount was entirely at the judges' discretion. After about an hour the judges returned to the courtroom. Bareheaded, the presiding judge read out the six pages on which the sentence was set out, in accordance with Articles 45, 80, 309 and 64 of the Tuscan penal code.

Callisto Grandi was sentenced to prison with hard labour for twenty years at public expense. It was a severe sentence:[63] the year before, in the same court, a woman found guilty of killing her own children while in a state close to one of no awareness or free choice had received a five-year prison sentence.

So much the better, I will get back to work, commented Grandi, rubbing his hands in satisfaction.[64]

4

The Psychiatric Case

___

The psychiatrists' battles and defeats

So they had lost, and the defeat was galling. They had been shut up in that courtroom 'morning and evening for nine days, to what end?' wondered professor Livi; 'people who, after having spent years studying books and the human brain both living and dead, are still supposedly not able to distinguish, for God's sake, an imbecile from a sane man!'[1] He and his colleagues were indignant. Not only was the destiny of one wretch involved, they explained, but it was also 'a question of humanity . . . a question of science'.

The sentence pronounced on the accused affected them too and offended their dignity as doctors and men of honour. They could not let it pass. They had to react somehow. They decided to publicize their defeat and so published the most complete account of its kind in the *Rivista sperimentale de freniatria e medicina legale*. The whole affair was presented with great solemnity:

> We of the defence, we who have been defeated, derided and even calumnied, wish now to appeal rationally to another no less sacred and honourable court . . . the court of Science. And it is to this court that we offer the pages of this journal. Our first concern is to be submitted to its judgement.

Let the publication vanish without trace, swore the editor, if they were in the wrong.

There appeared five long instalments on the 'child killer' between January 1877 and December 1878. These included Grandi's crimes, the experts' enquiries, a commentary on the trial and on the evidence of experts and other witnesses.[2] A year later, Enrico Morselli turned it into one volume of over 180 pages, which was published to support the value of psychiatric evidence in courts of law. The book was dedicated to the memory of Carlo Livi, who had died in June 1877 from an illness which had struck him down as he was providing expert evidence for another trial.[3] The story of the cartwright of Incisa became an 'exemplary case' in the field. It was discussed at meetings and congresses of psychiatrists and referred to for many years in books on criminal anthropology or forensic psychiatry. The case was cited by Cesare Lombroso, naturally, and also by Krafft-Ebing and other famous students in the field, who all agreed that the subject presented a text-book case of mental deficiency.[4]

At first they had not expected to lose. On the contrary, a defence based on mental deficiency had looked easy, even obvious. Even before the experts made their diagnosis couched in scientific terminology, the newspapers had carried reports of Carlino's reputation in Incisa, where he was said to be a fool, abnormal. Besides, there had never been a subject whose deformities were so open to a somatic examination of madness. There could not have been a better subject. He seemed to be a walking example of the stigmata of abnormality. He could almost have appeared out of the anthropometric studies of an alienist, out of Lombroso's laboratory for example. That was what made the case so interesting. The appearance of the accused provided a perfect opportunity to prove how modern, objective psychiatry could alone provide superior expertise to the advantage of society in general.

All this came also in the light of recent contributions from the field of criminal anthropology. In the very year 1876, *L'Uomo Delinquente* appeared and was reviewed by, among others, the *Archivio giuridico* of Pisa and the *Archivio per l'antropologia*, which predicted great success for the book.[5] In other words, the whole cultural climate was at that time propitious for certain 'scientific battles', particularly in city circles, which were inclined towards positivism. In fact, the Grandi trial had attracted the interest of intellectuals before it even opened, not just the morbid curiosity of the common people.

There had even been encouraging signs that the usual obstacles had been overcome. *La Nazione*, for example, which reflected conservative and moralistic opinion, had judged the cartwright's guilt to be almost justified as an act of defence in the face of the children's attacks on him and the common habit of mocking the afflictions of others. And later, during the public trial, the leading journalist of the most influential newspaper, who was a lawyer as well, had taken the defence view that the accused was not responsible because of his illness. Many people were interested to know what science would make of that dwarfish, twisted murderer, and when the judge did finally call upon the experts there was a general sense of anticipation. And finally there was the fact that the general atmosphere was more receptive in Tuscany, whose modern, open penal code was a model throughout Europe. 'The ancient divisions between the temples of Asclepius and Themis have been removed,' Francesco Puccinotti had exclaimed optimistically years earlier when he taught forensic medicine. In September 1873 Bini wrote in *Nuova Antologia*: 'Nowadays no one would dispute the doctor's and particularly the psychiatrist's superior claims over the philosopher, moralist or jurist to be able to pronounce judgement on the normal and abnormal state of psychic functions.'[6]

Why then had they lost? Not that losing was anything new in itself. There had already been prosecutors who demolished expert evidence as 'abstractions and digressions by the doctors'. Now they had experienced for themselves the fact that the magistrates were not only ignorant of medicine but also had no desire to gain any knowledge or understanding of it. Also that several judges, both lay and robed, assumed the power to decide questions of sanity for themselves without reference to, and even in contradiction to, the doctors. So Carlo Livi complained. Everyone clung to the false belief that it was quite 'sufficient to be somewhat cultured and keep an open mind: enough in fact to have a little common sense'.[7] Nevertheless, after all their devoted work the defeat was painful. Their error had been to have faith and in fact they had been deluded. That was the mistake which the three psychiatrists admitted to, and according to them, it was the only mistake they made.

For their part the magistrates kept silent. They made no reply to any accusations and provocations. They carried on with their work as though nothing had happened, initiating other enquiries, leaving matters at the investigation stage or bringing cases to court before other juries. The administration of justice continued to follow its own rhythm and the customary wheels kept grinding. Once the case had been completed with no possibility of appeal, it was finished. There was no point in chewing it over and discussing all the 'ifs' and 'buts'. It sometimes happened that certain cases which had emotional appeal for the public were still discussed long after sentence had been passed and outside the restrictions of the courtroom. It was understood that given other circumstances and places and different magistrates, the proceedings and outcome of a particular trial might have been different. But what could be done about it? The matter was no longer their official concern: it no longer had anything to do with the deputy prosecutor Dini nor the examining magistrate Satti nor Mori Ubaldini nor the other court judges, who certainly all preferred to maintain professional detachment rather than offer any explanations for their conduct.

Apart from those directly involved, no lawyers made any comment on the Incisa case, although they were usually very involved in the debates currently raging in the specialist journals, the university faculties and in Parliament. But it would have been strange if they had commented. It was true that the central question in the Grandi case was closely tied to the various problems surrounding the issue of responsibility, which was currently of paramount importance in the drafting of the new penal code. But the line adopted in court against the cartwright provided no clarification on this point, only further ambiguities. Those who were proposing to adopt the Tuscan legislative model as having greater potential than the Sardinian-Italian one and being more appropriate to modern scientific thought, would certainly not have found the Grandi case of any use since the psychiatrists, themselves men of science, were protesting about the way the judges had conducted the trial. It is not surprising therefore that there was silence about the case from legal circles, in contrast to the great clamour coming from the psychiatrists and criminal anthropologists. There was also the fact that the lawyers held long-established status which the positivist scientists had only just achieved. Their positions were unequal and, in a sense, in competition.

Given time, the relationship would change. The positivist school of thought gained prominence in the field of legal philosophy. With experience the magistrates learned that it was not only possible but to their advantage to draw on expert opinion when dealing with mental illness. On the other hand, by the beginning of this century the psychiatric experts were complaining that they were called to court to give evidence on matters which had nothing to do with their expertise and which the law and the judges ought to be able to resolve.

Meanwhile, however, once the trial was over, in December 1876, none of the lawyers or magistrates gave any further attention to the Grandi case. It seemed to concern only the psychiatrists who had lost. And the way that group went about demonstrating its concern displayed the typical reactions of those who are offended, arrogant, victimized and incapable of self-criticism. Everyone else was to blame, the judges in particular as well as the jurors, who were biased, ignorant and presumptuous. These people were not worthy of attention in their opinion, and science itself remained unaffected. Giuseppe Lazzaretti said as much in consolation to a colleague whose expert advice had been similarly ignored in another criminal trial.[8]

The verdict of science was superior and detached from any other rationale. But this self-sufficiency and detachment could not in practice be reconciled with the desire to provide evidence in the court-rooms where a different discipline reigned supreme and where they could not avoid coming into contact with the common sense they so despised. It was not enough simply to make claims for the superiority of science when its actual results were proving inadequate. Something was amiss within the ranks of the psychiatrists themselves, however much they failed to recognize the fact.

One point at least was clear, or ought to have been. The most distinguished of Tuscan lawyers admitted that he would willingly have 'turned a deaf ear', but he could not fail to respond to the letter addressed to him publicly on 20 May 1875 from his 'illustrious colleague', the psychiatrist spurred by a case in which a patricide had been condemned to life imprisonment even though his lack of responsibility was acknowledged.

Certainly the magistrates ought to have paid more respect to the experts' opinions, and Francesco Carrara added that there was really no need to consult a professor such as himself on that point. But the main problem was essentially 'medical', and he put it to the anguished Carlo Livi: the psychiatrists should agree among themselves to show the legal profession the causes and varieties of madness as well as the means of identifying it. Even if the judge did leave such questions to the experts, as was hoped, more often than not they could not agree among themselves and put forward opposite or disparate opinions,[9] all in the name of science. Who should be listened to? The psychiatrists were asking that the judge and jury should simply accept their expert evidence. But, warned the *Rivista penale* in January 1877, such a constraint would 'place the rule of law at the mercy of the oscillations of science'.[10] This was the element that seemed to be uncertain, subjective and untrustworthy.

Carrara suggested that there might be another jury made up of scientists whose only task would be to decide on the accused's responsibility. The editorial opinion of the review was that it would be better to abolish the system of separate experts appearing for the prosecution and defence and to establish one single panel of experts. This was in fact adopted after 1913 when the new penal code effectively did away with the deplorable spectacle of experts contradicting each other in trials, which both debased the legal proceedings and forced the experts into predetermined roles.[11]

However the problem was to be resolved, the disagreement between the forensic scientists was disturbing, since it demonstrated that they were unable to fulfil their own promises. Every time, including in the Grandi case, they announced that their judgement was final, incontrovertible, would clarify all doubts about the accused and stood above the vagaries of public emotion and opinion. They claimed that their scientific judgement stood above moralism and even legal speculation. And yet they always ended up contradicting each other. How was it possible in the circumstances not to doubt their claims of certainty and the supposed objectivity of their knowledge?

Unless of course their disagreements sprang from the bias of whichever side they were representing. If that were the case, it would be dishonourable but basically less damaging to the principles of science, which could not be expected to answer for the particular sins of its less noble exponents. This hypothesis seemed satisfactory. The nature of the 'medical problem' lamented by Carrara was moral and economic rather than fundamentally theoretical. And if that were the case, procedural reform should prove to be sufficient remedy to the problem. Meanwhile, he warned the medical experts that they must not be open to temptation, they should speak the truth and not sell themselves for money, especially the defence experts, who were not paid by the court as the prosecution ones were. To avoid suspicion and to 'clarify their position', Morselli pointed out that neither the experts nor the lawyers had received a cent for defending the wretched cartwright.[12]

In the Grandi case the experts had disagreed, and their lack of unanimity, no matter how predictable it was, indeed their aggression towards each other, had made a bad impression on the public and the jury, as Yorick noted. Particular damage was done to the defence case, which was based entirely on psychiatry. The fact that certain elements of the argument were contrived by the experts solely to support their opposite conclusions can actually be proved in part. For example, in order to refute the defence's diagnosis of imbecility, Lazzaretti and his colleague had laid heavy emphasis on the murderer's cunning. But Lazzaretti himself had been the first to state in his study, *Le affezioni mentali*, that it was only too easy for certain sick people to appear to be imposters or cunning 'to common eyes'. In such cases their apparent malice was caused by insane passions. The 'skilled magistrate' should be aware of this and be able to distinguish the symptoms of illness. Carlo Morelli warned against 'the unfortunate confusion between affliction and perfidy in the administration of justice'.[13] Another example of Lazzaretti's contradictory expertise is that little was said about freedom of choice in the case of the Incisan murderer, and what was said was not particularly apposite. Elsewhere, however, Lazzaretti stated that even imbeciles had a degree of initiative and will which, however, were motivated by instinct and passion rather than choice, and that therefore the lawyers who defined such people as indubitably responsible were mistaken. Even people who were merely 'simple-minded' could hardly be held fully responsible (though in classifying Grandi as simple-minded, Morelli had assumed him to be responsible), and he recommended extreme caution in making judgements even of people who were less seriously ill. For a viable diagnosis of the accused's mental state Lazzaretti urged, among other methods, an examination of his language and writings – whereas, paradoxically, he had preferred not to consider Carlino's.

There were also some unacknowledged contrivances in the defence evidence. For example, the defence experts placed great emphasis on cranial measurements and on a somatic and anatomical approach about which Livi and Bini were usually as diffident as Morelli and Lazzaretti. Morselli, meanwhile, had already taken a psychological approach, of which he was to become Italy's first exponent. The prosecutors relied on an organicist argument to discredit the defence. That became the theoretical centre of their disagreement.

According to the psychiatrists, the experts' disagreements did not stem purely from their loyalty to the prosecution or the defence. The true issue involved scientific competence, a dimension to the argument of which the men of law were not aware. As far as they were concerned, you only needed a degree in medicine to be able to serve as an expert witness, just as the Justice Minister Raffaello Conforts had decreed.[14] But the truth was that only specialists could judge an individual's mental state and decide whether he was sane, pretending or an irresponsible madman. There was a wide gap in skill and in theoretical and practical training between a psychiatrist and an ordinary doctor.

Francesco Bini planned to address this very question in November 1875 at the Florentine Istituto di Studi Superiori, when he introduced his thirty-first course in clinical mental illness. But books alone were not sufficient: at the outset of his career, when he suddenly found himself in charge of more than 400 psychiatric patients, even he did not know where to turn. Clinical experience and contact with sick people were indispensable, but so was contact with families, magistrates and the appropriate authorities. In previous decades psychiatrists had been able to gain sufficient scientific knowledge within asylums. Now, however, they had to acknowledge that if they remained enclosed in institutions, isolated from others, their new ideas and knowledge would not gain sufficient esteem to overcome ignorance and prejudice. They wanted to come out into the open therefore, to use their skills in society and to be appreciated, especially in the courts. Bini wanted to devote his course to 'imputability within madness' in November 1876, when the Grandi trial was imminent. He had to be careful, for to many people the questions were controversial and cases were always suspect, since 'those who have not observed and studied them will not readily admit their importance ... in civil and criminal matters.'[15]

Although they had been named as experts by the judge, both the modest Dr Morelli and the esteemed professor of forensic medicine, Lazzaretti, certainly lacked the necessary skills – at least, in Livi and Bini's opinions, compared with themselves, both of them directors of asylums for over ten years. Even the twenty-four-year-old Morselli was convinced that he knew more about madness, since he had seen so much of it at the Reggio Emila asylum where he trained. The three defence experts tried to establish throughout the trial that they were better qualified than the others: they hinted at the fact, they stated it clearly and they repeated it. Morselli even wrote down that one of the prosecution doctors appeared to be ignorant of 'the true, direct relationship between anthropology and psychiatry', and he supported his assertion by referring to the number of times the said doctor criticized (with little knowledge) modern anthropological studies of biological criminality and craniology. As for Lazzaretti, he had 'to confess to never having directed an asylum nor ever having been in charge of lunatics'.[16] This was why the defence and prosecution experts could not agree, and the defence experts supported their diagnosis by constantly assuring everyone in court – the public, the jury and the magistrates – that any other real psychiatrist would have agreed with them.

Bini was right. The problem was not so much how to define mental illness – there were plenty of manuals on the subject – but rather of establishing who was able both to recognize such an illness and to see the significant implications of the legal verdict: the psychiatrists or the doctors. The dilemma was particularly clearly presented in the Grandi case, in which one group was on the side of the defence and the other on the side of the prosecution. But once again, matters were in fact more complex than they appeared at first.

The banner of organicism

The psychiatrists had two things to prove: that they were able to satisfy the needs of the legislators and that they were better fitted to do so than anyone else, including doctors, whose presence in court had long been established. They were therefore fighting on two fronts. On the one hand, there was the battle for scientific progress against traditional metaphysics and judicial powers; on the other, they were fighting for the autonomy of the new academic professional discipline against the claims of general medicine.

Italian psychiatry began its ascendance in the 1870s. The Società Freniatrica organized publications and conferences, and the psychiatrists issued their own manifesto of the scientific renewal. There were certainly various different opinions, doubts and cross-currents within the psychiatrists' ranks, but they presented a united front to the world which even historians have often mistakenly accepted. In order to shake free of a metaphysical tradition, they adopted certain beliefs and practices which were typical of the prevalent climate of positivism and which reflected the values of pure science: determinism and naturalism, a quantifying approach and principles of continuity and causality in various forms of evolutionism which were more or less misunderstood. There were special applications in the fields of anthropological and psychiatric research, particularly with regard to morbid heredity, revised Morelian degeneracy and Mantegazza's neogenetic version of atavism. There was also interest in the much more famous theory of Lombroso, who in 1871 announced that he had discovered a cranial depression in the skull of the brigand Villella not normally found except in many criminals and some prosimians. He identified this feature as the organic stigma of human biological and moral inferiority.[17]

Criminal anthropology was categorized by the psychiatrist Lombroso, who purported to distinguish on organic grounds certain abnormal classifications: the delinquent type, for example, the lunatic, and others which suited 'positivist science's' aim to manage the social problems of anomalies. He built up a theory which was not new, although it was radical and systematized and based on the scientific approach manifested by organicism.[18]

It would appear that in the late nineteenth century, to be 'credited as sufficiently scientific', that is to say in line with 'true positivist direction', the psychiatrists had to prove that they were organicists. This was remarked upon by Morselli in 1914.[19] The fact that some of them officially declared themselves to be organicists, however, did not mean that they acted as such in their clinical work or that they held such theoretical convictions. In any case, there were many variations and distinctly different beliefs, which all tended to be mixed together into the category of 'organicist': the theory that all mental activity is due to brain secretions, for example, a drawing of parallels between the physical and psychic phenomena and the theory which left the metaphysical questions open but sought to ascribe physical characteristics to mental states.

However, despite the fact that it included such diverse approaches, it is undoubtedly true that the organicists' success lasted for a long time, largely because of its ambiguities. That the success of the more extreme theories was not due to any scientific validity is obvious and not only in the light of today's judgements. There were plenty of critics even in the last century, and several revisions of theory were made in the light of empirical errors. Autopsies on the corpses of lunatics, for example, disproved the theory that every psychic aberration was necessarily matched by a pathological anatomical sign. Morselli presented this finding at the Società Freniatrica's second congress in September 1877.[20] It was clear that theoretical assumptions were often unverifiable if challenged or applied to real individuals, since they were based on invisible or unknown factors. Yet Lombroso suggested that 'it is dangerous to seek the reasons for the reasons for the facts,' that is, the cause of the presumed anomalies in bone structure found in criminals and lunatics. Moreover, when experimental observation was possible, the results of all the calculations, statistics and deductions did not always yield the expected results. And it was not always possible to protect the theory and explain this away as the result of mistaken measurements or the unsuitability of the subject or a confusion of data.

It was a waste of time to insist too much on the physiological basis of mental illness. This was said even by the Società Freniatrica with reference to the use of the craniometer in psychiatric diagnosis. The accusation was particularly levelled at Lombroso, who must have been aware that most of the objections to his 'uomo delinquente' were objections to the anatomical approach which he deemed essential. Because of this, and in order to establish that his was 'a treatise on criminal psychology', he began, from the second revision of his work and then gradually in the subsequent editions, to draw on theories other than the organicist one of 1876, although this remained his main approach. Furthermore, he increased the number of criminals measured to 1279 in the 1878 edition. He still came under serious attack, however;[21] even the French pupils of Broca, who were convinced craniologists, found Lombroso's methods unacceptable. Paul Topinard's contention was that Lombroso did not say: Here is a fact which suggests certain inferences to me, let us see if I am mistaken and let us proceed with the experimental research and verify the facts.' Rather, he started by proposing the conclusion, then looked for proofs to support his theory, which he defended blindly to convince himself. His approach was more that of a lawyer than a scientist.

Nevertheless, organicism endured, brandishing itself like a banner. There was no lack of other contemporary theories which were less crude and reductive, but the power of the organicist propaganda was considerable, even dominating in the courts. One careful and articulate observer had this to say:

> Seen from afar, it has all the appearance of a solidly based scientific edifice... with a great display of scientific demonstration and erudition in all branches of human knowledge and beyond... of sensational discoveries, of wisdom drawn from the fields of anthropology, biology, ethnology, psychiatry, sociology and numerous other modern disciplines whose names alone command reverence, with all the computations of skulls and human brains, of craniometric compasses and dynamometers, of electrical and photographic equipment, with everything in fact to strike the imagination and make one believe that they possess a body of knowledge which is arcane and yet at the same time totally devoid of... solid facts.[22]

Experts in the field used the language of initiates, discoursing in the tones of those who had received a revelation; for an example, one has only to study the rhetoric used by Morselli in court. They were the ones who saw the truth, who knew what others did not, because they were the ones with the necessary skills. The penal code required a technical opinion, a 'judgement of fact', and what facts could be more concrete than physical signs on the face, skull and body? What facts could be more objective, since they could be measured with instruments? The psychiatrists employed methods, statistics and rules and consequently drew conclusions which were logical and simple to them, however confusing they might be to the non-expert listener.

For the psychiatrists, the main thing was to confront public opinion with scientific opinion and remove the ability of the former to make judgements. To this end the organicist theories seemed most efficacious. Andrea Varga, head of the psychiatric college, had observed that the general public tended to look for vague moral reasons for insane actions. They looked for motives which were in some sense psychological, such as delusions of love, jealousy, fear or suffering. The psychiatrists had to objectively prove the physical causes or at least the organic links between moral and physical symptoms, although these were frequently hidden.[23] If they were not able to do this then anyone could claim to be able to identify a lunatic.

It was because of the danger that psychiatry's authority might not be recognized that it was necessary for everyone to wave the banner of organicism, even those who 'admitted the truth', that nothing was really known about the organic roots of psychosis. Those who preferred the psychological to the anatomical-physiological approach nevertheless had to show the flag: it was important to present a united front. Even Livi, whom Lombroso had identified as being typically resistant 'to the new anthropological-psychiatric school', when he was offended by the magistrates refusal to accept his expert judgement explained that psychiatrists should use 'the anatomical knife, the microscope, chemistry, the ophthalmoscope, the thermometer, the algometer, the dynamometer, the craniometer . . . to demonstrate the reality of this hundred-headed monster called madness'.

What did the judges understand of all this?[24] Organicism not only served to present the 'strong image' of psychiatric science against common sense and the philosophical traditions of the law, but the label also conferred legitimacy and exclusivity to the psychiatrists as medical specialists. Once it had been established that the various forms of mental or moral aberration and even criminality all arose from within the nervous system, and that these defects, like other illnesses, would manifest their own symptoms, hereditary factors and chemical or organic lesions, then the psychiatrists' skills were obviously required. In fact, the physiological model of aberration seemed to recur and fluctuate in Europe and America according to the demand for expert evidence.[25]

Physiognomy: scientific rationality and common sense

There was a drawback inherent to the organic school, which is admitted even by those who are well disposed to it. More often than not, criminals and mental defectives did not display textbook characteristics nor match up to the physiological types therein. Conversely, those characteristics could often be found in well-balanced people. Mantegazza launched an attack and stated that in the 'necromantic cabal of modern criminal anthropologists', it was certainly possible 'to find sixty or more anomalies in one single criminal's skull, only to discover that the poor vessel had contained the brain of the most perfect gentleman or innocent dimwit'.[26] And worse still, the cranio-anthropological descriptions provided in the manuals were applicable to living persons.

Carlino, however, had the perfect 'physique du rôle', though that was clearly not the reason why his fellow countrymen thought him an idiot nor why the psychiatrists judged him to be insane. They could have reached their conclusions without needing to conduct all those physiological examinations. Such tests, however, could serve to convince others that the scientific verdict was true, demonstrable and based on factual evidence. Grandi was an exemplary case for being measured and analysed with the approach. His body could be used perfectly to display the rigour, objectivity and skills of the psychiatrists. The proofs they presented to the public said more about them, in fact, than they did about Grandi.

The trial had caused a great sensation and the psychiatrists' words were eagerly awaited. They carried considerable prestige in that lively cultural climate, with its faith in science, 'in which Florence can claim to be the cradle of modern psychiatry', as Morselli proclaimed. There was prestige for the whole group and personal prestige in particular for the youngest of them, who was looking for a good position (which was in fact immediately offered when he was nominated the extremely youthful director of the asylum at Macerata). Altogether, here was an opportunity not to be missed.

In the circumstances it is easy to understand why even Professors Livi and Bini added their weight to the organicist strategy, even though they were normally worthy followers of Bufalini and Puccinotti in their aversion to and scepticism of it. At first, too little attention had been given to physical causes, now there was too much. Bini warned his students in 1879 against the 'craze for ascribing too much importance to anatomical lesions, for however much the psychiatrists have recently attempted to link the various manifestations and types of madness to established anatomical lesions, they have been unable to firmly establish such a link'. He added, however, that 'were the link to be proved, it would certainly furnish the most secure basis possible'.[27] In the case of the deformed dwarf it was worth looking for such a link by means of 'the external signs' as he cautiously called them – the brachycephaly, convergent crossed eyes, optic muscular spasm, dwarfism, lack of head and body hair, stupid expression and vacant look. He admitted, however, that these features merely illustrated a hypothesis and provided no demonstrable proof.

Morselli, the novice, was the most enthusiastic and ardent supporter of the organicist theory, which he propounded in his role of psychiatrist and expert on modern thought. 'We are not among those who ascribe exaggerated meaning' to the pathological, organic, craniological symptoms, he stated. Nevertheless, it was on this that the certainty of his expertise was based. The facts were there in Grandi's recorded physical deformities: 'I defy them to be refuted since they are objective in that sense.' And there were certain laws which only other modern psychiatrists could understand: 'In every instance where the morphology and functioning of the organs departs from the norm, science considers that there are lesions in the delicate, complex structure of the nervous system, and every day brings new discoveries in this rich and widely unknown field.'[28] For this reason, as we have already seen, he examined and interpreted the smallest physiological signs, drawing on the very recent theory of atavism, on the hypothesis of correspondence between the parts and the whole, and on Morel's theories of degeneracy and the hereditary aspects of alcoholism and neurosis, which were commonly assessed more in terms of morals than clinically. Since Grandi had committed those terrible crimes, he also drew on theories of cerebral localization and psycho-physical parallelism to explain that 'his imperfect brain lacked the organs governing the sense of morality'.

When the prosecution experts commented that with 'anthropology and statistics' it was possible 'to ascribe any meaning one chooses to the facts', they were not mistaken. They invoked the 'analytical methods of Galileo and Bufalini'. Lazzaretti launched the typical accusation that they had started from an a priori concept, a 'preconception inspired . . . by Grandi's physical deformities', according to the public prosecutor. Morelli warned them severely that they should pay more attention to brains and less to skulls. He insisted on treating the defence experts as anthropologists (with no complaints from them on that score) rather than psychiatrists, probably because of their constant referral to recent anthropological trends. But that whole discipline was flawed. Even Mantegazza had said so, and he added 'more against the modern theories which consider criminality to be an effect of cerebral organization'.

Bini attempted for 'several hours' to answer such criticisms, but we do not know how; Livi was not at that particular hearing, and his presence was probably missed. In compensation, Morselli was more arrogant than ever. The young man who had barely graduated felt 'the need to clarify certain deplorable errors which the honoured doctor has incurred' – the honoured doctor who was thirty-six years older than him – errors not so much concerned with the wretched cartwright but concerning science, anthropology and psychiatry, which could not be understood by the uninitiated. He affirmed the superiority of psychiatric skills and praised the objectivity of responses inspired by organicism, which he appeared not to doubt in the slightest. It hardly seemed possible that this was the same young man who had just publicly expressed to Mantegazza his own disatis-faction with craniometry, with the obsession for quantifying and with materialist reductionism. This pupil of Carlo Livi was a follower of the 'new psychological school' (as he himself repeated when he discussed again the expert evidence in the Grandi case at the psychiatric congress),[29] and yet here in court, in front of the judges and the public, he seemed to be adopting the mantle of a follower of Lombroso.

The author of *L'Uomo Delinquente* was certainly interested in the case, so much so that in his museum of criminal anthropology in Turin he mounted Grandi's autobiographical 'novel', reproduced lithographically by the Florentine publishers P. Smorti & C., in its own smart display case with a revolving base. This was the same work which had been rejected by the judges and published by Yorick in *La Nazione*. It remains there to this day, along with an unpublished photograph of Carlino with his sly look, wispy moustache and little pointed beard, evidently taken after his hair had started to grow in prison. Over the photograph is written 'From the Collection of Enrico Morselli' in his own hand, probably when he wanted to present it to Lombroso. It is not known whether Morselli received direct help from Lombroso in preparing his expert evidence, but it is of no great importance. The child murderer's trial demonstrates how in certain circumstances there were good reasons to adopt the somatic approach inspired by organicism without necessarily implying a profound belief in it.

None of this greatly helps us to understand why the psychiatrists were defeated. On the contrary, it raises other questions, particularly in this case when, unusually, the whole structure of the argument was based on the clearly demonstrable objective proofs of the accused's deformity. However, just as the theory's success bore no relation to scientific value, nor, obviously, can its failure be explained simply in terms of its inherent truth or falsity. Paradoxically, the organicist approach adopted by the defence experts failed precisely because it was relatively easy to apply in Carlino's case.

The psychiatrists claimed to be able, thanks to their exclusive skill, to discern that which ordinary people, including magistrates and doctors, could not see. But the fact that Carlino was deformed and bald and dwarfish and had six toes was clearly visible to one and all – it was for this after all that the boys had teased him. The same applied to his mental deficiency, which everyone in town knew about. No one needed learned scientists to tell them the obvious nor to provide detailed descriptions measured in centimetres.

However, when the scientists put forward the conclusions which they had deduced from statistics and anthropological laws, then other people were left in the dark. There were, after all, plenty of deformed wretches around who never hurt a fly. So why should the one who murdered his neighbours not be held responsible? Particularly one like the cartwright of Incisa, who had previously led a blameless life living and working like everyone else. Many people asked themselves what being physically deformed had to do with murdering children.

People needed some other reason. Even if it were proved that every external abnormality always hid a cerebral lesion, it was absurd to assume that every murderer or suicide was psychotic because of that. Carlo Livi had clarified the point in his treatise, *Forensic phrenology*, in which he criticized 'the organologist' Gall, 'famous decipherer of skulls and brains'. Livi had explained that internal lesions and physiological abnormalities were also found in illnesses which left the mind and will unaffected.[30] The emphasis which the psychiatrists laid on facts which were obvious to everyone only made it more obvious how little they actually provided in the way of explanations.

The same could be said for organicist reductionism in general. Its widespread acceptance was partly due to the fact that it was close to ordinary common sense, which it had 'made scientific' rather than rejected. Lombroso was aware of this: 'Never has the expression "there is nothing new under the sun" been more clearly borne out, because the truths discovered by the new schools of thought, even the most controversial theories, are founded on popular sayings and belief.'[31] The scientists Thompson, Benedikt and Camper had only provided a body of theory to ideas which were already in general circulation, particularly the criminal anthropologist, who liked to pretend he was Hamlet: 'The sad wounds which they could not help, having no choice in their provenance.'

In a manual published by Hoepli devoted to the Lombroso school of thought. *Guida per i giudizi medico-forensi nelle questioni di imputabilità*, the psychiatrist Giuseppe Antonini asserted that the contents were neither revolutionary nor personal. The popularizer told his readers that advanced ideas abounded in Morel, in Gall, in Lavater's phrenology, in the physiognomy of the 1500s, and above all in popular wisdom.

> You too will have come across men whose high forehead, lively eye and harmonious expression have made you exclaim, 'he must be an intelligent man', whereas at the sight of a man with a deformed face, low wrinkled brow, snub nose, receding chin and awkward gait you have judged, 'this man is an idiot.'[32]

The *Uomo Delinquente* also contained several regional proverbs and old sayings which the author had deliberately chosen to show how the truth of his anthropology was rooted in popular consciousness.

But there were risks attached to such a comparison, namely that particular school of scientific knowledge would not be regarded as superior and indispensable and that it would not be explanatory. This was in fact the case. 'Considerations of . . . deformed or limbless people' was the content of one of the very popular 'useful and entertaining' books published in Florence by Salani in 1871 called *Deformities and conditions in men and women and their meanings*. There too, physiognomy and skulls were said to hold clues to character, morals and intelligence. But when it came down to details, there was little agreement. The high forehead, for example, was not in fact a good sign: those who have it 'are often lazy and ponderous and resemble cattle'. A rounded forehead on the other hand belonged to the quick-tempered and miserable. Intelligence, wisdom and cunning were indicated by a medium-sized head. Wicked madness was particularly signalled by the eyes: if they were sunken (as Carlino's apparently were) the man was 'malicious, short-tempered, had bad habits, was audacious, cruel, untruthful and proud'. If the eyes were prominent on the other hand, the individual was 'loquacious, lacked judgement, was mad or a liar'.[33]

At least popular belief did not pretend to have the coherence or absolute certainty which science claimed for itself and it was certainly less rigid. In novels, the ugly and deformed were not necessarily the wicked characters; on the contrary, they were often poor creatures in need of love. They were often – as in the monster of Zelinda – hiding noble souls and sometimes noble birth beneath their exteriors. The same applied to the character of the fool. Without ever achieving the heroic and magic heights of the truly mad, the fool was often imbued with a mixture of absurd naivety and cunning which served to diffuse difficult situations and either showed up the mean nature of ordinary people or unmasked their wickedness with childlike innocence.[34]

This genre, with all its variety and popular tradition, did not always agree with the precepts it borrowed from scientific texts (in themselves contradictory). And neither corresponded in any way to real individual cases, not even the Grandi case. Everyone told the story in their own way. Where positive proofs were not possible, it was the duty of science to provide negative ones, to prove that the assertions of the judicial authorities or of common sense were not infallible.

Lazzaretti's advice, therefore, was to stick to 'cautious formulas'. Regarding physical signs, he himself doubted whether there were reliable, recognizable signs even in cases of habitual sodomy, let alone that pederasts had distinctive physical characteristics, as Tardieu and of course Lombroso claimed. And yet even the Paduan teacher devoted pages to the physiological symptoms of idiots and cretins, listing the details: runny eyes which were often squint, large cheeks, fat lips, high ears set far back, few body hairs and dirty head hair. Morselli constantly pointed out that some of these physical characteristics matched the cartwright's. Carlo Morelli recalled how the great Chiarugi observed physical aberrations in lunatics, but 'he could not directly ascribe the causes of madness to any one feature in particular'. Pucinotti, who was his teacher as well as Livi's and Bini's, maintained that the anatomical-physiological signs of imbecility were mainly the inequality between the right and left side of the brain as well as a small cranium (Carlino's was disproportionately large), on which point at least everyone was agreed – Esquirol, Pinel, Gall and Brown. But he admitted that in reality the possible variations were endless. In 1877 even Andrea Varga concluded that 'Seeking to base a diagnosis of imbecility on the configurations of the skull, the more or less acute facial angle, a badly placed or misshapen ear or unruly hair which is untamed by the comb . . . is a waste of time.'[35]

Physiognomy and physical abnormalities did not in themselves indicate if a murderer was cruel or manic (that is, a responsible criminal or an irresponsible lunatic). The fact that the psychiatrists relied on this evidence was not sufficient to lend supreme authority to their judgements. What counted – and this is stating the obvious – was the significance ascribed to such characteristics on the basis of other considerations, scientific or otherwise. The psychiatrists did not succeed in convincing people that their own interpretations of these features were in any way better than the interpretations of non-experts. They attacked every one, particularly the jurors, and the Lombroso supporters would have liked to have seen the jury abolished although more liberal legal professionals supported it. The psychiatrists were also disdainful towards the witnesses, at least when their evidence did not coincide with their own diagnosis or contradicted it. This in its turn generated several equivocations.

At first sight, the psychiatrists had thought they were dealing with 'moral insanity', an illness where the intellect functioned more or less normally but the sense of morality was absent, paralysed or perverted. The definition was proposed by the British scientist Prichard, whose works Livi was disseminating at the time. Prichard was not really an 'organicist' at all, yet he was frequently invoked in psychiatric-forensic cases which were otherwise inexplicable, this in turn invariably unleashing enormous 'doctrinal and practical dissension between magistrates and doctors'.[36] Perhaps it was to avoid this that Grandi's defence experts chose instead to adopt the completely different diagnosis of imbecility, though this nosographic classification did not coincide with common sense. The term 'imbecile' was widely used in everyday language, but in a sense which differed from the legal and medical definitions, which in their turn were different from each other and also had inherent internal differences. In common parlance, 'imbecile' was synonymous with inanity, ignorance or stupidity. It meant someone of feeble brain, unable to absorb learning, who gets into all sorts of trouble and 'moves one to pity' – characteristics which did not match well with a murderer who was well able to take care of himself, as the relevant testimony emphasized.[37]

On the question of morality and suspected madness, Lazzaretti recognized that 'the public voice and rumour, that is, people's general opinion . . . constitutes an element of proof which is apt at least to influence the judge.' Morselli, however, stood against the people of Incisa, who appeared in court 'representing the least educated and most biased of common people', whose words 'the serious and respectable representatives of the law' seized on and brandished like a weapon to oppose the theories of science. He stated that since the jurors understood 'the language and attitudes of the common people . . . rather than the voice of science, which speaks clearly and yet is not understood', they did not realize how much more valuable were the studies of 'three specialists than the opinions of many townspeople and the other three doctors'.[38]

For the psychiatrists it was a point of principle: on the one hand stood the errors and prejudices of common sense, and on the other the truth of their own science, which proceeded by deterministic method to an equation between physical characteristics, mental illness and lack of responsibility for the crime, with the logic of transferred characteristics so that the third premise equalled the first. In contrast to this rigid, positivist rationality, which by definition admitted no objections or interlocutions, the classic legal rationality appeared altogether broader and more complex. In its basic principles at least, whatever might occasionally transpire in practice, it depended on the discretion of the court, on the particular judges and jurors involved and on the whole collection of variable factors which made each trial a case of its own. If nothing else, the judgements of the law always presupposed listening to diverse opinions, imposed cross-examination, and above all did not maintain that the verdict was a matter for autocratic experts but saw it as closely connected with the values of morality and justice adhered to by the general public.

Even when it came to the question of the accused's imputability, it was not only a question for science. The code established that those of unsound mind were not deemed to be responsible for certain actions, because it assumed that society rejected the idea of punishing people who acted without true choice, from madness, constraint or because they were under the age of responsibility. But it still happened that in certain cases, when the crime had been violent enough to revolt a whole town, the people demanded and expected a severe sentence. Nevertheless, the psychiatrists concluded that the reason for their defeat was the judges' lack of understanding.

Freedom, constraint or otherwise

The Grandi case can be interpreted as a typical example of disagreement between magistrates and psychiatrists, a conflict which led to the famous clash between the classical school of law, led by Francesco Carrara, and the positivist school, represented by Lombroso, Ferri and Garofalo. The threads of conflict in the Grandi trial which lend support to this hypothesis are outlined in general terms in the ample literature on the subject. The conflict between the two philosophies was clear: rationalism and the metaphysics of free will on the one hand, and naturalism and the laws of causality extended to the world of humans on the other. At the centre lay the issue of free will as against determinism, which the two schools of thought were unable to resolve; this was the real sticking point when it came to defining imputability.[39]

In 1877 Enrico Ferri devoted his thesis on jurisprudence to the question, which was developed further in a volume published the following year. He urged, 'Study the problem for two years with devotion and good faith, as I did. Experience the defeats, as I did, when I found my most cherished, long-held illusions demolished at every step.' His bitter conclusion was this: that between the doctrine of free will and that of scientific determinism, 'tertium non datur'. Therefore, free will did not exist or at best it belonged to the realms of theory, and was negated by social statistics and the observation of human affairs. Ferri claimed to have rejected emotional judgements and to have relied solely on reason, a feat of which, so it seemed to him and others, not everyone was capable – certainly not the classical jurists nor the magistrates. At the Florence Court of Assizes, Morselli accused those jurists of bringing 'to the weighty problem of human responsibility the ancient burden of metaphysics or the biased voice of emotion'.[40]

The positivists maintained that the only admissible freedom was physical freedom, i.e. the absence of obstacles to the completion of an action. Man was only free to *act* or not; he was never free in regard to his *will*. The moral freedom to will one thing rather than another independently of any cause or motivation was unacceptable from a scientific point of view. The physiologist Aleksandr Herzen, Jr. explained in Florence that this was because science had to eliminate all unpredictable, random elements. It was necessary that human actions, like natural phenomena, should follow constant laws which could be seen in terms of cause and effect.[41] Even crimes were the inevitable result of certain known or as yet unknown conditions, which meant that the individual, however free, could not have acted otherwise. For classical jurists on the other hand, moral freedom was an essential precondition of the rule of law and the right to punish. Only if he is free and rational can man determine to act, given certain conditions, in one way rather than another, and he is therefore responsible for himself before his neighbours.

The acknowledgement or denial of so-called free will depended on two different requirements, one moral, the other scientific. Ferri asserted that the two were not irreconcilable, though the doctrinal positions which supported them seemed incompatible, maintaining that the input of determinism furnished a more solid basis, even for ethics. 'The adversaries argue as though they were dealing with irreconcilable opposites, whereas in fact they are making statements which can co-exist very well without damaging each other.' So assured Mario Calderoni in a work produced at the University of Pisa and enthusiastically reviewed in the *Rivista sperimentale di freniatria*. Freedom, causality, will were all words with a multiplicity of meanings which had become confused with use. 'Liberum arbitrium' indicated 'the ability to select a preferred course of action from diverse choices.' It excluded coercion, not causality, just as causality itself did not exclude free will, but merely the idea that it sprang from no cause whatever.[42]

It is necessary first to establish exactly what the classical school really believed rather than simply ascribing to them a belief in absolute freedom without cause, as Ferri had done. Carrara believed that man had 'partial freedom' from physical laws, including those of his own body, as a requirement for living with moral laws as well.[43] In legal, as well as everyday ethics people are not seen as mere bodies which act purely on the basis of mechanical determinism. What counts are individual choices and intentions, and it is necessary to establish whether someone committing a crime has done it on purpose, accidentally or from constraint. Judges did not pronounce on the metaphysics of free will in individual trials so as to establish the concrete application of the concept. Nor did the supporters of the scientific approach invoke the doctrine of determinism to explain all forms of human behaviour, to the point of not being able to distinguish between voluntary and involuntary actions. However much the debate continued at the theoretic level, it did not affect its actual practical applications, which proceeded as normal.

This was especially so in cases where the question of the accused's imputability arose. In such cases freedom of choice, instead of being presupposed as an essential faculty of human nature, was, according to the same penal code, considered to be absent. On the other hand, it was admitted that freedom of choice was present in normal individuals by the very experts who undertook to demonstrate scientifically that the perpetrator of a crime was out of the ordinary, a madman, and therefore not a criminal. The one constant factor within the wide varieties of madness seemed to be the individual's inability to act otherwise, which Francesco Bini equated in legal and philosophical terms with the loss of free will. Livi agreed.

In debating the proposed new penal code many psychiatrists,

apart from the organicists and determinists considered that it was more in keeping with medical knowledge to address the dominant value of freedom of choice as a requirement for imputability rather than the question of awareness, which the legislators tended to favour. Even in Grandi's defence the expert evidence reached the conclusion that 'free will ... is not present in him and therefore he lacks the necessary condition, the main element required for him to be held responsible.'[44] In the psychiatrists' assessment of unimputability, the concept of determinism which effectively came into consideration in this case, as it did in general, was not the same as that involved in the debate against the liberalism of the classical school. It was a less explicit form of determinism, which held that the crime committed by an individual was due, in a cause and effect analysis, to the dangerous nature of a criminal or lunatic type.

Another difference between the classical and positivist schools concerned the object of judgement itself. For the classicists this was the crime itself as a legal entity, whereas for the positivist criminologists and psychiatrists it was the criminal or dangerous lunatic who was submitted to judgement.

The scientists emphasized the point to establish further the indispensable nature of their own function. Not only were they able to make more objective, truthful and scientific statements than the magistrates, but they were also able to say more useful things, which the others had not even thought of. The judges limited themselves to evaluating and apportioning the appropriate punishment for the crime committed. They were on the scene after the event and made no provision for protecting society from further crimes, because they judged criminal actions to be completely random and unpredictable. The determinists claimed that this was the fault of the doctrine of free will without cause. They themselves, on the other hand, favoured some protection of society. Since they focused their attention on the particular individual concerned rather than the deed, they were able to establish his propensity for crime, his 'tendency ... to commit criminal acts' either with full responsibility or, equally dangerously, with irresponsible criminal insanity.

The psychiatrists regarded Grandi as an extremely dangerous congenital idiot, whom they would have liked to incarcerate in an asylum for the rest of his life. The actual sentence, unheeding of the scientific viewpoint, had instead condemned him to prison. The psychiatrists warned of the risks: once the murderer had served his sentence and returned to freedom, 'the fathers and mothers of Incisa must go in fear once again.'

But apart from the question of protecting society, was it really true that the classic legal wisdom did not address the question of the criminal himself at all? Was it only modern criminologists who provided a knowledge of the individual's character? Did the different forms of judgement which the psychiatrists claimed were so misunderstood and for which they were defeated, really come down simply to a focus on the real individual instead of abstract principles? Once again, it is necessary to look at the alternatives to the scientific approach on the one hand and the speculative approach on the other, polemically treated by the positivists and persistent in historiography.

The fact that Carrara had placed the definition of the crime itself as a legal entity at the centre of the debate did not minimize the importance which both legal theory and practice attributed to the subjective elements of the crime, including an enquiry into individual motivation. The masters in the field, Gian Domenico Romagnosi and Pellegrino Rossi, had warned that only the least evolved of penal systems limited themselves to considering nothing but the crime itself and its objective consequences. It was always necessary to take into account other variables, such as possible 'internal causes' and how 'different psychological degrees of wickedness' might inspire the same crime, and consequently the degree 'of public danger' involved. In view of this, a committee of magistrates, psychiatrists and anthropologists had in 1867 reviewed the project of classifying the causes of delinquency already proposed by the Sardinian states ten years earlier.[45]

A criterion of motive was necessary even to be able to establish the sentence, which varied for the same crime according to whether the act was premeditated or not. Better still, it was suggested that these criteria be measured according to 'the normal nature of the motives' which had pushed the individual to break the law. This concept thus recognized that there were differences inherent in the idea of premeditation itself. 'Psychological motives' were referred to; these could be of social origins when the criminal subscribed to the 'errors, prejudices and passions common to the people among whom he lives'. This would be said, for example, of the brigand Musolino. The motives could also be entirely idiosyncratic and related to the intellectual, spiritual or physical life of the murderer, as the *Rivista penale* explained in an article in 1875.[46] An identical crime could be committed by various people or one person repeatedly and in different circumstances for many different reasons. The judges had to distinguish between the crime which was ultimately committed and the criminal's motives. And given that the crime itself was the same, sentence should be modified according to the criminal's motivation.

This was clearly even more important where there was a suspicion of non-imputability. In such cases the code clearly directed the magistrates to turn their attention to the author of the crimes and not the crime itself, as they were accused of doing by the positivists. No penalty was imposed by the court even in the most atrocious crime when the accused was considered to have been incapable of understanding or exercising his free will at the moment when the crime was committed.

Why? 'No reason'

In the need to understand why, for example, a murderer had killed, judicial enquiries should have been linked with scientific enquiries, which always sought to discover the truth about the accused – instead of the two being in conflict, as seems to have been the case. It was this very need to understand which led the lawyers and the particular judge on a case to turn to the experts if the accused's motives were outside the bounds of normal psychology and criminal logic. But what answers did they receive when they looked for advice?

The psychiatrists had stated that the essential question was not 'what action should be punished', but 'who is this person we are judging'? Just as in clinical practice, the problem to address was not the illness itself but the individual and his personal characteristics. 'Individualization and differentiation' were the basic tenets of the scientific and criminal anthropological approach adopted by the positivist school. This was claimed by adherents at the time and recently confirmed by the historians David Garland and Michel Foucault.[47]

One thing is clear, however. The supposed 'specialists in motivation', asked why a specific person in certain circumstances and at a particular time and place had committed a particular crime, were effectively able to offer little or nothing in the way of explanations. And they were even less able to do so the more they deployed powerful theories like organicism and natural determinism, since they became too preoccupied in establishing the superiority of their particular skills. To declare that a man had attacked a preselected or random victim because he belonged to the category of 'born criminals' who were, according to Lombroso, biologically inclined to crime, did not say very much about the murderer's personality, nor about his reasons for that specific action. To say that a young man had killed because he was an imbecile, as was said of Carlino, did not help in understanding why he had done it, why at that particular time and place, why he had picked on children and why those particular four.

People wanted the answers to these questions. The judges wanted to know. The prosecutor did at least provide some explanation for the incredible events. Grandi had acted out of revenge – that deplorable motive. He had been reduced to furious behaviour by all the insults and, being himself weak and prevaricating, he had chosen creatures even weaker, who had fallen easily into his trap. What else did the experts have to add? What other explanation could they offer, since they maintained that the accused was not responsible? There was no motive, no 'plausible explanation' for the cartwright's criminal actions, stated the psychiatrists. That was precisely why he was mad.

The medical diagnosis with its legal implications was drawn from two main elements: first from the act itself, which was deemed 'inexplicable', and only secondarily from the organic structure and physiological and anatomic aspects of the accused, interpreted according to the laws of atavism and from the supposed correspondence between physical and mental anomalies, which was not always proven. By naturalizing aberrations and presenting them in a deterministic framework, the *individual* was transformed into an abstract *type*. His individuality was taken away and he was labelled as a 'variety of the human species'. Even the attention focused on his body, something so tangible and concrete, was of such a nature as to eliminate all individuality and to miss all possible significance. A person did what he or she did – killed, stole or sold herself because of some organic defect or hereditary factor, because of some biological arrest or reversal which placed him in a lower class of the animal kingdom.

In the experts' evidence on mental deficiency, the development of organicist deterministic theories served greatly to defeat their own purpose. Far from offering interpretations, it negated, twisted and minimized any meaning which might have appeared from the evidence or from the accused's interrogation. Carlino had justified himself with 'most frivolous reasons', which were 'so stupid and puerile' that they were enough to prove his mental illness on their own, asserted Morselli. His crimes came under the heading of 'unprecedented crimes, which cannot be explained . . . without assuming a horrendous perversion of moral sense and an absolute lack of emotions'. The criminal also lacked morality and feelings, but he always pursued his own interests. The imbecile like Grandi, on the other hand, 'had no motive, not a single one' for his actions.

Bini stated that 'the lack of awareness of committing a crime is regarded by everyone as an extremely powerful indication of an unsound mind.'[48] But in 1875 there were formal protests made in Parliament against those medical experts who, when a crime appeared to be inexplicable, simply got up and declared that the accused was mad.[49] Lazzaretti, for example, found the idea of a murder without motive inconceivable, because even lunatics have reasons for their actions which, however irrational and wild, still constitute a motive. When a crime appeared to have been committed 'without any reason whatever', the judges classified it as *ad lasciviam*, 'solely from evil intent'; an example would be the case of a murderer who, simply to check whether a firearm is working and accurate, fires shots at an innocent passerby. Lombroso insisted on stating that the expression 'brutal wickedness' only made sense if it meant madness, and it was thus that one of his patients ended up with a life sentence.

The code was perfectly clear, even if Morselli did not know it or misinterpreted it. During the Grandi trial he suggested that 'when the law cannot explain such atrocious crimes with any motive other than wicked brutality, then it looks to science for help.' But the Florence Court of Cassation in 1868 and that of Naples in 1874 had both confirmed that not only the absence of responsibility but even 'the excuse of partial mental deficiency is inappropriate to murder committed with no other motive than brutal wickedness', although these could be aggravating factors.[50]

In declaring that Carlino had done everything from insidiously trapping the victims to burying four children alive over two years without any motive whatsoever, the psychiatrists did not incline the judges to agree with them that he was unfit for punishment. Nor, certainly, did it placate the anger of the townspeople or the pain of the parents. The psychiatrists had failed to provide any explanation about the man who had been harmless enough before the crimes. They had not explained how he had become so dangerous nor why he had committed such ghastly deeds. In other words, they failed to provide the answers the magistrates looked to them for. This was possibly the main reason why they had been ignored and defeated.

But it was not the only reason. Some blame was certainly due to the fact which Carrara deplored in his open letter to Carlo Livi – that the medical profession could never agree among themselves.

The arguments did not follow clear distinctions of attitude between prosecution and defence nor of skills between psychiatrists and general practitioners. They were far more diffuse and entrenched and resulted in outcomes which some supported and others opposed; and their disagreements did not stop at diagnosis.

Livi, naturally, declared that he was in complete agreement with his colleagues in the Grandi case. A closer examination, however, shows that he supported a different line which in fact conflicted with what Morselli had previously stated. Morselli had discoursed at length on the somatic analysis and atavistic interpretation of Carlino's imbecility. Livi did not even wish to address the question. Rather he sought to explain, given that the murderer was mentally deficient, why he had been obsessed with revenge. Far from denying, like the other two psychiatrists, that the murderer had any motives at all, Livi asserted that his motivation was in fact so strong that he could not have acted in any other way. This, he claimed, meant that Grandi was not responsible because in his condition he had no choice in his behaviour.

He urged the court to listen and interpret what emerged from Grandi's confession and from the evidence. The words 'dwarf', 'Baldy' 'twenty-one-toes' recurred throughout the constant insults he suffered, and he could not bear it any longer. He was undoubtedly dangerous, but this was not a natural feature inherent to his biological illness but one which appeared suddenly because of the negative relationships in his daily surroundings. In fact, when he had left his natural surroundings and gone away to do some work in another area, the need to kill had not overcome him for months and months. He was seized by it, as by an 'organic need' for survival, as soon as he got back to Incisa and found himself in the same situation. The psychiatrist declared, 'It is certain that if the wretched man had been in some country family where nobody came to torment and endlessly mock him he would have lived peacefully and quietly with simple good will and without harming anyone.' He would have been an imbecile, inferior to his neighbours, but he would not have been wounded and driven to wickedness by the cruelty and indifference of others.

Livi raised the question of collective responsibility, particularly on the part of those, such as the priest and even the children's parents, whom Carlino had turned to for help in removing the torments which deprived him of 'peace at work and peace of mind'. He had received no help from those people nor even the compassion which was his due. It was at that point that he became obsessed with the idea of seeking his own justice, and he was unable to ignore it. A normal person would have reasoned with himself and tried to overcome the impulse, but that young man had been different since birth. He lacked the reason and will to control the passions he felt, 'love, anger, jealousy, revenge'. His feelings were the same as other men's but stronger, obsessive, a 'blind dizziness'.

In 'the name of human dignity' Morselli had rejected 'any identification with him'. He was a monster not a man. Livi, on the other hand, said that in the same conditions and given the same illness, 'I who am speaking and all those listening in court would have done the same. This you must never forget: we would all have done the same!'[51]

But people did want to forget. They wanted to distance themselves from so much horror. At the beginning they hadn't even thought that the children's disappearance could be the fault of anyone in Incisa; it was the waters of the Arno they had said straight away. But the river was dry. Then it must have been some gypsy, a brigand who had sold the children – certainly it was some stranger from who knows where. When they discovered instead that it was that young man whom everyone knew well, whom everyone trusted, and that it had all happened right there in their midst, then they turned on him. Of course it was him, the proud, evil hypocrite. He was a good-for-nothing braggart, different from other people. He didn't even sleep with women, he didn't get on with his family, who were good people, who hadn't known anything about it even though they lived and worked, brothers and brother-in-law all together, in the same workshop where the corpses were lying, barely covered with a handful of earth.

Nobody realized. Nobody understood. And anyway what was there to understand? Even that young doctor had said during the trial, 'It is not possible to understand, it is inconceivable.' Apparently it was all because he had been badly formed by nature, something inside him didn't work properly. Who else was to blame? What was that newspaper in Florence on about? That he shouldn't have been teased. But that was kids' stuff. And that the adults ought to have helped him. What! He was the one who was always trailing along behind the children. He used to chase them with a broom and threaten them. People were at work, they had better things to do all day than be keeping an eye on children's games. Anyway, not even the defence lawyers had paid any attention to that, no matter what some citizens started saying in *La Nazione* about the murderer being a victim too. It was time to put an end to it all. As soon as the court had sentenced him everything would go back to the way it was before. Let daily life go on in peace without any attacks or fears: that, above all, was what the people of Incisa wanted.[52]

In such a general climate of opinion, Livi's call to reconsider the whole affair and to identify with the accused and understand his desperation at his constant torments cannot have been well received. It went against the need the townspeople felt to exorcize the evil that had been bred in their midst. Not that the psychiatrist was simply shifting the blame onto the community, like those moralizing press articles had done by pointing the finger at the ignorance and wickedness of the whole populace. Nevertheless, since he did not believe that Grandi's violence was an inherent part of his imbecility, Livi was looking for reasons why the sick man had become so dangerous. Moving away from the rigidity of naturalistic determinism, the explanation for his behaviour necessitated a critical look at the world he lived in, his experiences and his relationships with others.

The three defence experts all reached the same conclusions: that the murderer could not be blamed. But their arguments were quite different, and on one crucial point they drew different conclusions. Livi's psycho-pathological analysis ascribed a certain degree of responsibility to the wider community, whereas Morselli and Bini's naturalistic reductionism removed any such responsibility and was thus more acceptable to the community in its need to absolve itself of any guilt. Thus, the ability to explain offered by the first approach was precisely why it failed, whereas the very inadequacies of the second approach opened up spaces which allowed for consensus.

Because Carlino was manifestly an ideal example to confirm the doctrine of stigmatized aberrations, the process and outcome of the trial set the pattern for future contradictions by the school of Lombroso. Despite its scant scientific value, which was obvious from the beginning in 1876, the positivist criminological school was destined to gain considerable fame even beyond Italy and Europe. Not only was it popular despite its theoretical weaknesses, but that popularity actually depended on them. It was rooted in the inability or refusal to collect and explain the meaning of sickness and violence within a living context. By depicting a dangerous type, either criminal or mad, with an aberration which was unavoidable and motiveless, it removed all responsibility for these tragedies from the deprivations of poverty and suffering. The deeper a society examined itself to understand why so many terrible crimes and sicknesses occurred despite the glories of progress, the less able it would be to resort to simple, deterministic explanations. The success of such simplistic diagnoses goes far beyond their scientific credibility; in fact the two almost appear to operate in inverse proportion, and they still return in updated form today.

Compared to the end of the nineteenth century, psychiatric and legal structures have certainly changed. Attitudes have also changed among the general public and in the field of science: we know more and are somewhat less prejudiced about criminal lunacy. And yet it is not enough; even today we would not know what to say or do if faced with the affair of the child killer. Today's sociological reductionism for every ill in society is not an alternative to nineteenth-century biological determinism, but simply a variation, with a different emphasis and an equally unsatisfactory theoretical basis.

Carlino's thoughts

What happened to Carlino? – twenty years in prison. He had immediately announced that he was pleased he had to work, and 'now I'm even happier because I'm a government mechanic'. He had derived a certain satisfaction from the trial, 'to see himself looked at and listened to "by the whole of Italy and especially those thieves from Incisa who will crease up with rage and envy" to see him being part of the Government'. Just so long as he did not have to return to his town to be humiliated as usual – they had never given him any justice – and suffer his usual life at the hands of those ignoramuses. The main thing was that they hadn't sent him to an asylum. When he had learned that that was the defence's intention he was offended, because in 'asylums they tie people up', he knew that. Prison was better. But 'thieves go to prison and he was no thief' was what came into his mind from time to time.[53] Anyway, the carabinieri and the judges must know that, they had treated him very well from the start, with a mounted escort, guns loaded and chains on his wrists when they came to fetch him with the carriage. He had been flattered.

> Because Carlo Grandi of Incisa, when I was in the coach when they conducted me as soon as we arrived in Florence. The carabinieri. They told the driver to go by the Via dei Fiorentini. Because Carlino is afraid. Because he has a good brain, Carlino. Carlo Grandi. Cheer up the King's carabinieri told me Cheer up young man we are at the Murate. Cheer up Carlino. Goodbye said the King's carabinieri. Goodbye brothers of the King but I told them you have saved my life. Brothers of the King the Lord bless you from the heavens. All of you. Poor and rich his soldiers of the King. Long live the King's flag hurrah.

He remembered that day well. And then at the Murate he was visited by

> The Lord Judges of Florence. The young Carlo Grandi of Incisa will do me the pleasure of redirecting me because I have a good brain and good judgement. Tell the Lord Judges of Florence. And I will die with a good brain and judgement to say to the Lord Judges of Florence. And death, to the one who stole from my cartwright's workshop. Death Incisan thieves. Death thieves. The day has come Incisan thieves end of prison. Incisans you will die thieves. You will die prison thieves. You will die in prison. Carlo Grandi is cheerful like in his own home cheerful. Like a gentleman. Long live the King and his soldiers. Long live justice that we willingly serve the King Victor Emmanuel King of Italy. Cheerful soldiers of the King. And we are soldiers. Sons of the King of Kings. My soldiers long live the judge of earth. Hurrah. Hurrah. The fatherland and our King of Kings. Hurrah.

His fellow townspeople cannot have understood all this but he kept repeating:

> Oh men of Incisa have judgement. But I Carlino of Incisa have a good brain and judgement. The mayor of Murate told me. You are a good boy young Carlo of Incisa. Incisans have judgement for the children of 10, 11, 12, 13, 14. Oh fathers and mothers of families you are wicked souls, big and little people of Incisa.
> Oh people of Incisa send your sons to the town school. You are pigheaded. Your children have more judgement than you.
> Oh fathers and mothers you are pig-headed. It will go from bad to worse Oh fathers and mothers of families. Because your children do not have judgement and because they are wicked in much. To tell the gentlemen judges of Florence. The people of Incisa are half thieves. Incisans even stole from me the Incisans my tools from my workshop. Fine Incisan thieves. Incisans it is not true. Incisan thieves yes yes we are fine thieves. Poor children of God. Good 8 and 9 year olds.

This, in a few lines and with many mistakes, is what the famous *Novel of Carlo Grandi* consisted of. Four pages in all, with which he was very pleased, but which the judges had not allowed as evidence.[54] He had even illustrated it in pen and ink. First the bridge over the Arno at Incisa, all highly decorated and inscribed 'Long Live Jesus'. Underneath he had drawn a man in a boat who was perhaps himself. And at the end there was another figure, probably himself again, working a machine with wheels and ropes on which another four figures stood next to each other, the children one imagines, all the same height and all wearing hats on their heads.

He could not help thinking often of the children, poor things,

Romazio di

Carlo Grandi Incisano Poneva.
O Signoroni delli Incisa Abiate
Giudizio. Maio Caro Carlino I
Incisano A testa Fine Cache
Giudizio. Midisse il Margione
delle Murate Bravo Sei Giovane
Carlo Incisano Incisani Abiate
Giudizio Pei Bambini di Anni
10. 11. 12. 13. 14. O Padri o Madri di
Famiglia Siete Anime Cattive
Piccini e Grandi Incisano —
O Popolo Incisano Forni figliuoli
Mandatelli Ascuola Comunale
O Genitori di Famiglia. Siete
testa dura i Forni Bambini
Anno Piu Giudizio divoiari
O Padri e Madri Siete teste dure
Andera Male Pergio o Padri
e Madri di Famiglia pei vora
i Bambini nonanno Giudizio.
e Perche Sono Cattivi dimorto
Adi llo A Signore Giudice di
Firenze. Lia Incisani e
Sono Mezzi Ladri Incisani
Mianno Rubato acheame
lig A Incisani i Ferri di
Bottega Mia. Ladri Incisa
ni. Fini. Incisani nonevora
Ladri Incisani si si Siemo
Ladri Fini Poveri Bambi
nii di Dio. Boni di Anni 8. 9.

Signore Giudice di Firenze
J Giovane Carlo Grandi J
ncisano Mizara Piacie di
Ristradami Perche Io Otexta
Fine e Giudizio. Adillo Ki
Signore Giudice di Firenze.
E morino Kon testa Fine E
Giudizio Kadillo. K Signore
Giudice di Firenze. E Morte
chima Bubato Klla Mia
Bottega di Garratone Monte
Ladri Incisani Monte Ladri.
Evienuto Giorno Incisani
Ladri Fini. di Gallera Incisani
Morixte Ladri. Morirte Ladri
di Gallera Morixte i Gallera.
Carlo Grandi Incisantea
Le Kllegro Come Casa Sua K
llegro. Come un Signore E
Kiva i Re Ei suoi Soldati E
Viva La Giutizia. Chenoi
Sisserve Gollentieri il Re
vittorio E Manuelle Rediglia.
Soldati Kellegri di Re.
Enoiatri Soldati Siemo. Figliuo
li di Re dei Re Miei Soldati
Eviva il Giudice di terra
Eviva. Eviva. Lapania E
Notro Re dei Re Eviva

TESTA FINE. E GIUDIZIO

Di Carlo Grandi Incisano
Cittadini di Firenze. Sgiovava –
Carlo Grandi. Incisano Enominato
Pertuntta Ligttalia. Boni Cittadini
di Firenze Perche Carlo Grandi
Incisano quando Ero Io
Carrozza quando Micondussero Anpien
di a rinvanre A Firenze. I
Carrabinieri. Ligttissero Ai ventu-
rino Atronttta Pervia dei
Fioretini. Perche Carlo A Paura
Perche A testa Fine. Carlo.
Carlo Grandi. Allegro Miticie
vano I Carrabinieri di Re
Allegro Giovane Siemo Alle
Murate. Allegro Carlo. adio
Midimetro I Carrabinieri di
Re. Adio Fnatelli di Re
Maio Ligdini Miavente Larva-
ta La Mig vita, Fnatelli di
Re I Dio Ligtia Benedizione
dalle Cielo. Adutti Poveri
Cricki Soldati di Re Suoi.
E viva La Bandiera

Giovanni Carlino Incisano
te di 29 Agosto 1875.
Il Popolo Incisano era
Subberbinto Pei 4 Cadave
ni Bambini. Primo Anni 4
Secondo. Anni 4. emessi 4.
Nel teorizo. Anni 9. quanto.
Anni 9. Giovane Carlo
Grandi di Anni 24. Il
Popolo Incisano Mivolleva
Fadre Pezzeti adi 29 Agosto
. 1875.

TRIBUNAJE. DI FIGLINE
dise: Popolo Incisano
PACE
i R................no
No Pace. ..... uNale
Sivolle Nelle Mani Carlino
Incisano o popolo Incisano
crepade. Adio Ladri
INCISANI

FECE Vedi 25 Settembre
1875.

even if he did become confused over how old they were and what their names were. They had given him a lot of trouble, but even so it hurt him to think of them. At least 'those children are in heaven now and they are better off than Carlino,' he reflected occasionally.[55] He declared that he was sorry. They all pestered him about that, the judges and doctors and journalists and he never knew quite what to say. Yes, but no, because . . . He became agitated when they persisted with their questions and the same thoughts went round his head as he kept having to justify himself and explain 'Callisto Grandi suffers many ills and bears them patiently.' How long would it last?

On 10 October 1895 prisoner number 683 was released from the island of Capraia. How had he spent all that time? 'Well,' he told one journalist, 'I would never have left but when the sentence is completed they put us out.' They had taken him to Florence where, if he had understood rightly, they were looking for a place for him. He wanted them to take him to the mayor of the city so that he could explain personally what he would prefer. Unknown to him, however, matters were already arranged.

Five days earlier the mayor of Incisa had officially requested that Grandi be admitted to the charity workhouse in Florence or else 'held somewhere in the country', so long as it was 'very far from Incisa'. The town council undertook to pay a lira a day for his keep and any hospital bills he might incur. Police Chief Ciotti agreed. He supported the request in a letter to the director of the workhouse, Carlo Peri, and had it delivered as soon as the former prisoner reached the city. The guards had to take him straight to the main police station, and it was on that walk that Carlino had the unfortunate meeting with his neighbour. The director of the Montedomini workhouse said that he would refuse to receive Grandi in his institution even for just an hour. He said that he posed a danger for himself and for the 'family of inmates', comprising 150 young men and women who had heard of Grandi's arrival; there was consequently unrest, which was threatening to turn into serious disruption.[56] In accordance with their agreement with the public security authorities, Montedomini held 'beggars taken in to work' and 'harmless lunatics', and it was already overcrowded. The common good there would not be best served by 'a man out of prison, and particularly one who is mentally disturbed'. One official of the workhouse announced in a letter from Pontassieve that if 'such a miserable gift' was offered then he himself would leave his job the moment Grandi entered the institution.

For some time there had been criticism of the repressive and inhuman management of the workhouse, and an article in the weekly *La Battaglia* pointed out that this refusal to accept a man who had served his sentence was 'neither just nor logical'. But Carlo Peri was adamant. He suggested that the Police Chief turn instead to the lunatic asylum. He also referred to the suggestion that Grandi be held on a farm in the country, though after all the publicity surrounding his release and the press comments about his mental state, the director of Montedomini thought it would be difficult to find anyone prepared to take charge of him. The best suggestion he could come up with was to telegraph Egisto Vannini, the butcher at Borgo Buggiano, to see if he could offer Grandi work – although his trade did not seem best suited to a mass murderer. Perhaps this was part of the reason why, on 11 October, the Police Chief abandoned all current proposals. Another, more convenient solution was being developed.

During all this frantic search for a home for him, the inconvenient former prisoner had remained locked up in a cell. On the same day a registered doctor visited him and reported that Grandi was in 'an abnormal psychiatric state liable to prove a danger to society at any moment'. That had become the new language of the experts and judges for describing types like him, whether or not they were in fact a danger to society. A few hours later, on 11 October 1895, 'he was provisionally incarcerated' in the asylum of San Salvi.[57]

Beyond the gates there was a tree-lined avenue running parallel to the railway. Within the grounds stood the two-storeyed, whitewashed buildings. On entering these there were the stairs and wide corridors with light rooms to right and left. Let them see for themselves – the rooms were brand new, some even unfinished. The equipment and services were all modern. There were even special cells for the truly raving. Professor Eugenio Tanzi showed the visitors round in person. He was 'the worthy psychiatrist and asylum director' who had just been appointed in Florence to be in charge of the seven or eight hundred patients, a forty-year-old from Trieste, a pupil of that luminary of psychiatry, Enrico Morselli. He told the forty students of penal law who were his honoured guests that day that he would explain 'the truth of the various most common types of madness which were likely to present themselves to psychiatrists and followers of the anthropological-legal sciences'. He had eight inmates shown into the room and outlined the pathological nature of each. There was one old lady with uncontrollable erotic urges; a frequently committed lunatic covered in tattoos; an idiot whose symptoms were due to arrested development and rickets; one solid citizen with a persecution mania; two more suffering from progressive paralysis; and one with a religious mania who smilingly talked to God. Finally, and in great detail, Tanzi introduced the case which most interested the visitors: Callisto Grandi, 'killer of four children for reasons of wounded pride'.

Twenty years earlier, though they were too young to remember, this man had been involved in a sensational trial, which unfortunately ended in a verdict of guilty. From 1876 he had been in prison, but for some months now he had been here at San Salvi, permanently committed for imbecility as ordered by the court in Florence on 5 November 1895. He was suffering from 'paranoic megalomania, moral insensitivity, hypocrisy and congenital alopecia', but despite his previous crimes he was behaving well in the asylum, the director assured them. His main occupation was writing his memoirs and doing rough drawings of himself, the carabinieri and the children he had killed. Were there any questions about the case? The students might care to ask Grandi himself. He was vain and claimed to be very intelligent. He believed himself to be 'famous, admired by everyone and worthy of being venerated as a saint'. He would certainly be willing to talk.

Naturally, they asked at once. Certainly, he answered, he knew he had done wrong. But they had persecuted him, they never left him alone, not in his workshop, not anywhere. And he started to tell the story of his life, especially the early part when he was living in the town and they made him suffer, suffer so much. At the end he wanted to give some advice to those fine young people who listened to him so attentively: 'to be *good*, *devout*, not to keep bad company and to ... be like him who slept peacefully at night because, *poor thing*, he had never harmed anyone'.

Grandi had never really understood the whole business of being arrested, locked up in prison, then released, then shut up again in an asylum. If he was mad they shouldn't have put him in prison in the first place nor kept him there so long. And if, as the judges said, he wasn't mad, then they should have freed him as soon as he had served his sentence. That is what he told the students. Wasn't it logical?[58]

By then he was forty-four years old. When he died at San Salvi on 1 March 1911 he was nearly fifty-nine. He had spent twenty years in prison, sixteen in the asylum. There he was considered to be a model patient who, reported Professor Tanzi, 'was hard-working, docile and harmless, because nobody ever failed to show him respect'.[59]

Notes

Notes to chapter 1

1   Two articles on Grandi appeared in *La Nazione* in 1895: 'Lo "Strangolatore dei bambini"', 4 October, p. 2; 'L'ex-galeotto Grandi. Lo "strangolatore de' bambini". Particolari importanti', 10 October, p. 2. In *Fieramosca* in 1895 there appeared 'Dopo vent'anni di galera. L'uccisore dei bambini in libertà', 4–5 October, p. 3; 'Ancora Callisto Grandi. L'uccisore dei bambini', 9–10 October, p. 2; 'Callisto Grandi in Firenze', 10–11, October, p. 2.
2   'L'ex-galeotto'.
3   ACI, *Register of Marriages*, 1891, n. 14.
4   ACI, *Register of Births*, 1892, 21 January, n. 11; 1893, 6 March, n. 47; 1894, 11 February, n. 21; 1895, 21 June, n. 76; *Register of Deaths*, 1881, 2 September, n. 56. See also the ten-year *Index* of registers (I, 1866–75).
5   F. Bernocchi, *Storia di Pizzighettone* (Pro Loco, Pizzighettone, 1973).
6   ACI, correspondence from the mayor to the Florence prefecture on 15 July 1871, 26 March 1873, 21 September 1873, 30 April 1875, 11 March 1876; and the answering correspondence of 4 August 1871, 6 May 1873, 13 June 1877. The historical archives of Incisa suffered great losses from both a fire during the Second World War and the flooding of 1966. The remaining material is in very bad condition and is presently in the process of reorganization. There is, nevertheless, much more material than is listed in G. Prunai (ed.), 'Gli archivi storici dei comuni della Toscana', *Quaderni della 'Rassegna degli archivi di Stato'*, XXII (1963), pp. 123–4. All the documents I have consulted come from the ten files for 1870–9, which have not yet been reorganized or catalogued and are piled together in no chronological or other order.
7   ASF, Police files, b. 1, 'Atti di Polizia, Notizie, Questione. A.P.I.S.', 7 April 1872 and 'Rapporto informativo sulla Propaganda Internazionale', 7 May 1872, sent by the Public Security delegate in Figline in response to a request of 27 April made by the Police Chief in Florence. See E. Conti, *Le origini del socialismo a Firenze (1860–1880)* (Rinascita, Rome, 1950), pp. 124–7.

8   From the 1841 census, including figures on households, families, individuals, areas and professions. ASF, 'Stato Civile Toscano', 12110, Register 974, Community of Figline, Parish of Incisa Sant'Alessandro. The number of people was recorded by the priest Ferdinando Mini, as required by the Secretary of State on 12 November 1840. Successive dates can be found in ACI, I, the registries of 1866 onwards. For the intermediary period, see APSA, *Register of Marriages*, 1838–71. For a comprehensive picture, see M. Tarassi, *Incisa in Val d'Arno. Storia di una società e di un territorio nella campagna fiorentina* (Salimbeni, Florence, 1986), particularly pp. 105–26; A. Bossini, *Storia di Figline nel Valdarno Superiore* (Mori, Florence, 1964); and I. Bignati, *Sviluppo industriale e lotte sociali nel Valdarno Superiore (1866–1922)* (Olschki, Florence, 1984). For all local references, see G. Mori (ed.), 'La Toscana', in *Storia d'Italia. Le Regioni dall'Unità a oggi* (Einaudi, Turin, 1986), especially pp. 125–31 on share-croppers and day labourers and pp. 195–246 on the end of the nineteenth century.

9   ACI, 1873, 'Querele e denunzie', cat. XIV, 'Crimini e delitti', 5 February, 27 February. On 29 August was recorded only a denunciation *ad personam*: Giovanni Falorni had verbally and physically threatened Alessandro Bertelli, who was passing by on his way to the fair at Sesto Fiorentino, in front of his pregnant wife, who was frightened; on 5 October action was brought against a man from Reggello. For assaults, see documents of 23 November and 24 December.

10 ACI, 1870–9, 'Tabella indicativa delle materie di cui si compone in Nuovo Archivio Comunale', n.d.. According to the director, Giuseppe Raspini, no trace of the Grandi case could be found in the AVF papers, despite the importance of the event and the fact that both parishes were involved in the evidence from witnesses and the accused.

11 ASF, 'Tribunali di Firenze, Processi. Assise 1875' (referred to henceforth without title), b. 818 f. 275, 'Rapporto dei Carabinieri Reali', Pontassieve section; also the reports from the commander of the Figline station and the Public Security official of Figline, 23 August 1875.

12 'Cronaca della città', *La Nazione*, 27 August 1875, p. 3.

13 Against the drowning theory, see the interrogation of the witnesses in ASF, b. 818 f. 275; and the report from the prosecutor in Florence, 29 August 1875; cf. the 'Cronaca', *La Nazione*, 27 August 1875, p. 3. All meteorological information has been taken from *La Nazione*.

14 ASF, b. 85 f. 335, 31 August 1875, the witness Giovacchino Francalanci.

15 ACI, IV, 'Carteggio Affari Generali, 28 Sicurezza Pubblica', 1875. For applications of the law cited see the Interior Ministry's circular of 31 January 1874, section 2A, subsection 1A, n. 11 900. See also G. Bruscoli, *Lo Spedale di Santa Maria degl'Innocenti di Firenze dalla sua fondazione ai giorni nostri* (Ariani, Florence, 1900), pp. 136–51; and the health report on the province of Florence assembled in 1890 and reproduced in P. Sorcinelli, *Miseria e malattie nel XIX secolo. I ceti popolari nell'Italia centrale fra tifo petecchiale e pellagra* (Angeli, Milan, 1979), pp. 165–6.

16 'Dopo vent'anni di galera'; the journalist brought the events of 1875 forward by two years. See also 'L'uccisore dei bambini dell'Incisa', *Opinione Nazionale*, 30 August 1875.

17 See P. Bandettini (ed.), *La popolazione della Toscana dal 1810 al 1859* (Department of Statistics, University of Florence, 1961); annual figures for Incisa are on p. 107. In 1875, there were 260 deaths out of 3551 inhabitants, a substantially higher number than in 1860. For the ages and sexes of the deceased (the numbers of which do not generally agree with Bandettini's), see ACI, *Register of Deaths* for 1866 and later.

18 ASF, b. 85 f. 335, 31 August 1875, the witness Amerigo Turchi.

19 ACS, 'Min. Grazia e Giustizia, Uff. Sup. Pers., Fasc. Magistrati' (henceforth referred to as 'Min. G. G.'), b. 20 f. 28447. Apart from his other duties Chelini was also assistant magistrate at Montevarchi in 1866, secretary to the public prosecutor at Arezzo in 1867, and magistrate at Cervia, Russi, Budrio and Porretta between 1869 and April 1873. After Figline he was at Castelfiorentino from 1878 and at San Miniato from 1881. In 1883 he was a court judge at Cagliari and in February 1887 he took the post at Livorno. He died the following November.

20 ASF, b. 85 f. 335, where the other 'Esami di testimone senza givramento' are to be found (henceforth referred to without title). See those cited on 29 August 1875, all conducted according to Articles 171 and 172 of the penal code. The code recommended that the testimony be transcribed as accurately as possible (Article 173), and criticism was often levelled at the examining magistrate's habit of translating into 'select language and elegant style those expressions which though spoken in the vernacular' maintained 'their original and inimitable significance'; see G. Borsani and L. Casorati, *Codice di procedura penale italiano commentato*, (Pirola, Milan, 1873–83), vol. II, p. 214.

21 ASF, b. 85 f. 335, 'Rapporto del Pretore', 29 August 1875.

22 ASF, ibid., 'Rapporto dei RR. Carabinieri', Figline, 30 August (signed by Tedeschi); see also the report of the carabinieri of the periphery of Florence, 30 August. On the transfer to Figline, see the reports in *La Nazione* of 30 August and 1 September 1875.

23 ASF, ibid., 'Verbale de visu et repertum', 30 August 1875, from which all previous information has been drawn.

24 ASF, b. 818 f. 275, 'Verbale di autopsia', 1 September 1875, p. 15, which includes the witnesses' identification. See also ACI, *Register of Deaths*, 1875, suppl. 8–11, in which the councillor added the certificates relating to the four victims, which had been sent in by the examining magistrate.

25 ASF, ibid., 'Requisitoria del Procuratore generale'; 'Estratto di Requisitoria', 9 October 1875; and the declaration of notice to Grandi, 22 October 1875.

26 F. Benevolo: 'La riforma al Codice di Procedura Penale (il pubblico ministero e il giudice istruttore)', *Rivista Penale* XVI: xxxi (1890), pp. 405–17, especially p. 412.

27 See F. Ogliari and F. Sapi (eds), *Segmenti di lavoro. Storia dei trasporti italiani, XI: Toscana, Umbria, Marche* (Milan, 1971), vol. 1, pp. 124–6, where the timetable of the Florence-Terentola line is reproduced. On the construction of the railways and in particular of the station now called Santa Maria Novella in Florence, see I. Briano, *Storia delle ferrovie in Italia* (Cavalotti, Milan, 1977), vol. 3, pp. 117–32; see also *Treni nel verde. Strade ferrate in Toscana dalle origini a oggi* (Alinari, Florence, 1987).

28 ASF, IV.30, 'Carceri 1876', various requests from the prefecture in Florence; see the letter of 18 February 1876.
29 A note signed by one 'Orlando' in the reports of 29 and 30 August 1875.
30 ACS, 'Min. G. G.', b. 83 f. 31586.
31 ASF, b. 818 f. 275, 'Interrogatorio dell'imputato', 30 August 1875, signed jointly by G. Melegari, A. Satti and Fiumi, the court clerk; see also 'Certificato di povertà' of C. Grandi, 10 February 1876, issued by G. B. Sbrocchi of the Incisan mayor's office. See also 'certificato di penalità', with no charge, issued by the Correctional Court in Florence on 2 September 1875. Useful information on criminal sources is furnished by A. Groppi and M. Pelaja, 'Delitti e loro narrazione', *Percorsi del femminismo e storie delle donne*, supplement to *Nuova DWF*, XXII (1982), pp. 108ff. A critical acknowledgement of the recent researches in criminal history was initiated by E. Grendi in *Quaderni Storici*, 1980, nos. 44, 46, 49, 66.
32 Fortunato Burchi refers to Luigi Bonechi (Affortunato was his third name and Burchi was his mother's surname). Grandi made many other errors of time, date, place and names, which he corrected in part during further interrogations. The first part of the questioning, dealing with generalities, has been omitted here. A space has been inserted where, in the original, 'Int' indicated the unrecorded questions.
33 Grandi's errors were considerable: Amerigo Turchi and Fortunato Paladini were nine years old, Angiolo Martelli was seven and the two other children were both under four years old, not seven or eight. Copies of their birth certificates are in ASF, b. 818 f. 275, and are recorded in ACI registers.
34 ACS, 'Min G. G.', b. 85 f. 31586; information on A. Satti from the president of the Parma court, n.d.
35 Cf. E. Morselli, ed., *L'uccisore dei bambini Carlino Grandi. Relazione del processo e degli studi medico-legali* (Calderini, Reggio Emilia, 1879), henceforth referred to as *L'uccisore*.
36 ACS, 'Min. G. G.', b. 83 f. 31566, letter to the minister of G. G.', 1 February 1877. His subsequent duties were as prosecutor at Spoleto in 1878 and as deputy prosecutor at Catanzaro in 1886, then as councillor at the Court of Appeal at Aquila. He died in February 1892. The same documents contain all the information on the magistrate A. Satti.
37 On the attempted insurrection of 1874 and the trial see Conti, *Le origini*, pp. 172–86, who often draws information from the *Opinione Nazionale*; see the relevant article there of 13 and 15 August 1874.
38 'I processi politici e i doveri dei giudici istruttori', *Opinione Nazionale*, 29 October 1874, p. 1.
39 On Salvatore Battaglia, member of the management council of the Tuscan Workers' Federation and Republican Association, see Conti, *Le origini*, pp. 185–6.
40 'Dibattimenti nel processo per conspirazione ed internazionalismo innanzi alle Assise di Firenze', published by the lawyer Alessandro Bottero, Rome, 1875. See also the famous self-defence conducted by Francesco Natta, a mechanic who spoke of internationalist ideals and the miserable conditions of 'poor but honest labourers' in a speech which has often been reprinted in pamphlets. Among the very long accounts in *La Nazione*, see 'Processo di conspirazione detto dell' 'Internazionale', 1 September 1875.

41 ASF, b. 85 f. 335, testimony of Amerigo Turchi, 31 August 1875. The testimonies of Rachele Turchi, Sebastiano Turchi and the others mentioned can all be found, unless otherwise indicated, in the file 'Volume delle deposizioni dei testimoni'.

42 ASF, b. 818 f. 275, 'Reperto medico', 29 August 1875, signed by Dr Luigi Migliarini; the magistrate Chelini asked the same doctor for confirmation. See also 'Giudizio definitivo di Perito medico-chirurgo', 30 August 1875.

43 ASF, ibid., report from the Public Security officer, 31 August 1875.

44 ASF, ibid., autopsy report of 1 September 1875, p. 15.

45 ASF, ibid., report from the Public Security officer, 1 September 1875, to which is attached the 'fragment of writing'.

46 ASF, ibid., a note at the bottom of the transcript of the interrogation of the accused, 31 August 1875.

47 'Cronaca della città', *La Nazione*, 31 August and 1 September 1875; there were also a few lines in the editions of 2 and 3 September. See also the reports of 4 and 7 September.

48 There are two articles on the Grandi case in *Gazzetta d'Italia* on 31 August and 1 September 1875, then more news on 5 September.

49 'L'uccisore dei bambini all'Incisa', *Opinione Nazionale*, 30 August 1875, and 31 August with corrections. The discoverer of the murderer was not Bernardo Della Lunga (as he had boasted earlier to the journalists, including the one from the *Gazzetta d'Italia*), but Argenta Monsecchi.

50 *La Nazione* discussed the matter on 7 September 1875.

51 ASF, b. 818 f. 275, 'Verbale di perizia', 31 August 1875; 'Pianta geometrica', 1 September 1875, signed by L. D. Sarri; 'Verbale di autopsia', 1 September 1875, signed by the doctors Giaconi and Migliarini and by Satti and Melegari, p. 15; and the document sworn by Anacleto Bonechi and Assunta Burchi, 1 September 1875.

52 Diomira Francalanci had been called to give evidence by Chelini (ASF, ibid., 31 August 1875) but she did not appear.

53 This was reported by the witness in 'Perizia Calligrafica', ASF, ibid., 3 September 1875, where there is also O. Focardi's 'Esame di testimone con giuramento', 1 September 1875. The interrogation of V. Ceccherini is in ibid., 'Volume delle deposizioni'.

54 Borsani and Casorati, 'Codice di procedura penale', vol. II, p. 368. The whole of chapter IV concerns expert evidence.

55 ASF, b. 818 f. 275, 'Interrogatorio dell'imputato', 4 September 1875.

56 Borsani and Casorati, 'Codice di procedura penale', pp. 313, 494 and 173–4. A similar problem of divided loyalty applied not only to the examining magistrate but also to the prosecutor, who was equally an official of both the Police Department and the magistrature. For a lucid critique, see Benevolo, 'Le riforme', p. 417, which also includes the reforms proposed by Lucchini and others. The clear distinction between the role of impartial examining magistrate and prosecutor was particularly lacking in the system which operated in the Papal States and Lombardy-Veneto, but the confusion remained in the mixed system which derived from the Piedmontese code of 1859. Cf. G. Delitala, 'Codice di procedura penale', *Enciclopedia del dritto* (Giuffrè, Milan, 1960), vol. VII, pp. 284–7.

57 Borsani and Casorati, 'Codice di procedura penale', vol. II, pp. 502–5, and vol. III, pp. 109–10.

58   Both in the prosecutor's report and the deposition, ASF, b. 818 f. 275.
59   See F. Carrara, *Programma del corso di diritto criminale dettato nella R. Università di Pisa. Parte speciale, ossia Esposizione dei delitti in genere con aggiunta di note per uso della pratica forense*, 9th edn (Cammelli, Florence, 1912), pp. 133–9 and 225–7; see ibid., 1st edn (1863), pp. 309 on brutal murder.
60   ASF, b. 818 f. 275, 'Ordinanza di rinvio alla Corte d'Appello', 7 September 1875, p. 6.
61   Testimony of Tito Brachetti, 1 September 1875, in the presence of Satti and Melegari. When they told Grandi they did not believe his story of a man in the woods, he answered, 'I'm not telling fairy stories. You'll see if they are fairy stories. If that bad man doesn't take them tomorrow (Sunday, 29 August), some other boy will disappear.' So said the witness Ceccherini. See also the depositions of F. Luti and A. Benucci.
62   ASF, b. 818 f. 275, 'Nomina di difensore', 7 February 1876.

Notes to chapter 2

1   See Yorick, 'Cronaca giudiziaria... Causa contro Callisto Grandi,' per omicidio premeditato e continuato, e per tentativo di omicidio, *La Nazione*, 19 December 1876; see also the report of the trial in an unsigned article of the day before.
2   ASF, 'Ass. Firenze Sent. 1876, Verbali 16', the entire 'Verbale di dibattimento in causa Grandi', hearings from 18 to 29 December 1876, excluding the 24th and 25th. On the magistrates, see the documents in ACS, b. 23 f. 28 809, G. Mori Ubaldini; 'Min. Grazia e Giustizia, Uff. Sup. Pers., Fasc. Magistrati' (henceforth referred to as 'Min. G. G.'), b. II f. 27 455, F. Petrucci; b. 382 f. 42 180, A. Bonini.
3   *Regolamenti per il collegio degli avvocati toscani e Regolamento per i procuratori dei Tribunali del Granducato* (Granducale, Florence, n.d.).
4   Yorick, 'Cronaca', December 1876.
5   *L'uccisore dei bambini Carlino Grandi. Relazione del processo e degli studi medico-legali* (Calderini, Reggio Emilia, 1879), henceforth referred to as *L'uccisore*, p. 66.
6   See the lengthy commentaries on the relative articles of the penal code (especially articles 304, 305, 317) in G. Borsani and L. Casorati, *Codice di procedura penale italiano commentato* (Pirola, Milan, 1873–83), vol. IV (1879), pp. 95–164; cf. also for the principle of orality and for article 49 of the law of 8 June 1874.
7   It was the prosecution's duty to establish the circumstances and the accused's state of mind, which made him fit for trial. On this point see articles 440–1 of the Penal Procedure Code, with comments, in Borsani and Casorati, *Codice di procedura penale*, and articles 235–6, when the question arose during initial investigation and the intervention of expert witnesses was requested.
8   ASF, 'Tribunali di Firenze, Processi. Assise 1875' (referred to henceforth without title), b. 818 f. 275, the note at the foot of the page of 'Interrogatorio all'imputato', 7 February 1876, signed by G. Mori Ubaldini, T. Grossi and Carlisto Grandi (*sic*).

9   ACS, 'Min. G. G.', b. 176 f. 35 738, Sante Dini, from an anonymous letter.
    As a result of this complaint and others in 1880–1 about a scandal in
    which he had been involved, Dini was transferred in March 1881. There
    are no precise details available on the lawyers, as I was not permitted to
    consult the archives at the Ordine di Firenze. For their personal details and
    qualifications, see *Indicatore generale della città di Firenze* (Galleotti e
    Cocci, Firenze, 1876).
10 ASF, b. 818 f. 275, the request for expert evidence of 1 March 1876. See
    also that of Dini of 7 March, with a reply from Mori Ubaldini.
11 ASF, ibid., 'Istanza di rinvio', 10 September 1876, with a note of Mori
    Ubaldini's reply.
12 See the report in *La Nazione*, 7 September 1875. When included in the
    text, details of the article are not repeated in the notes.
13 For the close relationship between the director Bianchi and Lambruschini
    and Ricasoli, see 'Bianchi Celestino', in *Dizionario Biografico degli Italiani*,
    (1st. Enc. Ital., Rome), vol. X (1968), pp. 73–5. See also C. Pazzagli,
    'Prime note per una biografia del barone Ricasoli', in *Studi di storia
    medievale e moderna per E. Sestan* (Olschki, Florence, 1980), vol. II, pp.
    903–56. On the contradictory ethos of the books published for children
    and the populace which had a high profile at that time in Florence, see the
    first chapter of A. Faeti, *Guardare le figure. Gli illustratori italiani dei libri
    per l'infanzia* (Einaudi, Turin, 1972), pp. 11–62. For an overview of the
    whole field, see G. Gentile, *G. Capponi e la cultura toscana del secolo XIX*
    (Vallecchi, Florence, 1922), with a chapter on Lambruschini. See also F.
    Baldasseroni, *Il rinnovamento civile in Toscana* (Olschki, Florence, 1931);
    A. Gambaro, *La critica pedagogica di G. Capponi* (Laterza, Bari, 1956);
    and on the vast output of G. Spadolini (ed.), see *Ricasoli e il suo tempo*
    (Olschki, Florence, 1981).
14 C. Collodi, *Gianettino. Libro per i ragazzi della quarta classe elementare*,
    ed. R. Mariani (Bemporad, Florence, 1900), pp. 74–7 (1st edition: Paggi,
    Florence, 1875). For his emphasis on the Florentines see C. Lorenzini, *I
    misteri di Firenze. Scene sociali* (Fioretti, Florence, 1857) and *Occhi e nasi
    (ricordi dal vero)* (Piaggi, Florence, 1881). See also F. Frabboni, 'Collodi,
    autore di libri scolastici?', in *Pinocchio oggi. Atti del convegno pedagogico*
    (National Collodi Foundation, Pescia, 1980), which includes a wide biblio-
    graphy. For a biography, see F. Tempesti, 'Chi era Collodi', in *Pinocchio*
    (Feltrinelli, Milan, 1972), pp. 7–49. On the parallel reputations of Lorenzini
    and di Ferrigni (Yorick), 'Princes of Tuscan humour', see especially the
    testimony of E. Cecchi in 'La Firenze d'allora', in Yorick, *Su e giú per
    Firenze* (Barbera, Florence, 1925), pp. 1–17.
15 See 'Morandi Luigi (1844–1922)', in A. De Gubernatis (ed.), *Dizionario
    Biografico degli scrittori contemporanei* (Le Monnier, Florence, 1879), vol.
    II, pp. 737–8.
16 'Comunicazione dal pubblico', letter from R. Chelini in *La Nazione*, 23
    September 1875.
17 'La proposta Morandi', letters from L. Morandi, B. Bianchi and A. S.,
    ibid., 27 and 29 September 1875.
18 Concerning which, see the convincing arguments produced by S. Timpanaro,
    'Anti-leopardiani e moderati nella sinistra italiana', *Belfagor*, XXX (1975),
    pp. 129–56, 395–428, and XXXI (1976), pp. 1–32, 159–200; see also

Belfagor (Ets, Pisa, 1982), especially pp. 49–96; cf. U. Carpi, *Letteratura e società nella Toscana del Risorgimento. Gli intellettuali dell' 'Antologia'* (De Donato, Bari, 1974). See also A. Salvestrini, *I moderati toscani e la classe dirigente italiana (1859–1876)* (Olschki, Florence, 1965).

19 In *L'uccisore*, p. 52, are reproduced the writings of Grandi from 29 August 1875, the day he was discovered. For the passages quoted and information following, see pp. 8, 22–4, 56 and 71.

20 Paolo Scoti, mentioned by Yorick in 'Cronaca', 24 December 1876.

21 F. D. Guerrazzi, *La battaglia di Benevento* (Volpi, Livorno, 1842), p. 6 (1st edition 1827–8); see also *Memorie di F. D. Guerrazzi* (Poligrafia italiana, Livorno, 1848) and *Note autobiografiche* (Le Monnier, Florence, 1899). Notice of the production of *Veronica Cybo* was in *La Nazione*, 2 September 1875.

22 F. Fedi's preface to F. D. Guerazzi, *Scritti scelti* (Giachetti, Prato, 1904), pp. vii–viii; see also C. Lombroso, *Nuovi studi sul genio* (Sandron, Milan-Palermo-Naples, 1902), pp. 157–201. The quotation is from F. D. Guerazzi, 'La vendetta paterna', in *Novelle* (Soc. Ed. Toscana, San Casciano, 1930), pp. 3–4; compare with the passage in Grandi's confession to the magistrate. Recent critical contributors are in the minutes of the symposium, *F. D. Guerazzi nella storia politica e culturale del Risorgimento* (Olschki, Florence, 1975).

23 *L'uccisore*, p. 71. There was great press coverage of the murderer studied by Lombroso. The most popular bookshop in Florence produced a booklet of the press articles in the form of pamphlets such as are sold at fairs. See *Vincenzo Verzeni detto lo strangolatore di donne condannato ai lavori forzati a vita dalla corte d'assise di Bergamo il di 9 Aprile 1873* (Salani, Florence, [May 1885]).

24 Actually, the edicts against reading the Bible were abolished in 1757; in 1765 Antonio Martini began to translate it into the vulgate order. Running to many editions, this was published by the diocesan press of Florence in 1787–92 and was approved by the Accademia della Crusca, which remained critical of the previous translation by Giovanni Diodati. See C. Guasti, 'Storia aneddota del volgarizzamento dei due Testamenti fatta dall'ab. A. Martini', *Rassegna nazionale*, VII:xxv (1885), pp. 235–82. (For his influence in Tuscany see *Raccolta di omelie, di lettere pastorali e di sacri discorsi dell'illustriss. e reverendiss. monsignore A. Martini arcivescovo di Firenze* (Moüche, Florence, 1788–1811), 4 vols. In the nineteenth century, up until the 1870s, other publishers of the Bible in Italian were, in Florence: Passigli, Ducci, Pagni and Borghi; at Prato: Vannucci and Giachetti; see also *Bibbia. Catalogo di edizioni a stampa 1501–1956* (Ist. Centr. per il Catal. Unico Bibl. Ital., Rome, 1983), which includes anthologies and indexes. Among these, see *Storia del Testamento Vecchio e Nuovo con spiegazioni estratte dai Santi Padri che molto edificano e servono a ben ordinare i costumi di ogni genere di persone* (Vannini, Prato, 1853).

25 See also L. A. Parravicini, *Giannetto* (Maisner, Milan, 1880), 60th edn, pp. 3–25 (1st edition 1837); and P. Thouar, *Il libro del fanciulletto ad uso delle scuole elementari* (Paggi, Florence, 1876), 11th edn, pp. 18–42; for 'true goodness', see pp. 75–7. Cf. M. Raicich, 'I libri per le scuole e gli editori fiorentini del secondo Ottocento', in *Editori a Firenze nel secondo Ottocento. Atti del convegno*, ed. I. Porciani (Olschki, Florence, 1983), pp. 297–340.

26　See also P. Thouar, 'Raccontini morali', in *Nuova raccolta di scritti per fanciulli* (Paggi, Florence, 1868), vol. III, pp. 10–19, commissioned for use in schools by P. Dazzi; also *Il fanciullo buono e il fanciullo cattivo* (Paggi, Florence, 1878), p. 50, the 2nd Florentine edition approved by the schools council. For biographical and critical notes on the author, see A. Gambaro in *Enciclopedia italiana* (Ist. Enc. Ital., Rome, 1949), vol. XXXIII, *ad vocem*; and Faeti, *Guardare le figure*, pp. 19–23.

27　*L'uccisore*, pp. 52 and 54. The arguments are in P. Thouar, *Letture graduali con nuovi raccontini per fanciulli* (Paggi, Florence, 1871), 12th edn, p. 30; and Parravicini, 'Gianetto', vol. I, pp. 176–8.

28　'*L'uccisore*', p. 51.

29　I. Nieri, *Vita infantile e puerile lucchese* (Forni, Bologna, 1976), from the Livorno edition of 1917, pp. 116 and 128–9 (1st edition, 1898).

30　See A. Niceforo, 'La struttura interna dell'Io nel pensiero della scuola italiana di criminologia', *Giustizia penale*, XLV (1939) para. I, lines 48–68. See also L. Ferriani, *Minorenni delinquenti (Saggio di psicologia criminale)* (Kantorowicz, 1895), p. 7, which includes the opinions of various authors; also P. Mantegazza, *Fisiologia dell'odio* (F.lli Treves, Milan, 1889), pp. 23–5 and chapters II, VI, VII, and id., *Fisiologia del dolore* (Paggi, Florence, 1880).

31　In the various newspapers quoted and in *Fanfulla* (I, 16 June 1870), founded by the Milanese G. Augusto Cesana, Giovanni Piacentini and the aristocrat Francesco de Renzis, who left the project in 1876; see B. Righini, *I periodici fiorentini* (Sansoni, Florence, 1955), 2 vols *ad vocem*. For notes on the editors and contributors, see A. De Gubernatis, *Dizionario Biografico*.

32　On the pattern of interest in phrenology in Italy, see C. Pogliano, 'Localizzazione della facoltà e quantificazione: frenologia e statistica medico-psichiatrica', in *Follia psichiatria e società*, ed. A. De Bernardi (F. Angeli, Milan, 1982), pp. 330–49. Tagliavini talks about the Phrenological Society but exaggerates the extent of its expansion: A. Tagliavini, in V.P. Babini, M. Cotti, F. Minuz and A. Tagliavini, *Tra sapere e potere. La psichiatria italiana nella seconda metà dell' Ottocento* (Il Mulino, Bologna, 1982), pp. 77–134. See also the reports of the Anthropological Society in its publication *Archivio per l'antropologia e l'etnologia*, in which see E. Pardini and V. Rossi, eds, 'Indice dei cento volumi 1871–1970', vol. 1975.

33　Morselli, in *L'uccisore*, pp. 45–7 and 74.

34　On Martinati and the question of Florence there are many references in E. Conti, *Le origini del socialismo a Firenze (1860–1880)* (Rinascita, Rome, 1950). On the same subject and on the society of free-thinkers to which Herzen and Schiff belonged, see G. Verucci, *L'Italia laica prima e dopo l'Unità* (Laterza, Rome-Bari, 1981), pp. 211 and 219. For the evolutionist ideas of Martinati and his group, see 'Che cosa è il socialismo', *Fascio Operaio*, 1 December 1872.

35　The letter was published on 24 September 1875. For the abolition, see C. Livi, 'La pena di morte al lume della fisiologia e patologia', *Riv. sper. fren.*, I (1875), pp. 209–35; id., *Contro la pena di morte, ragioni fisiologiche e patologiche* (Mucci, Siena, 1862). See also the treatment by Livi's pupil, Morselli, in 'Dell'influenza della pena sui detenuti dedotta dalle statistiche disciplinari carcerarie'; 'Contributi alla psicologia dell'uomo delinquente', para. I, *Riv. sper. fren.*, III (1877), pp. 316–31.

36　On Conti's forty years at the Institute, where he ended up being isolated from the prevailing positivist climate, see A. Olivieri, 'L'insegnamento della filosofia nell'Istituto di Studi Superiori di Firenze 1859–1924', *Annali dell'Istituto di Filosofia*, IV (1982), pp. 111–47; and G. Gentile, 'Il misticismo di A. Conti', in E. Garin (ed.), *Storia della filosofia italiana* (Sansoni, Florence, 1969), vol. II, pp. 203–6.

37 The information on Mantegazza's inactivity is given by E. Ehrenfreund, 'Bibliografia degli scritti di P. Mantegazza', *Arch. antr. etn.*, LVI (1926), p. 84. Schiff's problems began when a young English woman on holiday in Florence accused him in 1873 of torturing his laboratory animals. The story ricocheted from the English press to the Italian newspapers and grew considerably in the process. Schiff's colleagues, who, like himself, were members of the Animal Protection League, gave up their membership to show their support of both Schiff and scientific research. See P. Guarnieri, 'M. Schiff: Experimental Physiology and Noble Sentiment in Florence', in N. Rupke, *Vivisection in Historical Perspective* (Croom Helm, London, 1987), pp. 105–24.

38 On the damage, not solely economic, which followed the publication of the provisional capital's accounts, see A. Mari, *La questione di Firenze* (Paggi, Florence, 1878). Apologetic but well substantiated is the work by Jarro (pseudonym of G. Piccini), *Vita di Ubaldini Peruzzi* (Paggi, Florence, 1891). See also various notes and the bibliography in the recent volume of *Storia delle città italiane* by G. Spini and A. Casali, *Firenze* (Laterza, Rome-Bari, 1986). Cf. E. Garin, 'L'Istituto di Studi Superiori di Firenze (cento anni dopo)', in *La cultura italiana tra '800 e '900* (Laterza, Rome-Bari, 1976), pp. 29–69; and especially U. Peruzzi, *Relazione sull'ordinamento e ampliamento dell'Istituto* (Le Monnier, Florence, 1874).

39 P. Villari, 'La filosofia positiva e il metodo storico', in *Il Politecnico*, s. IV, 1 (1868), pp. 1–29 and in *Saggi di storia di critica di politica* (Cavour, Florence, 1868), p. 31.

40 The titles of Mantegazza's courses are in Olivieri, 'L'insegnamento', p. 125. G. Landucci treated the subject of Mantegazza and the cultural climate of Florence in *Darwinismo a Firenze. Tra scienza e ideologia (1860–1900)* (Olschki, Florence, 1977) and also in the chapter on Mantegazza in *L'Occhio e la mente. Scienza e filosofia nell'Italia del secondo Ottocento* (Olschki, Florence, 1987), pp. 137–206, with biographical notes and appendices, pp. 281–8.

41 This remark is recorded by A. Herzen himself in *Gli animali martiri e i loro protettori e la fisiologia* (Bettini, Florence, 1874), p. 24. His aforementioned lecture was reproduced in full in a book of the same title together with Lambruschini's letter (Bettini, Florence, 1869).

42 See A. Filippi, 'La storia della scuola medico-chirurgica fiorentina', *Riv. di storia delle scienze mediche e naturali*, XVII (1926), pp. 145–51, 234–59 and 1274–87; cf. A. Cazzaniga, *La grande crisi della medicina italiana nel primo Ottocento* (Hoepli, Milan, 1951), chapter VII. See also F. Mariotti (ed.), *Ricordi di M. Bufalini sulla vita e opere proprie* (Le Monnier, Florence, 1876), and in particular M. Bufalini, 'Sul metodo scientifico e specialmente sull'induzione', *Sperimentale*, XXVI (1874), pp. 45–62 (and XXVIII (1875), pp. 361–416 on his memorial service). On the Tuscan psychiatrists, see F. Stok, *L'officina dell'intelletto. Alle origini dell'istituzione psichiatrica in Toscana* (Il Pensiero Scientifico, Rome, 1983).

43 'Istruzioni', *Arch. antr. etn.*, III (1873), pp. 322–35, especially pp. 320–1; for the quotation criticizing the French, see Mantegazza's review of Paul Topinard, *L'Anthropologie* (Paris, 1876), in *Arch. antr. etn.*, VI (1876), p. 391.

44 On this central figure in Italian positivism see P. Guarnieri, *Individualità difformi. La psichiatria antropologica di Enrico Morselli* (F. Angeli, Milan, 1986), which includes a biography and bibliography of his writings. There is a chapter devoted to Canestrini in G. Pancaldi, *Darwin in Italia. Impresa scientifica e barriere culturali* (Il Mulino, Bologna, 1983), pp. 149–208.

45 Published by Chiusi, Milan, 1865–8. For a biography and list of works see E. Morselli and A. Tamburini, 'La mente di C. Livi', *Riv. sper. fren.*, V (1879), pp. i–xlvii and VI (1880), pp. i–xxxiii, respectively. See also S. Anceschi-Bolognesi, *Una luce fra le grande ombre. Carlo Livi per i nudi di mente* (Emiliano, Reggio Emilia, 1979). On San Lazzaro see the *Gazzetta del frenocomio di Reggio Emilia*, I (1875), founded by Livi himself; among the many recent publications see 'Per un museo storiografico della psichiatria', *Riv. sper. fren.*, CIII (1979), suppl. I and II. Livi resigned from the asylum at Siena when they denied him autonomy over religious administration; see the *Statuto organico e regolamento ... di San Niccolò in Siena* (Siena, 1874), including historical accounts.

46 On Livi's successor as governor at Reggio from 1877 to 1905, when he moved to Rome, see G. Guicciardi, 'A. Tamburini. La sua vita e il significativo di essa', *Riv. sper. fren.*, LV (1920), pp. v–xix.

47 For a new and well-substantiated interpretation see R. Villa, *Il deviante e i suoi segni. C. Lombroso e l'origine dell'antropologia criminale in Italia (F. Angeli, Milan, 1985)*; see also the indispensable monograph by L. Bulferetti, *Cesare Lombroso* (Utet, Turin, 1975); also chapter V of Pancaldi, *Darwin*. The field work in Tuscany is described by Lombroso's daughter, G. Lombroso Ferrero, *C. Lombroso. Storia della vita e delle opere* (Bocca, Turin, 1915), pp. 152–3.

48 Gina Lombroso (ibid., pp. 102–3) gives her own version of how Mantegazza attacked Lombroso for his measurements of the pain threshold in 'Sull' al-gometria. Nota critica', *Rendiconti Ist. lomb.*, XXV (1868), 16 April; for other criticisms see further. On the Milanese school of Verga and Biffi, see F. De Peri, 'Il medico e il folle: istituzione psichiatrica, sapere scientifico e pensiero medico fra Otto e Novecento', in *Storia d'Italia. Annali 7* (Einaudi, Turin, 1984), pp. 1080–92.

49 On disagreements with Livi, see E. Morselli, 'Come nacque la Rivista di Freniatria', *Riv. sper. fren.*, XLI (1915), pp. xxxvi–xlv.

50 On the importance of quantifying types within the positivist discipline with special reference to psychiatry and psychology, criminal anthropology and forensic science, see P. Guarnieri, 'Misurare le diversità', in the display catalogue at the Istituto e Museo di Storia della Scienza, *Misura d'uomo. Strumenti, teorie e pratiche dell'antropometria e della psicologia sperimentale tra '800 e '900* (Florence, 1986), pp. 120–71.

51 See E. Morselli, 'Sui crani antichi esumati nel modenese (Lettera al Prof. Mantegazza)', *Arch. antr. etn.*, II (1872), pp. 339–46, and id., 'La neogenesi. Lettera al Prof. Mantegazza', with reply, vol. III (1873), pp. 165–94 and 195–7. Then followed both their major propositions: E. Morselli, *Critica e riforma del metodo in antropoligia fondate sulle leggi statistiche e biologiche*

dei valori seriali e sull'esperimento (Botta, Rome, 1880); P. Mantegazza, 'La riforma craniologica. Studi critici', *Arch. antr. etn.*, X (1880), pp. 117–35. On the anatomist from Modena, see A. Carrucio, *Dei meriti speciali del cav. prof. P. Gaddi* (Vicenza, Modena, 1873).

52 The whole account is in *L'uccisore*, pp. 18–61; the passages quoted are on pp. 18, 42, 55 and 57.

53 See also ibid., the measurements on pp. 34 and 39; descriptions and photographs of the instruments are in *Misura d'uomo*, pp. 151–3.

54 *L'uccisore*, p. 60; for the previous quotation, p. 48.

55 His father, Giuseppe Grandi, a cartwright 'of wretched condition', himself son of the cartwright Tommaso and the spinner Violante Ceccherini, was born on 14 April 1820 and died on 12 May 1861. In February 1846 he married the widow Caterina, a seamstress, who was born on 21 July 1822 to the carter Niccolò Falugi and the spinner Stella Grifoni. The Grandis were left with five children (one girl died in 1855): Ernesta, born in 1847 and married to the cartwright Antonio Bellacci; Callisto, born in 1852; Guido or Mariano, born in 1853; Violante and Tommaso, born in 1856 and 1859. At the time of the trial Ernesta and Antonio already had five children: ten-year-old Maria Umiliana, eight-year-old Luisa, five-year-old Fiammetta, three-year-old Ersilia and one-year-old Giuseppe. Carlino's mother lived to the age of eighty-three and died in Incisa on 16 November 1905. See APSA, *Register of Births and Marriages*, for the dates relating to the Grandi in-laws. For details of deaths, see respectively ASF, 'Stato Civile Toscano', 1861, Incisa, f. 2197, a. 16; and ACI, *Registro atti di morte* 1905, a. 71. For details of the children and grandchildren see the relevant registers and ASF, 'Stato Civile Toscano', 1847, Figline, f. 991, a. 76; 1849, Figline, f. 1055, a. 151; 1851, Figline, f. 1119, a. 405; 1853, Incisa, f. 1178, a. 132.

56 See the entry on Bini in P. Grachi, *Dizionario del vernacolo fiorentino etimologico, storico, aneddotico, artistico* (Bencini, Florence-Rome, 1878), p. 22. For the biography, see B. Sadun, *F. Bini* (Pisa, 1899) and De Gubernatis (ed.), *Dizionario biografico, ad vocem*. (See also P. Grilli, *Del manicomio fiorentino diretto dal cav. prof. F. B. Tavole e annotazioni statistiche* (Murate, Florence, 1869), and Stok, *L'officina*, pp. 42–70.

57 See 'Cenni sulla vita del Prof. Giuseppe Lazzaretti', in *Annuario R. Univ. degli studi Padova* (Randi, Padua, 1883), pp. 73–4, and L. Pasqualigo, *Osservazioni e appunti critici sull'opera di medicina legale di G. L.* (Longo, Este, 1881).

58 See the translator's preface to *Delle malattie mentali considerate in relazione alla medicina all'igiene e alla medicina legale. Opera dell' Esquirol*, 1st Italian version translated by C. Morelli (Cecchi, Florence, 1846–8), vol. I, pp. ix–xlviii. See also C. Morelli, 'Della pazzia in rapporto ad alcuni elementi della civiltà', vol. II, pp. 247–57.

Notes to chapter 3

1 See *Adriano Salani, tipografo editore fiorentino* (biographical notes) (Salani, Florence, 1910); and E. Faccioli, 'Un editore popolare di orientamento

moderato: Adriano Salani', in *Editori a Firenze nel secondo Ottocento. Atti del convegno*, ed. I. Porciani (Olschki, Florence, 1983), pp. 367–80. Also in the same volume, G. Tortorelli, 'La letteratura popolare', pp. 493–501, and in particular E. Ghidetti, 'Un aspetto della letteratura popolare in Toscana: i misteri', pp. 341–66. For information on bandit stories, see S. Romagnoli 'Il brigante nel romanzo storico italiano', *Archivio storico per la Calabria e la Lucania*, XLII (1975), pp. 177–212.

2　See 'Documenti ricordi e aneddoti raccolti dai figli', in P. Ferrigni, *Uomini e fatti d'Italia* (Le Monnier, Florence, 1921), pp. v–lxiii. Yorick wrote *Tribunali umoristici* (Salani, Florence, 1902). Like him, other lawyers often edited the stories of *Processi celebri di tutti i popoli*, for example, or *Processi celebri contemporanei italiani e stranieri*, published respectively by Sonzogno of Milan and Ernesto Anfossi of Naples to satisfy the curiosity not only of the general public but, according to them, lawyers and psychologists.

3　See Yorick, 'Cronaca giudiziaria . . . causa contro Callisto Grandi, per omicidio premeditato e continuato, e per tentativo di omicidio', in *La Nazione*. The articles signed by Yorick are from 19 to 29 December 1876, and are referred to later in the text.

4　On Carolina Invernizio – 'name dear to civilized Florence . . . excellent but modest writer . . . good little housewife', see G. Davico Bonino and G. Ioli, (eds), *Carolina Invernizio* (Gruppo Ed. Forma, Turin, 1983), which includes the long list of her works. See also the recent collection of her stories, *Nero per Signora*, with an introduction by R. Reim (Editori Riuniti, Rome, 1986).

5　See ACS, the documents of S. Dini already cited, with letters to Ricasoli of 11 October 1871, and others of 9 September 1872. Various documents concern his unpopularity in Florence (already indicated); his alleged favouritism towards his son, also a lawyer in the same city courts; and finally the incident which resulted in his immediate transfer to Bologna in 1881, i.e. his insulting of the lawyer Riccardo Giovacchini during a summing up, and the resulting libel action and conviction that ruined Dini's reputation. He had entered the judiciary at Arezzo in 1843 and ended up as president at the Court of Appeal in Venice in 1887, years during which he suffered seriously 'from nerves'.

6　One of the few in that collection which are not in the Biblioteca Nazionale Centrale di Firenze, nor is it to be found in the archive of the Salani publishing house (partially saved from flooding in 1966 and later restored, thanks to some of the employees), which does not include the nineteenth-century pamphlets.

7　See the brief reports of 18, 19 and 30 December 1876 in *La Gazzetta d'Italia*, which was naturally more concerned with the Nicotera trial. See also the rather more detailed reports of the 'Cronaca cittadina' in *Opinione Nazionale*, 18–22, 24, 26 and 29–30 December 1876.

8　On this, see the entry on Ferrigni in A. De Gubernatis (ed.), *Dizionario Biografico degli scrittori contemporanei* (Le Monnier, Florence, 1879), vol. I, pp. 440–2.

9　Borsani and Casorati commented on the role of the presiding judge on several occasions; see G. Borsani and L. Casorati, *Codice di procedura penale italiano commentato* (Pirola, Milan, 1873–83), vol. IV and V in the section devoted to the judiciary in court, and L. Lucchini, 'Corte d'Assise', in *Digesto italiano*, VIII:iv (1899–1903), pp. 22–72. See also A. Marongi, 'Corte d'Assise (storia)', in *Enciclopedia di diritto* (Giuffrè, Milan, 1962), vol. X, pp. 774–83. Essential primary sources apart from the penal code are the judges' rules of 1865 and the law of 8 June 1874, on which more later.

10 See ACS, 'Min. Grazia e Giustizia, Uff. Sup. Pers., Fasc. Magistrati' (henceforth referred to as 'Min. G.G.'), b. 23 f. 28 809, which is rather scanty and does not even include the usually admirable judgements.

11 See Borsani and Casorati, *Codice di procedura penale*, vol. V, pp. 262–4, and the interrogation of the accused in ASF, 'Tribunali di Firenzi, Processi. Assise 1875' (referred to henceforth without title), b. 818 f. 275, of 7 February 1876.

12 On the three basic rules of penal judgement see Borsani and Casorati, *Codice di procedura penale*, vol. IV; on the lack of consensus see vol. V, pp. 10–11. Before 1865, all judges at the Court of Assize had to belong to the Court of Appeal, not only the president. On the two magistrates, see ACS, 'Min. G.G.', b. 382 f. 42 180 and b. 11 f. 27 455, respectively. Bonini, a landowner, practised advocacy from 1853 to 1855. He was a magistrate at various Tuscan posts including Galluzzo, Volterra, Manciano, Carmignano, Campi, Scansano and Grosseto and then later in the Marche. After leaving Florence he was a judge in Naples in 1883, then at San Miniato, Lucca and Florence again, where he ended his career as a councillor at the Court of Cassation in 1903. Petrucci was a barrister from 1847 to 1856 and a judge at Camerino, Ravenna, Forlí, Ancona etc. He died in Florence in 1882.

13 It should be remembered, however, that neither the prosecutor Melegari nor the magistrate Satti, who were involved in the initial investigation, were Tuscans. For information on the judges at the committal session, see ACS, 'Min. G.G.', b. 8 f. 27 330. A small landowner born at Bibbiena in 1807, Carlo Migliorini graduated from Pisa, worked on the criminal circuit of Florence, was a barrister in 1834, deputy prosecutor at Grosseto in 1838 and from there pursued a slow but secure career at Pistoia, Siena, Arezzo and Lucca until he became councillor at the Court of Appeal in Florence in 1860. Here the judgement of his superiors was that he had 'scant intelligence, a very superficial knowledge . . . adequate practice in criminal law, average application, excellent moral and political conduct'. He died in 1882. In the same year, the same superiors gave high praise to Leopoldo Puccioni, 'one of the best judges in Florence'; see ACS, 'Min. G.G.', b. 342 f. 41 299. Born in Siena in 1825, he practised as an independent lawyer in Florence from 1848. He was raised to the tribunal in Florence in 1862 and became president in 1869. In 1871 he was an Appeal Court judge, was transferred to Rome in 1879 and retired in 1900 at the age of seventy-five as a senator and honorary president at the Court of Cassation. There are no documents on Francesco Piccini, Raffaello Soldani or other members of the Court of Indictment.

14 Carrara also praised him in 'Giuseppe Puccioni e il giure penale', in *Opuscoli di diritto criminale* (Giachetti, Prato, 1878), 3rd edn, vol. I. For a full reconstruction, P. Grossi has filled the gap by drawing on frequently scanty sources in *Stile fiorentino. Gli studi giuridici nella Firenze italiana*

1859–1950 (Giuffrè, Milan, 1986), pp. 3–74, on the late Grand-Ducal period. On jurisprudence at Siena, which he taught from 1878 to 1881, see the previously cited Luigi Lucchini, *L'università. Le istituzioni culturali in Siena* (S. Bernardino, Siena, 1935), pp. 21–32. On the teachers of the Florentine school, see A. Mazzacane, 'Carmignani Giovanni e Carrara Francesco', in *Dizionario Biografico degli Italiani* (Ist. Enc. Ital., Rome), vol. XX (1977), pp. 414–21 and pp. 664–70; see also V. Papini, *La figura di F. Forti nel primo Risorgimento italiano* (Deputazione subalpine di storia patria, Turin, 1967).

15 See M. Tabarrini, *Degli studi e vicende della R. Accademia dei Georgofili nel primo secolo di sua esistenza. Sommario storico* (Cellini, Florence, 1856), including a list of members; see also *Catalogo delle memorie e communicazioni scientifiche contenute negli atti accademici a tutto il 1923* (R. Acc. dei Georgofili, Florence, 1934). On the lawyers who frequented the Vieusseux circle see 'Rapporto degli studi praticati all'Accademia dei Nomofili', in *La Temi. Giornale di legislazione e giurisprudenza*, III (1851).

16 The reference is obviously to the judges at the Court of Appeal and the Indictment Court in the case against Grandi. For the regulations prescribed for barristers and prosecutors, and the qualifications required for the judiciary, see the collection of 'Leggi e circolari del Granducato di Toscana dal 1836 al 1852', Bibl. Giurisp., Università di Firenze.

17 One of the main obstacles to a unified penal code was precisely the question of the death penalty. Should Tuscany reintroduce it or should the Kingdom of Italy abolish it? Carlo Cattaneo was one of the first to highlight the paradox in the *Politecnico* of 1860. The legal proposals put forward by Mancini in 1864, including abolition, were approved in Parliament but rejected by the Senate. In Vigliani's proposal ten years later, the death penalty was incorporated. See E. Brusa 'L'unificazione penale e la politica', *Rivista penale*, I (1874), pp. 24–37, and A. Buccellati, 'La pena di morte e il Senato italiano', *Rivista penale*, III (1876), pp. 5–31. For a complete picture, see E. Pessina 'Il diritto penale in Italia da C. Beccaria sino alla promulgazione del codice penale vigente (1764–1890)', in *Enc. diritto penale italiano* (Soc. Ed. Lib., Milan, 1966), vol. II, pp. 541–768; also briefly C. Vassalli 'Codice penale' in *Enc. diritto* (Giuffré, Milan, 1960), vol. VII, pp. 261–70. For an assessment of opinion at the time, see 'Il progetto del codice penale italiano e i lavori della commissione ministeriale', *Rivista penale*, III:iv (1876), p. 512. See also by B. Paoli, a member of the commission and of the Court of Cassation in Florence, *Esposizione storica e scientifica dei lavori di preparazione del codice penale italiano dal 1866 al 1884* (Niccolai, Florence, 1885).

18 See the penal code, Articles 281, 282, 284. Records of the ten hearings which took place between 18 and 29 December 1876 are in ASF, 'Assise Firenze, Sentenze 1876, Verbali 16'.

19 On the functions of the charge session, which was held in camera and based its decisions on the public prosecutor's report without hearing the accused or witnesses, see Borsani and Casorati, *Codice di procedura penale*, vol. III, pp. 324–477, and especially Article 441 of the penal code.

20 For the handwriting expert's evidence, see p. 44. Carlino's words are in *L'uccisore dei bambini Carlino Grandi. Relazione del processo e degli studi*

medico-legali (Calderini, Reggio Emilia, 1879), henceforth referred to as *L'uccisore*, pp. 68 and 71.

21 P. Ferrua emphasizes this in *Oralità del giudizio e letture di deposizioni testimoniali* (Giuffrè, Milan, 1981), pp. 67–144. Borsani and Casorati, *Codice di procedura penale*, vol. IV, pp. 95–164, stress the importance of orality. It is the spoken word which makes direct examination of proofs possible together with all those eloquent gestures and expressions. The judges base their judgement on what they themselves have seen and heard.

22 *L'uccisore*, pp. 68–70.

23 See Articles 235 and 236 of the penal code, and the commentary by Borsani and Casorati, *Codice di procedura penale*, vol. II, pp. 496–7. For information on the council chamber, vol. III, pp. 109–13 and 167, with discussion of mitigating circumstances. On the charge session see vol. II, p. 324. The question of the best time during a trial to present expert evidence has often been discussed. Today's current theories on the question are almost diametrically opposed to those prevalent in the late nineteenth century, but the frame of reference is also very different. For information about the current revision of concepts of non-imputability, state of mind and danger, see the recent publication from the Centro Studi e Iniziative per la Riforma dello Stato, *La perizia psichiatrica tra medicina e giustizia* (Rome, 31 January 1986), particularly G. L. Ponti, 'Imputabilità e malattia: orientamenti nel dibattito', and E. Marzano and R. Canosa, 'Proscioglimento per totale infermità senza ricovero in manicomio giudiziario'.

24 The Cassation of Turin, 5 June 1871, was very clear on this. See Borsani and Casorati's commentary in *Codice di procedura penale*, vol. IV, pp. 188–9.

25 ASF, b. 818 f. 275, 'Nota dei testimoni', signed by S. Dini. That of 8 September 1876 includes the motives.

26 See ACS, 'Min. G.G.', b. 315 f. 43 897, on Melegari. Born in 1841, he entered service in 1865, was first a judge at Castiglione delle Stiviere then Public Prosecutor at Brescia and in 1866 was at Rocca San Casciano, from which he wrote complaining about how far he was from his parents. From 1871 he was in Florence for eight years and eventually, after various transfers, ended up at Brescia. From there a series of anonymous letters were sent to the Minister protesting that Melegari was 'always at Medole and leaving other people here to do his work, him with twelve thousand lire . . . if he were a poor "Travet" he would already be dead and buried.'

27 ASF, b. 818 f. 275, 'Istanza per ammissione di testimoni', 3 March 1876. See also *L'uccisore*, pp. 75 and 78–9, and Yorick, 'Cronaca giudiziaria', 23 December 1876, in which he calls the town doctor Pietro Migliorini instead of Luigi Migliarini.

28 For information on Satti, see pp. 29–32 and ACS, 'Min. G.G.', b. 83 f. 31 586. Born in Garfagnana in 1825, he studied for five years at the legal college of Reggio Emilia then at the University of Modena. In 1851 he was clerk at the Criminal Court for the Duchy of Modena and in 1859 court clerk at Grosseto. He was in Florence for six years from 1872, from which he sent many polemics to Spoleto, Catanzaro and L'Aquila. He died in 1892 while councillor at the Court of Appeal.

29 See *Il Codice Penale Toscano Illustrato* (Cino, Pistoia, 1855–7), vol. I, Articles 34 and 36, with commentaries; see especially pp. 277–84 and

306–7. For a contrasting theory, see Paoli, *Esposizione storica*, pp. 93–103. For a reply, see C. Civoli, 'Della imputabilità e delle cause che la escludano o la diminuiscono', in *Enc. diritto penale italiano*, vol. V, pp. 1–191.

30 L. Lucchini, 'Studi intorno al Progetto 24 febbraio 1874 di un nuovo codice penale italiano', *Rivista penale*, I (1874), pp. 529–55, especially p. 535, including the criticism of Article 62's lack of scientific basis. This article introduced the phrases 'unsound state of mind' and irresistible 'external forces'. In 1876 Article 59 referred to 'states of folly' and 'awareness of committing an offence'. See 'Il progetto del codice penale per l'Italia', *Rivista penale*, III, part V (1876), pp. 369–71, in which is traced the 'Testo del progetto ministeriale allo studio della Camera', pp. 375–8. See also 'Sunto dei pareri della Magistratura delle Facoltà di Giurisprudenza . . . dei cultori di scienze mediche . . .', *Rivista penale*, IV:vi (1877), pp. 483–512, and articles by Bini and Morelli, Lombroso and Tamburini.

31 See the interventions of Pescatore and Maggiorini in 'Atti parlamentari italiani (sunto dei resoconti ufficiali). Senato . . .', *Rivista penale* II (1875), pp. 486–9.

32 See G. Lazzaretti, 'Studi intorno al progetto 24 febbraio 1874 di un nuovo codice penale italiano', *Rivista penale*, I (1874), pp. 405–10.

33 B. Paoli *Nozioni elementali di diritto penale* (R. Ist. sordo-muti, Genova, 1875), 2nd edn, p. 40, and the chapter beginning on p. 33.

34 On the methods of interrogating witnesses, see Articles 302 and 305 of the penal code, with commentary by Borsani and Casorati, in *Codice di procedura penale*, vol. IV, pp. 413–16.

35 On the role of expert witnesses in the penal code, see ibid., vol. II, pp. 357ff and vol. IV, pp. 413–14. For the sentences of Cassation see E. Pacifici-Mazzoni and S. Coen (eds), *Repertorio generale di giurisprudenza civile, penale, commerciale . . . Supplemento degli anni 1876–80* (Un. Tip. Ed., Turin, 1884), part II, Turin, 21 February 1868; Catania, 8 September 1878 and Florence, 22 June 1878.

36 ASF, b. 818 f. 275, 'Istanza per l'ammissione di periti', 1 March 1876.

37 See F. Bini, *Sulla imputabilità nella pazzia e nella ubbriachezza, secondo gli articoli 61, 62, 64 del progetto di nuovo codice penale* (Le Monnier, Florence, 1876), pp. 12–15.

38 For the distinction between a juror ('giudice di fatto') and judge ('giudice togato'), see L. Lucchini, 'La separazione del fatto dal diritto nei giudizi della corte d'assise', *Pel cinquantesimo anno di insegnamento di E. Pessina* (Trani, Naples, 1899), vol. II, pp. 91–105.

39 See Article 399 of the Penal Procedure Code, amended by the laws of 30 June 1876, when it was no longer assumed that every witness was a believer; the oath was based on moral and legal values and the religious oath was only taken by believers.

40 See Articles 285–7 of the Penal Procedure Code in Borsani and Casorati, *Codice di procedura penale*, vol. II, pp. 310–13.

41 For this and subsequent evidence, see *L'uccisore*, pp. 78–91, the reports quoted by Yorick; and ASF, b. 818 f. 275, 'Istanza per ammissione di testimoni', 3 and 4 March, signed by C. Galardi and E. Papasogli.

42 See the notices in *L'uccisore*, p. 151, and G. B.'s obituary of Chiarino

Chiarini in *Riv. discipline carcerarie in relazione con l'antropologia*, VII (1877), p. 64.

43 See the records of the court hearing held on 22 December 1876, the reports by Yorick of 24, 26 and 27 December. On the teacher, see APCLF, 'Atti diversi', 1873, f. 133 n. 73, 'Carte riguardante la nomina di P. Scoti...', especially the letter from Inspector Pietro Dazzi to Carlo Peri of 17 September 1873. For further information, see ibid., 1876, f. 138 n. 10. I would like to thank Dino Donati for pointing out these documents to me. He is presently engaged in research in the archives of Montedomini.

44 ACI, letters from P. Scoti to the mayor of Incisa, 16 May 1871 and 16 November 1871.

45 *L'uccisore*, p. 95; the same was quoted by Yorick in his chronicle of 24 December. On 30 December, while *La Nazione* reprinted the prisoner's writings, *Opinione Nazionale* gave a so-called 'translation... dictated by Carlo Grandi in person'.

46 For accounts of all the expert evidence, see *L'uccisore*, pp. 90–136 (Morselli), 137–43 (Livi), 144–69 (Bini) and 170–3 (summaries of Morelli and Lazzaretti).

47 See ibid., p. 132.

48 See also the full accounts chosen by Bini, ibid., p. 166, which referred above all to Lazzaretti, 'Studi intorno al progetto'.

49 Article 94 of the Penal Procedure Code: 'There is no crime if the accused was in a state of absolute imbecility, madness or pathological rage when the act was committed nor if it involved irresistible force.' For the arguments surrounding this, even in future proposals, see Paoli, *Esposizione storica*, pp. 100–3. See also the section on irresistible force and passion in *Repertorio generale di giurisprudenza civile, penale, commerciale... Supplementi*, 7 April 1869, pp. 1325–6; 22 June 1877 and 21 May 1879, p. 1305.

50 See Lazzaretti, 'Studi intorno al progetto', especially pp. 407–8, and 'Le affezioni mentali', pp. 11 (n.) and 13–22.

51 In the file of official reports, see 'Ordinanza di rigetto d'istanza defensionale', 27 December 1876.

52 Until the law of 8 June 1874, n. 1937. In Article 494 of the penal code of 1865, the summary came first and the presiding judge's power was consequently limited. See L. Casorati, *La nuova legge sul giurí* (Giachetti, Prato, 1874), p. 379. For criticism see L. Franceschini, *Osservazioni e proposte su alcune questioni di procedura penale* (Foligno, 1907), pp. 68 and 135ff. More recently, see Ferrua, 'Oralità del giudizio', especially pp. 104–9. For Vigliani's opinion and the opposite views of Mancini, Michelini, Della Rocca and Puccioni, see *Atti Parlamentari. Camera. Discussioni* of 20 March 1874, p. 2539. See also F. Carrara, 'Questioni ad occasione della giuri', in *Opuscoli*, vol. V, pp. 345–430, especially pp. 366–80. See also *I giurati e la libertà. Prolusione al corso accademico di diritto penale dell'a.a. 1874–75* (Lucca, 1874); A. Stoppato, 'Il presidente della corte d'assise', *Rivista penale*, XXIII (1886), p. 141; F. Benevolo, 'Le riforme al codice di procedura penale. Il dibattimento', *Rivista penale*, XXXVII (1893), p. 414.

53 Text of and commentary on the laws of 8 June 1874 on the appointment of jurors and the procedure in judgements before the Court of Assize are in *Rivista penale*, I (1874), pp. 158–68, 333–9 and 449–68 (especially Article 494 on questions regarding imputability). See also 'Relazione minis-

teriale alla legge dell'8 giugno 1874', *Atti Parlamentari. Camera. Documenti*, session 1873–4, n. 50. The jurors were drawn from a list of eligible citizens compiled by the mayor of each commune then sent to the district prosecutor, who composed another list to forward to the president of the court. There the lists were revised, then sent to the president of the nearest central court who, with two other judges, established the final list. See M. Giammarco, *La giuria popolare nella cultura giuridica italiana tra Otto e Novecento*, chapter 2 in the collection of graduate theses in the Faculty of Law, University of Florence, 1983–4; this unpublished thesis was discussed with P. Costa.

54 See in ASF, b. 818 f. 275, the 'Nota dei giurati ordinari e supplenti estratti all'udienza civile del dí 25 November 1876', for the fourth fortnight of the fourth session of the Florence circuit of 11 December 1876, including details of their qualifications and addresses. These fourteen jurors were drawn for the Grandi case: Emilio Bettarini, subscriber, Sesto, Petriolo; Domenico Beisso, teacher, Florence; Giuseppe Sabatini, college professor, Castello San Niccolò, Pistoia; Enrico De Mari, secretary at the finance ministry, Florence; Raffaello Nebbiai, subscriber, Florence; Guido Dainelli, engineer, Florence; Pietro Del Gamba, accountant at the civil and military ministry, Florence; Emilio Calvi, employee at the Biblioteca Nazionale, Florence; Ulisse Casalini, employee at the audit office, Florence; Leopoldo Rugiadi, town councillor, Cerreto Guidi, San Miniato; Ciro Folli, secretary at the finance ministry, Florence; Aurelio Lomi, landowner and ceramic manufacturer, San Bartolomeo, Pistoia; Giuseppe Renzi, town councillor, Reggello, Figline; Attilio Pratesi, accounts clerk at the Roman railways, Florence. The lists relating to the previous court sessions when the trial was originally due to take place are also available.

55 See *Atti Parlamentari. Camera. Discussioni* of 13 March 1874, pp. 2265ff, especially pp. 2271 and 2279. For criticism of the limited value of such jurors in terms of true popular representation, see proponents of the so-called juridic socialism, for example A. Pozzolini, 'L'idea sociale nella procedura penale', in *Archivio giuridico* (Modena, 1878). Conversely, the vigorous opposition of the positivist school is exemplified by C. Lombroso, U. Ellero and E. Ferri, who preferred the scientific skill of the few to the ignorance of juries and wanted to abolish 'groups of grocers, barbers and labourers', as R. Garofalo protested in *Criminologia: studio sul delitto e sulla teoria della repressione* (Bocca, Turin, 1891), p. 425.

56 From a rich survey of trials involving psychiatric evidence in Great Britain, R. Smith provides the framework in *Trial by Medicine. Insanity and Responsibility in Victorian Trials* (Edinburgh, 1981).

57 The law of 18 February 1874 provided for the care of poor lunatics and replaced the law of 20 August 1865. On the specific criteria and disputes see F. Bini, 'Se debbeno essere compresi fra i mentecatti gl'imbecilli e gl'idioti', in *Riv. beneficienza pubblica e istituti di previdenza* (Milan, 1876).

58 ASF, 'Sentenze 1876, Verbali 16, Fascicolo delle questioni proposte ai giurati nella causa Grandi Callisto', with related replies. Cf. sentences of the Court of Cassation, Florence, 9 July 1881: G. Mori Ubaldini, *Annuali della giurisprudenza italiana*, XV, part I, section 2.

59 See G. Manfredini, 'La questione escludente l'imputabilità proposta ai

giurati toscani'. Cf. also Carrara's comments with the same title in *Rivista penale*, II:iii (1875), pp. 535–44, and IV (1876), pp. 51–3.

60 See *Il Codice Penale Toscano Illustrato*, vol. IV, section I, chapter I on murder; F. Carrara, *Programma del corso di diritto criminale dettato nella R. Università di Pisa. Parte speciale, ossia Esposizione dei delitti in genere con aggiunta di note per uso della pratica forense*, 9th edn (Cammelli, Florence, 1912). vol. I, chapter II; id., 'Pensieri sul progetto del Codice penale italiano del 1874. III. Articolo 365. Premeditazione', *Giornale delle Leggi*, V (1874), pp. 146–7; and B. Paoli, 'Studi intorno al progetto di un nuovo codice penale italiano' *Rivista penale*, I (1874), pp. 11–23, and ibid., *Esposizione storica*, pp. 9–43.

61 See Cassation of Florence, 24 February 1869, 15 February 1872 and 3 May 1876, in *Annali della giurisprudenza italiana*, respectively III (1869), p. 1, section 2, pp. 64–5; VIII (1873), pp. 17–18 (where there is also the decision of the Cassations of Turin, Palermo and Naples, which came out against it on 22 June 1870); and X (1876), pp. 1 and 229–31.

62 On the jurors being forbidden to consider any penal consequences, see Article 498 of the law of 8 June 1874. See also 'Sui manicomi criminali. Interpellanza Righi' of the parliamentary reports of 14 April 1877, in *Rivista di discipline carcerarie*, VII (1877), pp. 336–47, and the minister P. S. Mancini's reply, pp. 347–59. For the psychiatrists' point of view (Lombroso, Biffi, Bonacossa, etc.), see A. Tamburini (Livi's pupil who posed the question again at the meeting of the Italian phreniatric society in September 1877), 'Dei manicomi criminali e di una lacuna nella odierna legislazione', *Rivista di discipline carcerarie*, VI:viii (1878), pp. 440–56, and also 'Sulla necessità di garantire la società dagli alienati pericolosi dichiarati non imputabili', *Rivista penale*, IV:viii (1878), p. 260ff. In 1876 Virgilio Gaspare, a follower of Lombroso, opened the first criminal lunatic asylum at Aversa. For an account of this see A. Manacorda, *Il manicomio giudiziario. Cultura psichiatrica e scienza giuridica nella storia di un'istituzione totale* (De Donato, Bari, 1982); see p. 21 on the fate (including their release) of those found unfit to plead for mental reasons before 1891.

63 ASF, 'Corte di Assise, Firenze, Sentenze 1876, n. 17'. The minister received a request to confer a decoration on Dini, 'who deserves public recognition for the energy and ability with which he performs the duty of public prosecutor' (in ACS, 'Min. G.G.', personal documents, letter of 24 December 1876). For the text of and commentary on the articles, see *Il Codice Penale Toscano Illustrato*, Article 64: 'When the protagonist is in a mental state close to that defined in Article 34 as entirely excluding fitness to plead, the courts are authorized to administer *a*) a less severe form of sentence if the sentence is statutory and *b*) a reduced sentence or a less severe one if the crime carries a dicretionary sentence.' On the judges' power to alter or reduce sentence, see the Cassation of Florence, 22 January 1876, referred to by Bianchini in *Annali della giurisprudenza italiana* (Niccolai, Firenze, 1876), Cassation penal material, pp. 105 and 135.

64 *L'uccisore*, p. 180.

Notes of chapter 4

1 *L'uccisore dei bambini Carlino Grandi. Relazione del process e degli studi medico-legali* (Calderini, Reggio Emilia, 1879), henceforth referred to as *L'uccisore*, p. 3.

2 'L'uccisore dei bambini Carlino Grandi', *Riv. sper. fren.*, III (1877), pp. 144–57, 352–69, 590–643, and IV (1878), pp. 515–75, 730–40.

3 See A. Tamburini's obituary in *Arch. ital. per le malattie nervose*, XIV (1877), pp. 276–84.

4 See C. Lombroso, *L'uomo delinquente in rapporto all'antropologia, alla giurisprudenza ed alla psichiatria*, 5th edn (Bocca, Turin, 1897), vol. II, pp. 9, 13, 19, 31, 37. Cf. R. von Krafft-Ebing, *Trattato di psicopatologia forense in rapporto alle disposizioni legislative vigenti in Austria, in Germania ed in Francia* trans. Lorenzo Borri, assistant at the Faculty of Legal Medicine, Istituto di Studi Superiori, Florence (Bocca, Turin, 1877), pp. 97–9. Also V. Mellusi, *L'amore che uccide. Studio di psicopatologia criminale* (Turin, 1911) p. xxi; E. Tanzi, *Psichiatria forense* (Vallardi, Milan, 1911), p. 346; E. Tanzi and E. Lugaro, *Trattato delle malattie mentali* (Soc. ed. libr., Milan, 1916), vol. II, pp. 796–9; S. De Sanctis and S. Ottolenghi, *Trattato pratico di psicopatologia forense, per uso dei medici, giuristi e studenti* (Soc. ed. libr., Milan, 1920), p. 886; G. Moglie, *La psicopatologia forense ad uso dei medici, dei giuristi e degli studenti* (Pozzi, Rome, 1938), p. 197; E. Altavilla, *Il delinquente. Trattato di psicologia criminale* (Morano, Naples, 1949), p. 231.

5 See the review initialled A. R. in *Arch. antr. etn.*, VI (1876), pp. 380–9, and that of doctor E. Fazio in *Arch. giur.*, XVI (1876), pp. 628–34. It should be remembered that certain parts of *L'uomo delinquente* were first published in the journal *Rivista di discipline carcerarie, in relazione con l'antropologia, col diritto penale e con la statistica*, edited by M. Beltrani Scalia (an Interior Ministry official who campaigned for penal asylums). See also the reviews by 'Un Medico' in *Riv. Disc. Carc.*, I (1876), pp. 472–7.

6 F. Puccinotti, *Lezioni di medicina legale*, 5th edn (Antonelli & C., Livorno, 1847), p. 8, and F. Bini, 'Gli alienati secondo i progressi della medicina e della legislazione', in *Nuova Antologia* (Florence, 1873).

7 C. Livi, 'I periti alienisti nel foro. Lettera al Prof. Comm. Francesco Carrara', *Riv. sper. fren.*, I (1875), pp. 256–9.

8 See *Di alcuni pregiudizi in medicina legale. Memoria del Prof. Filippo Pacini. Lettera del Dott. G. Lazzaretti* (Prosperini, Padua, 1877), extract in *Gazzetta medicina italiana. Province venete*.

9 See 'I periti alienisti nel foro. Risposta del Prof. Comm. F. Carrara alla lettera del Prof. C. Livi', dated 13 June 1875, in *Riv. sper. fren.*, I (1875), pp. 320–4. Another problem which was discussed concerned partial responsibility, the social and penal consequences of which Carrara defended (especially outside Tuscany where the death penalty existed), though Livi refuted it on scientific grounds.

10 See 'Nota della direzione', *Riv. penale*, III:vi (1877), p. 437, which comments on the article by F. Franzolini, 'La follia parziale alle corti d'assise', *Riv. penale*, III (1877), pp. 417–37, which is full of the usual criticisms of magistrates.

11 With the new code's requirement for two experts in the case of any disagreement, the judge could call on a third expert (Articles 208 and 211–15 of the Penal Procedure Code). See F. P. Gabrieli, 'Perizia (Diritto processuale penale)', in *Nuovo Digesto Italiano* (Turin, 1939), vol. IX, pp. 884–92. Even that was a restriction of critical rationality raised by the positivist school, of which M. Nobili discusses other aspects in 'La teoria delle prove penali e il principio della difesa speciale', in *Materiali per una storia della cultura giuridica*, ed. G. Tarello (Il Mulino, Bologna, 1974), vol. IV, pp. 417–55.

12 *L'uccisore*, p. 63.

13 See C. Morelli, 'Della pazzia in rapporto ad alcuni elementi della civiltà', in *Delle malattie mentali considerate in relazione alla medicina all'igiene e alla medicina legale. Opera dell'Esquirol*, 1st Italian version (Cecchi, Florence, 1846–8), vol. II, pp. 247–57, and G. Lazzaretti, *Le affezioni mentali, considerate nei loro rapporti colle questioni medico giudiziarie* (Barachi, Florence, 1861). For the various comparisons see, respectively, pp. 187–93, 182–4, 148 and 126ff.

14 The minister gave this reply to a particular parliamentary intervention on 7 May 1878, which denounced the nomination of experts without any criteria by the judges in charge court and at the trial. See 'Interrogazione dell'on. Umana sui periti medici nei giudizi penali', in *Riv. pen.*, VI:ix (1878), pp. 259–60.

15 F. Bini, 'Importanza dell'insegnamento clinico della psichiatria' *Arch. ital. malat. nerv.*, XIII (1876), pp. 36–61, especially pp. 57 and 38.

16 *L'uccisore*, pp. 170–1 and n, and 172.

17 See C. Lombroso, 'Esistenza di una fossa occipitale mediana nel cranio di un delinquente', *Rendiconti del R. Ist. Lomb. di scienze e lettere*, IV (1871), s. II, pp. 37–41, presented in the Società Frenetica's journal edited by Livi, Morselli and Tamburini; see also ibid., 'Della fossetta occipitale mediana in rapporto collo sviluppo del vermis cerebellare', *Riv. sper. fren.*, II (1876), pp. 121–30. For an account of the fetish discovery, see ibid., 'Come nacque e come crebbe l'antropologia criminale', in *Ricerche di psichiatria e nevrologia, antropologia e filosofia, dedicate al Prof. E. Morselli* (Vallardi, Milan, 1907), pp. 501–10. On this theory of Lombroso's in line with Darwinism, see G. Pancaldi, *Darwin in Italia. Impresa scientifica e barriere culturali* (Il Mulino, Bologna, 1983), pp. 268–76. On the opposite position, which was dominant in Florence, see 'L'elezione sessuale e la neogenesi. Lettera del Prof. P. Mantegazza a Carlo Darwin', *Arch. antrop. etn.*, I (1871), pp. 306–25. This is also commented on in 'La neogenesi. Lettera di E. Morselli al prof. P. M.', *Arch. antrop. etn.*, III (1873), pp. 195–7. For an interpretation of Morel in Italy, see S. Nicasi, 'Il germe della follia. Modelli di malattia mentale nella psichiatria italiana di fine Ottocento', and for a criticism of historiography rooted in organicism see P. Rossi (ed.), *L'età del positivismo* (Il Mulino, Bologna, 1986), pp. 309–32.

18 On the extent and survival of the Lombrosan ideology, see F. Giacanelli's introduction to G. Colombo, *La scienza infelice. Il museo di antropologia criminale di C. Lombroso* (Boringhieri, Turin, 1875), pp. 7–32.

19 See E. Morselli's overview of the past to inaugurate his journal, 'Ciò che vuole essere la psichiatria', *Quaderni di psichiatria*, I (1914), pp. 1–13.

For an articulation of the concept of organicism, see S. Moravia, 'Il problema mente-corpo nelle posizioni dell'illuminismo', and V. Babini, 'A proposito delle concezioni "organiciste" ', pp. 331–50, in the proceedings of the congress *Passioni della mente e della storia*, ed. F. M. Ferro (Vita e Pensiero, Milan, 1989).

20 See E. Morselli, 'Sull'anatomia patologica della pazzia', *Riv. sper. fren.*, III (1877), p. 746. Alternatively, see the discussion in *Arch. ital. malat. nerv.*, XIV (1877), pp. 418–23.

21 See C. Lombroso, *L'uomo delinquente*, 2nd edn (Bocca, Turin, 1878), chapter II and the preface; for the passage quoted, see pp. 21 and pp. 3–4, and in the fifth edition, the reply to criticism in the preface, I, pp. i – xxxi. 'Never... should a diagnosis be based upon' craniological data: many lunatics' craniums could equally well belong to sane people and vice versa. This was the conclusion of the committee (Verga, Amadei, Morselli, Tamburini, Tamassia) nominated by the third psychiatric congress to consider these problems. See G. Amadei, 'Delle migliori misure craniometriche da prendere sugli alienati', *Arch. ital. malat. nerv.*, XVIII (1881), pp. 268–79. See also P. Topinard, 'L'anthropologie criminelle', *Revue Anthr.* 3rd ser., vol. II (1887), pp. 658–91.

22 L. Lucchini, *I semplicisti (antropologi, psicologi e sociologi) del diritto penale. Saggio critico* (Turin, 1886), p. viii.

23 See A. Verga, 'I medici spuri e i medici legittimi delle alienazioni mentali, o il vulgo e la medicina mentale', *Arch. ital. malat. nerv.* III (1866), pp. 376–89, and ibid., the preface, I (1864), pp. 3–10.

24 C. Livi, 'I periti alienisti', p. 258. The criticism of C. Lombroso, *L'Uomo delinquente*, 2nd edn, pp. 586–90 was especially aimed against a debate of 1871 concerning expert evidence, when Livi declared that he should have saved himself the pointless effort of taking all the anthropometric measurements of the accused who, though insane, appeared perfectly normal. The best place for them was 'rather in a Public Security official's notebook than as medical expert evidence'.

25 He puts this forward as an explanation for the wavering between the physiological and moral models in nineteenth-century English psychiatry. See also A. T. Scull, 'From Madness to Mental Illness: Medical Men as Moral Entrepreneurs' and 'Mad-Doctors and Magistrates. English Psychiatry's Struggle for Professional Autonomy in the Nineteenth Century', *European Journal of Sociology*, respectively, XVI (1975), pp. 218–51, and XVII (1976), pp. 279–305.

26 P. Mantegazza, 'Di alcune recenti proposte di riforma della craniologia', *Arch. antr. etn.*, XXIII (1893), p. 51.

27 F. Bini, 'Definizione e classazione delle pazzie', samples from the Istituto di Studi Superiori, in *Arch. ital. malat. nerv.*, XVI (1879), pp. 210–41, especially pp. 225 and 226. See also ibid., 'Intorno alle cagioni della pazzia', pp. 310–41. From the ample documentary evidence on Livi and Bini's hostility to organicist reductionism, see Stok, *L'officina dell'intelletto. Alle origini dell'istituzione psichiatrica in Toscana* (Il Pensiero Scientifico, Rome, 1983), pp. 37–41.

28 *L'uccisore*, p. 100. All subsequent quotations come from this source, particularly pp. 99–136. There is no official record of the replies, and only that of Morselli is published in part, on pp. 174–6.

29 See E. Morselli, 'Sulla cosí detta pazzia morale', *Arch. ital. malat. nerv.*, XVII (1880), pp. 591–600, the debate at the third psychiatric congress. For the reservations concerning organicism, see what has been said here about the anthropological circle in Florence (particularly p. 85–8).

30 See Livi, *Forensic phrenology – Forms of insanity considered within the criminal context* (Chiusi, Milan, 1865–8), pp. 21–2. There is an important discussion of the four methods by which to establish whether a suicide or murder had been committed by unrecognized madmen or by sane people.

31 Lombroso, 'Come nacque', p. 501. The same allegiance to common sense was manifested by Maudsley, the British psychiatrist who was most well known in Italy at the time. He was famous as an organicist but with many contradictions: among other things he stated that it was unnecessary to seek proof of inherited criminal tendencies since they were already abundant proofs in the proverbs, in the Bible, in Horace and in Goethe. See H. Maudsley, 'Heredity in Death and Disease', *Fortnightly Review*, XXXIX (1886), pp. 648–59.

32 G. Antonini, *I principi fondamentali della Antropologia criminale* (Hoepli, Milan, 1906), p. 2 and chapter 2; this manual was approved by Lombroso. See also ibid., *I percursori di Lombroso* (Bocca, Turin, 1900). For the conflict with popular opinion, I have referred to Lombroso, *L'uomo delinquente*, 5th edn, pp. 308–12.

33 See *Indovinelli onesti e curiosi da passar via l'ozio e la malinconia, con discorso sulla Complessione, Costumi, Infermità e Condizioni dell'Uomo e della Donna e pronostico perpetuo di quello che deve succedere ogni anno, ed altri avvertimenti per conservarsi sani, aggiuntovi altre bellissime curiosità* (Salani, Florence, 1871), pp. 33–7. It should be remembered how widely spread and popular these Salani editions were.

34 There are other examples from the period with a regional context and variations; see V. Imbriani, *La novellaja fiorentina. Fiabe e novelline stenografate in Firenze dal dettato popolare* (Forni, Bologna, 1969, edn Livorno, 1871), especially 'Zelinda e il mostro', pp. 319–27, and 'Il matterugiolo e il savio', pp. 594–9. On imbecility, see also C. Lapucci, *La Bibbia dei poveri. Storia popolare del mondo* (Mondadori, Milan, 1985), pp. 120–4 (here I would like to thank the author for help on popular culture).

35 A. Verga, 'Frenastenici e imbecilli', *Arch. ital. malat. nerv.*, XIV (1877), p. 233. For the other references see in reverse order in the text, Puccinotti, 'Lezioni di medicina', pp. 260–2; Morelli, *Delle malattie*, p. xxiii; Lazzaretti, 'Le affezioni', pp. 174–6; and id., *Di alcuni pregiudizi*, p. 6.

36 This difficulty was also immediately pointed out by Franzolini, 'La follia parziale', p. 417. A pupil of Bini's introduced the three at the psychiatric congress; see P. Grilli, 'Sulla pazzia morale', *Arch. ital. malat. nerv.*, XVII (1880), pp. 458–73. The lively debate (pp. 571–600) was joined by Verga, who related Lazzaretti's disagreement with Livi and Morselli as he was reconsidering the Grandi case. See C. Livi, 'Della monomania in relazione col foro criminale', *Riv sper. fren.*, II (1876), pp. 394–415, 639–60.

37 In Verga's classic definition the imbecile was 'incapable of governing himself'; see 'Frenastenici', p. 231, in which Livi, Bini, Morselli and many

others clearly did not agree. According to the legal tradition, it was only the 'complete imbecile' who was unfit in civil actions, not 'the simple-minded', who were deemed to have sufficient understanding, as Lazzaretti explained in 'Le affezioni', pp. 126–7. See also the entries 'Imbecille' and 'Imbecillità' in N. Tommaseo (ed.), *Dizionario del sinonimi della lingua italiana*, 2nd edn (Reina, Milan, 1851); 7th edn, Vallardi, Milan, 1886–8. See also G. Rigutini and P. Fanfani, *Vocabolario italiano della lingua parlata* (Cenniniana, Florence, 1875), and B. Melzi, *Il vocabolario per tutti*, 17th edn (Treves, Milan, 1894).

38 *L'uccisore*, pp. 24–6. For Lazzaretti's 'Le affezioni', see p. 143.

39 See U. Spirito, *Storia del diritto penale italiano da Cesare Beccaria ai nostri giorni* (Sansoni, Florence, 1974), 3rd edn revised and expanded (1st edn 1924), chapter VI: 'Le critiche alla scuola positiva e gli eclettici'; see also chapters III–V on the three protagonists and the conclusion. Cf. E. Ferri *La teorica dell'imputabilità e la negazione del libero arbitrio* (Barbera, Florence, 1878), p. 12. Ferri was Ardigo's pupil at school and Pietro Ellero's at the University of Bologna. In 1879 he became a lecturer at Turin, where Lombroso was working. See V. Accattatis's critical introductions to the recent editions of, respectively, E. Ferri, *Sociologia criminale* (Feltrinelli, Milan, 1979), 1st edn 1880, pp. 9–51; and G. Bovio, *Saggio critico del diritto penale* (Feltrinelli, Milan, 1978), pp. 9–36, wherein the editor maintains that there was a certain amount of agreement between the two schools. See also A. Baratta, 'Filosofia e diritto penale. Note su alcuni aspetti dello sviluppo penalistico in Italia di Beccaria ai nostri giorni', *Riv. inter. filos. dirit.*, XLIX (1972), s. 4, pp. 29–54.

40 *L'uccisore*, p. 19.

41 See A. Herzen, *Analisi fisiologiche del libero arbitrio umano*, 2nd edn (Florence, 1870), which was highly praised by Ferri; and id., 'Arbitrio libero', in *Enc. medica ital.* (Vallardi, Milan, n.d.), vol. I, pp. 11 and 1603–14.

42 M. Calderoni, *I postulati della scienza positiva ed il diritto penale* (Ramella, Florence, 1901); then in O. Campa (ed.), *Scritti* (La Voce, Florence, 1924), vol. I, pp. 33–167; for the quotation see p. 53 and 61. The review was by Calderoni's mentor, the psychologist and psychiatrist G.C. Ferrani, in *Riv. sper. fren.*, XXVIII (1902), pp. 405–7. There are ample references to the recent discussions of those themes in P. Borsellino, 'Libertà, giustificazione della pena e metodo delle discipline penali in Calderoni', *Riv. crit. stor. filos.*, XXXIV (1979), pp. 316–48.

43 See the relationship between physical and moral laws which together with the laws of logic and justice constituted the norm in F. Carrara, *Programma del corso di diritto criminale dettato nella R. Università di Pisa. Parte speciale, ossia Esposizione dei delitti in genere con aggiunta di note per uso della pratica forense*, 9th edn (Cammelli, Florence, 1912), pp. 9ff. There are useful references to the false opposition of science and morality in penal law and on the question of responsibility in particular in H. L. Hart, *Punishment and the Elimination of Responsibility* (Univ. of London, Athlone Press, London, 1962). See also H. Fingarette, *The Meaning of Criminal Insanity* (University of California Press, Berkeley, 1972),

especially chapter II; and R. Smith, 'Expertise and Causal Attribution in Deciding between Crime and Mental Disorder', *Social Studies of Science*, XV (1985), pp. 67–98.

44 *L'uccisore*, p. 168. See also Bini, 'Definizione', p. 216, and Livi, 'Della monomania', p. 640.

45 See 'Atti ufficiali della Sesta sessione del Congresso Internazionale di statistica e proposta di Programma', presented by Pietro Maestri, Dir. Stat. Gen. of Regno (Barbera, Florence, 1867), p. 49. Among other members of the committee were A. Melegari, S. Biffi, S. Mancini, P. Mantegazza and the chancellor G. De Falco.

46 See F. Von Holtzendorff, 'La psicologia dell'omicidio', *Riv. pen.*, II (1875), no. 3, pp. 125–50; and T.R. Schütze, 'Le disposizioni sulla imputabilità nella moderna legislazione penale', ibid., vol. II, pp. 417–23, and vol. III, pp. 333–41. On motivation, see M. De Mauro, 'La libertà del volere ed il Codice penale italiano', and U. Conti, 'Nuove ricerche intorno a moventi a delinquere', both in *Pel cinquantesimo anno di insegnamento di E. Pessina* (Trani, Naples, 1899), vol. II, respectively pp. 117–31 and 313–39.

47 See D. Garland, *Punishment and Welfare. A History of Penal Strategies* (Gower, Aldershot, 1985); the rather unoriginal chapter on criminological science, focusing on the Italian school, is on pp. 73–111. See also M. Foucault, stimulating as always, 'About the Concept of the "Dangerous Individual" in 19th Century Legal Psychiatry', *Intern. Journ. Law and Psych.*, I (1978), pp. 1–18. On this question and on the contrast between the two schools of thought, I refer to P. Guarnieri, 'Alienists on Trial: Conflict and Convergence Between Psychiatry and Law (1876–1913)', *History of Science*, xxix (1991), pp. 393–410.

48 *L'uccisore*, p. 155; the other quotations are on pp. 121, 116 and 44.

49 The protest of the magistrate Pescatore was reported polemically by G. Ziino in 'Della pretesa mitezza de medici nelle questioni di psichiatria forense', *Riv. sper. fren.*, I (1875), pp. 200–8. On the inevitable reason to commit crime, see Lazzaretti, *Corso teorico pratico di medicina legale. Opera adottata nelle Università per l'insegnamento agli studenti di medicina e di legge*, 3rd edn (A., Padua, 1879): 'Libro VI. Medicina legale in relazione al diritto penale', p. 37, and the whole section on murder, pp. 28ff.

50 On brutal wickedness see the two Cassations of Naples of 14 August 1874, and of Florence on 28 August 1868, in E. Pacifici-Mazzoni and S. Coen (eds), *Repertorio generale di giurisprudenza civile, penale, commerciale ... Supplemento degli anni 1876–80* (Turin, 1884), *ad vocem*; also the commentary in *Il Codice Penale Toscano Illvstrato*, p. 282. With reference to Lombroso's position on the Vincenzo Verzeni case, see p. 88; on Morselli, who disagreed, see *L'uccisore*, p. 121.

51 *L'uccisore*, p. 142. The other quotations are from pp. 139, 140 and 121.

52 On the various common attitudes to 'criminal lunacy', some recent cases have suggested certain observations, for which see P. Guarnieri, 'Identificazione di un mostro', *Belfagor*, XLI (1986), pp. 102–7.

53 *L'uccisore*, p. 59.

54 In this transcription the order of pages has been reversed and the spelling corrected (unlike Morselli; see *L'uccisore*, pp. 52–3). It is reproduced

here from the table in the documents of expert evidence (my thanks to Sandro Bardi for the photographic work).

55 Carlino's ambivalent attitude and his constant thoughts about the children (his feelings towards the adults, 'the people' of Incisa, were consistently hostile) are repeated in his confession, in his autobiographical 'novel' and in the various quotations taken from *L'uccisore* (see pp. 40, 54, 59, 70 and especially 60, in addition to those already cited). His unpublished papers from his time in prison and the asylum have been lost, but the fact that he continued to talk about the children, write about them and draw them long after the crimes and even after he had served his sentence, is indirectly attested to by witnesses (from whom we also learn of his remorse). These testimonies are so heterogeneous and scattered in time (in the newspapers after his arrest, during the trial and after prison, from the witnesses and magistrates both in the investigation and in court, the expert doctors and the director of San Salvi) that it is not possible to draw a true picture of Carlino from the references available. This paragraph on his release from prison should be compared with the beginning of chapter I.

56 See letters without date or signature, but probably from the same Peri as in APCLY, 'Affari diversi', 1895, f. 170, ins. 57, containing all 'the means undertaken by the Police Department for the admission of Callisto Grandi and the decisive refusal of the workhouse directors to admit him'. The letter from the mayor of Incisa to Peri was dated 5 October and that of the Police Chief, 9 October. The letter from the official has an illegible signature and is dated the 11th. For information on that year's intake of 'harmless idiots' at Montedomini, see ibid., f. 170, ins. 24. See also 'L'ospizio di Montedomini e l'ex galeotto Grandi', in *La Battaglia. Giornale liberale monarchico*, VIII, 13 and 14 October 1895, p. 1.

57 ASF, 'Tribunali di Firenze Dementi,' 1895, b. 85, f. 335. The announcement that he had been admitted at San Salvi was in the newspapers: see 'Callisto Grandi in manicomio', in *La Nazione*, 12 October 1895, p. 2, and 'Il Grandi in manicomio', in *Fieramosca* 12–13 October 1895, p. 2. Alarmed notice of his release had also been given by *Riv. aper. fren.*, XXI (1895), p. 712. It should be remembered that an appeal had been launched in Incisa to provide help and comfort to Grandi's family, who were perceived to have borne 'not a blow but a great, immense, incomparable misfortune'. All those who knew his family held them up as 'exemplary for morality of habits, correct behaviour and love of work'. One of his brothers was especially respected – he was an organizer of the Incisan workers' association, leader of the orchestra and a town councillor. This was revealed in 'Ancora C. G. l'uccisore dei ragazzi', *Fieramosca*, 10 October 1895, p. 2; also included were letters to the journalist.

58 An account of the visit, with Carlino's words, was published in the journal edited by Enrico Ferri and prepared by one of his third-year law students. He concluded that Grandi's protest was so logical that it should have given the legislators and experts cause to reflect on the ambiguities of this difficult case; see S. Benedetti, 'Al manicomio di San Salvi', *La scuola positiva nella giurisprudenza penale*, VI (1896), pp. 446–8 (my thanks to Bruno Wanrooij for drawing my attention to this article). Even the newspapers had disclosed that Grandi was due to be released in

October 1895 and that this seemed an entirely reasonable assumption (whatever one's opinion); see the notes to chapter I.

59 Tanzi and Lugaro, *Trattato*, p. 797, where there is a photograph of Grandi and the 'moral testimony' he wanted to write on 10 May 1896, when he thought he was about to die of pneumonia. See the annual registers of 'Movimento generale della popolazione del Manicomio' in AOPF. The notice of his death and a diagnosis of 'paranoid imbecility' appears on 1 March 1911 (see also the Commune of Florence, 'Uff. St. Civ. Register of Deaths': G. C. 1 March 1911). The archives of the old psychiatric hospital of San Salvi were partially flooded in 1966 and are in the process of being reorganized under the direction of Signor Mugnai, for whose help I am grateful. Grandi's file is missing from the archives, nor can any of his many writings be found, not even at the ACTV, where part of the old asylum's clinical records have ended up. For information on the director of San Salvi, see E. Lugaro, 'E. Tanzi', *Riv. di patol. nerv. e ment.*, XLIII (1934), pp. i–xx.

Index